PENGUIN BOOKS

PETITE ANGLAISE

D1362846

Petite Anglaise

CATHERINE SANDERSON

PENGUIN BOOKS

PENGUIN BOOKS

Published by the Penguin Group
Penguin Books Ltd, 80 Strand, London WC2R ORL, England
Penguin Group (USA) Inc., 375 Hudson Street, New York, New York 10014, USA
Penguin Group (Canada), 90 Eglinton Avenue East, Suite 700, Toronto, Ontario, Canada M4P 2Y3
(a division of Pearson Penguin Canada Inc.)
Penguin Ireland, 25 St Stephen's Green, Dublin 2, Ireland
(a division of Penguin Books Ltd)
Penguin Group (Australia), 250 Camberwell Road, Camberwell, Victoria 3124, Australia
(a division of Pearson Australia Group Pty Ltd)
Penguin Books India Pvt Ltd, 11 Community Centre, Panchsheel Park, New Delhi – 110 017, India
Penguin Group (NZ), 67 Apollo Drive, Rosedale, North Shore 0632, New Zealand
(a division of Pearson New Zealand Ltd)
Penguin Books (South Africa) (Pty) Ltd, 24 Sturdee Avenue,
Rosebank, Johannesburg 2196, South Africa

Penguin Books Ltd, Registered Offices: 80 Strand, London WC2R ORL, England

www.penguin.com

First published by Michael Joseph 2008
Published in Penguin Books 2009
1

Typeset by Rowland Phototypesetting Ltd, Bury St Edmunds, Suffolk
Printed in England by Clays Ltd, St Ives plc

ISBN: 978-0-141-03119-4

www.greenpenguin.co.uk

Mixed Sources
Product group from well-managed
forests and other controlled sources
www.fsc.org Cert no. SA-COC-1592
© 1996 Forest Stewardship Council

Penguin Books is committed to a sustainable future
for our business, our readers and our planet.
The book in your hands is made from paper
certified by the Forest Stewardship Council.

for Mr Frog, and Tadpole

Prologue

I snap awake after three, maybe four hours of alcohol-saturated sleep. The events of the previous night swim into stark, shameful focus and I find myself unable to move; paralysed by guilt.

Tadpole, our daughter, is chanting. A low, plaintive murmur of 'Mummy, Mummy, Mummy . . .' travels along the corridor from her bedroom to ours. Left unanswered, her sounds will grow louder and more insistent, the volume rising in a hairpin crescendo. Someone will have to go to her and lift her warm, sleep-scented body from her bed into ours. A task I would relish on any other day.

My groan – and the protesting arm I heave across my face to blot out the daylight which infiltrates our room through slatted shutters – has the desired effect. The bed creaks as Mr Frog hoists himself upright and stumbles wordlessly in the direction of Tadpole's room. His silence conveys many layers of disapproval. That I'd stayed out into the small hours. That I'd returned so obviously tipsy, key fumbling ineptly in the lock. That I would doubtless not be in any fit state to drag myself to work.

I hear returning footfalls and moments later anxious fingers prise my arm from my face; a pair of grey-blue eyes gaze questioningly into mine.

'*Maman?*'

A wave of visceral love engulfs me, but I fight the urge to clutch my daughter to me, to bury my face in the back of her neck and inhale her milky, innocent scent.

'Mummy's got a bad, bad headache,' I mumble feebly, turning on to my side and burying my feverish face into the cool pillow instead.

But there is no pain, at least not in a physical sense. I am, quite simply, stricken with horror; aghast at the thought of the upheaval I am poised to inflict on our little family. Terrified that what I am contemplating can somehow be read in my face: a scarlet letter freshly branded on my forehead.

And yet, at the same time, every cell in my body vibrates at a higher frequency. I feel the blood thundering through my veins; the hair on my arms standing on end. My fear – fear of hurling myself headlong into the unknown – is shot through with giddy exhilaration. Never have I felt so guilty, nor so intoxicatingly alive.

I lie immobile while Mr Frog moves resentfully around the apartment, making no move to help as I hear him dress first Tadpole, then himself; pour breakfast cereal into her bowl.

Even before the front door slams accusingly closed behind them, I am itching to power up the computer. Spinning a web of words in my mind, I'm impatient to commit them to my blog while they are fresh and raw and new.

1. Snapshots

The day I created my anonymous internet diary, the *nom de plume* 'petite anglaise' instinctively sprang to mind, and felt so very right, so very natural, that I considered no other.

Ask any English girl who has ever lived in France, and I'm sure she'll tell you she has been called a *petite anglaise* at some time or another. It is a name loaded with meaning: an affectionate tone implies that the *anglaise* in question is not just English, but cute and English; a hint of lasciviousness makes her sound sexy, but also taps into a commonly held view that English girls are rather easy.

But there is another layer of meaning I've always found appealing: those two words summed up neatly everything I ever wanted my life to be. *Petite anglaise*: an English girl who has been translated into French; her life transposed into a French key.

For my pen name, or perhaps that should read *mouse* name, I took a liberty, dropping the '*la*' which should, by rights, precede it: *Petite* became my first name, *Anglaise* my surname. In a few whimsical clicks, an alter ego was born.

It's simple enough to identify what made these words such a perfect, obvious pseudonym. But I struggle to divine the source of my deep-seated desire to become a *petite anglaise* in the first place. What on earth could compel a girl to uproot her whole existence when she had never so much as tasted a genuine croissant? When her childhood holidays seldom took her beyond British shores, and her family tree was firmly rooted in Yorkshire? What was it that caused me to fall in love with the idea of immersing myself in a language and culture which were not my own? And why set my sights on France, in particular?

When Tadpole was born, I spent a sleepless night on the maternity ward gazing intently into her inky, newborn eyes, grappling to come to terms with the indisputable fact that this was an actual person looking back at me, not just a version of Mr Frog, or me, or both, in miniature. From the outset she seemed to know what she wanted, and I realized I could have no inkling of the paths she would choose to follow. But if I watch her life unfold carefully enough, perhaps I will see clear signposts pointing to who or what she will become. Because when *I* look backwards, ransacking my own past for clues with the clarity that only hindsight can bring, several defining moments do stand out. Moments charged with significance; snapshots of myself which, if I join the dots together, lead me unswervingly to where I stand today: from French, to France, to Paris and to *petite anglaise*.

My recurring daydream, as a child, had long been one of escape. As our Vauxhall Cavalier tore along the motorway, my legs wedged at an uncomfortable angle in the narrow space behind my father's seat, my stomach lurching with motion sickness, an image played across my shuttered eyelids. Closing my ears to the sound of my younger sisters bickering beside me on the back seat, I saw myself running. I parted fronds of wheat as I cut through fields, I sliced across people's gardens, leaped over dry-stone walls and streams.

It was as if there was somewhere else I wanted to go, but I didn't know, then, where this somewhere was. In the daydream, my course ran parallel to that of our car. My running self had no inkling of her destination.

A few days shy of my twelfth birthday, dressed in the navy uniform of Mill Mount Grammar School for Girls, my nylon, knee-length skirt crackling with static, I expectantly took my seat in an attic classroom. The wooden desk, scarred with many generations of graffiti, was at an unfamiliar gradient and I had to place my pen with care, just so, to prevent it rolling to the floor. Mrs Barker arrived and wrote her name on the blackboard, her resolutely English surname momentarily dampening my enthusiasm. '*Bonjour tout le monde!*' she said brightly, and with that, my very first French lesson began. I opened the well-thumbed *Tricolore* textbook which was to be my guide for many years to come, pushed my wayward glasses back up to the bridge of my nose, and bent my head studiously over page one.

France. Here was a destination to bend my running steps towards; a hook to hang my daydreams on; so alluring, so exotic, so tantalizingly close. No matter that school French lessons consisted of little more than endlessly rehearsed role plays and verb conjugations. No matter that my first extended stay on French soil would not take place for another six agonizing years. As I sat in a numbered booth in the school language lab, cumbersome headphones blocking out the English sounds of the world around me, I closed my eyes and pretended I was actually there. I yearned to taste the 200 grams of pâté I was instructed to buy in the grocer's shop; to visit the church or the town hall after quizzing a passer-by – invariably an elderly man wearing a beret – for directions.

'*Ecoutez, puis répétez!*' said the voice on the crackling tape at the start of every exercise. 'Listen, then dream' would have been more apt. I'd fallen hopelessly, irrationally, in love with the French language and, by extension, with France. And I'm at a loss to explain why, even now.

It wasn't until the summer before my eighteenth birthday that I finally boarded a coach at York railway station bound for Heathrow Airport, from where I would fly to France. As

I waved goodbye to my anxious mother, I took a series of deep breaths, trying to still the butterflies beating frantic wings against the walls of my stomach. It was hard to believe this was it, I was really going. Unzipping my rucksack with trembling fingers, I checked for the twentieth time that my passport was where it should be, wrapped around the tickets I had bought with money from my Saturday job serving cream teas to heavily perfumed old ladies. For years I'd argued bitterly with my parents every time the thorny subject of French exchanges was broached, indignant at their refusal to smooth my way. It was no good; they were unable to overcome their misgivings about welcoming a stranger into their home. But now, at last, I was of an age to take matters into my own hands. This trip to Lyons was to be my baptism.

For a whole fortnight I would stay with Florence and her family. I would sleep in a bed made up with French sheets. I would eat French food at their table, mopping my plate with a chunk of crusty baguette, just like the characters in the Pagnol books I devoured, or the actors in the handful of subtitled films I'd found in the local video shop. I would speak French, and only French, every single day for two weeks. For eighteen months I'd written Florence – whose details I'd stumbled upon by chance in the 'penpals' section of a *Cartable* magazine I'd found lying around in a classroom – long, painstakingly crafted letters, praying that one day an invitation would come. Florence always replied to my letters in French. She shared my obsession with The Cure, and in the photo she'd sent me her hazel eyes were circled with lashings of dark eyeliner, just like Robert Smith's. The dimples in her cheeks, the dusting of freckles across her nose, at odds with the moody image she was trying to project, were oddly endearing. Now we would finally meet. I was determined to love her in the flesh.

As I wheeled my suitcase out into the arrivals hall, suddenly overtaken by an echo of the shyness which had been the scourge of my early teens, a girl in dungaree shorts hurtled towards me.

'Cat-reen!' she exclaimed. *'C'est bien toi?'* I nodded, tongue-tied, savouring the sound of my name, in its French incarnation. How much prettier 'Catherine' sounded on her lips!

Florence was shorter than I had imagined, and her hair, as she leaned close to my cheek to administer my first ever French *bise*, smelled strongly of cigarette smoke. Her accent was like nothing I'd heard in any listening comprehension exercise in the language lab, and for days I had to beg her to repeat everything slowly, several times. My secret hope was that she would teach me local slang so authentic that my teachers back home would be flummoxed; my classmates mute with envy.

The welcoming committee Florence brought to the airport told me everything I needed to know about her happy-go-lucky existence: it consisted of an ex-boyfriend and two younger brothers, but no actual means of transportation. The plan, from what I could gather, was to take a bus to where her elder brother worked, in a nearby village post office. If he was around, he'd give us a lift; if not, we'd hitch a ride to her village. Her father, a widower, was working the late shift at the local sausage factory and wouldn't be home until dinner-time.

Thumbs outstretched, Florence and I stood on the grass verge while the boys hung well back with my unwieldy suitcase so as not to jeopardize our chances. Thank goodness my parents can't see me now, I thought, preparing to clamber into a French stranger's car, poised to become the subject of a cautionary tale used to deter future generations of exchange students. Remember that English girl? You know, the one who ended up dismembered and used as sausage filling?

But if there was any danger, I was past caring at that precise moment. Every sense amplified, I was too busy feasting on my surroundings: the cars with strange number plates which rumbled by on the wrong side of the road; the way in which Florence's brothers seemed to gesticulate with their hands, their arms, even their shoulders, when they spoke; the unfamiliar cadence of their sentences; the strumming of a thousand *cigales*, invisible in the scrubby vegetation around us. So caught up was I in the moment that when a car finally slowed to a standstill on the dusty road, it didn't register at first.

'Cat-reen, *réveille-toi*!' Florence cried, putting her hand on my arm and startling me out of my reverie. 'He is stopping, it is time to go!' She dropped her half-smoked Gauloise, scrunching it in a practised movement between the rubber sole of her tennis shoe and the dusty road, and bent her head to speak to the driver through his half-open window. After lengthy negotiations, we heaved my suitcase into the boot and clambered into the back seat with one of her brothers.

'*Et les autres?*' I asked, in my pidgin French.

'Oh, don't worry about them,' said Florence with a dismissive shrug. 'They'll hitch a ride of their own.'

As the car sped along, my eyes devoured every street sign, every yellow letterbox, every shopfront we passed. It was as if I had stepped inside the pages of *Tricolore*. Everything felt as alien and exotic as I had so desperately wanted it to. And yet, in spite of the unmistakable Frenchness of everything around me, there was a part of me that felt I belonged here. I wanted to hug myself with glee: I really did thrive on being out of context, just as I'd dreamed I would.

★

Three years later, when the 'year abroad' became the hottest topic of conversation towards the end of my second year of university, I never called it by that name. It was to be my 'year in France', with a couple of months in Germany tacked on at the end, to pay lip service to course requirements. I filled in an application to work as an English *assistante*, not caring which region of France I wound up in, although I did rule out Paris. With my small-town background, the sheer scale and intensity of the capital intimidated me. I would visit, and I suspected my path would lead me there eventually, but I wasn't quite ready for the City of Light, not just yet. I was assigned to a *lycée* in Yvetôt, a drab, uninspiring market town in austere Normandy, where my task was to 'teach' English conversation to groups of nonchalant denim-clad teens for a few hours a week. But the job – which I didn't particularly enjoy – was simply a means to an end. All that mattered to me was that I would spend nine whole months in France.

Home was a tiny attic room in a townhouse in nearby Rouen, rented from a school teacher and her piano-tuner husband whom I rarely saw. Much of my time, in those first weeks and months, was spent with other English *assistantes*, warming our hands on steaming cups of hot chocolate in smoky cafés, pining for absent boyfriends and mimicking our students' – and sometimes their teachers' – comical English accents. The experience fell short of my expectations at first: instead of total immersion in the language and culture, here I was speaking my mother tongue all day long to pupils, then hanging out with a crowd of fellow *anglaises* after hours.

One autumn Saturday, I was walking gingerly around the pedestrianized town centre with Claire, an English girlfriend, on cobbles made treacherous by their coating of damp, coppery leaves. Pausing at a street vendor's cart by the *Gros Horloge*, we bought scalding-hot, chocolate-filled *crêpes*, their

9

buttery slickness soaking through thin paper wrappers. As I took my first bite, Claire gave me a conspiratorial nudge, pointing out a tall boy striding towards us with a large Alsatian on a leash, flanked by a couple of shorter friends.

'You know that English teacher who invited me over for dinner with his family last week?' she said, pausing to swallow a mouthful of pancake. 'That's his son, Yann, over there. He's not bad, is he?'

As he drew closer I stared at the slim boy – obviously a student – with pronounced cheekbones, a Roman nose and moody smudges beneath his blue-green eyes. He wore a long dark-grey coat which emphasized his height over pale jeans and a *pull camionneur*, the zip-necked jumper which seemed to be compulsory wear for all Frenchmen that year. Suddenly self-conscious, I prayed I didn't have chocolate smeared around my lips. Yann wasn't just good-looking, he was gorgeous. Tall and dark-haired with an air of melancholy about him and, in some way I struggled to put my finger on, unmistakably French. In that single electric instant I knew that if Yann would have me, my university boyfriend, out of sight and mind back home, was history. Here, right before my eyes, was a compelling reason to upgrade to a French model; a passport to the French life I craved.

I saw Yann often over the next few weeks with Claire and the other *assistantes*, increasingly tongue-tied in his presence as I grew more and more besotted with him. Was it wishful thinking, or did the way he continually singled me out for attention – even if it was as the butt of his jokes – mean that he was drawn to me, too? A trip to Paris with Claire, Yann and a gang of his friends finally gave me the pretext I needed to find out for sure. And from the moment he slid into the seat next to mine on the train we boarded at Rouen station, I knew my instincts had not been wrong.

We kissed in semi-darkness, surrounded by slumbering bodies mummified in sleeping bags, on the tiled floor of a friend's apartment. I was euphoric. A French boyfriend: sexy, exotic, mine. I loved the way he pouted as he spoke his mother tongue; his range of expressive Gallic shrugs, every twitch of his slim shoulders speaking volumes. I loved the way he could casually throw a meal together in a matter of seconds; toss a salad in a perfect, home-made vinaigrette. With every kiss, with every evening meal at his parents' house, I inched one step closer to my goal: carving out a niche for myself in France, making it my home.

The first time I slept over we'd contrived a flimsy excuse: a late dinner with friends, a missed curfew for my rented room. No one was fooled, but Yann's parents played along gamely. En route to the kitchen to make coffee the following morning, clad only in a borrowed T-shirt, which Yann assured me was perfectly decent but felt quite the opposite, I slid along the walls, cringing with embarrassment, eyes downcast. Yann's father was sitting in his favourite chair by the window, pretending to read *Libération* but, from the way his newspaper twitched as I passed, I knew that he had witnessed my discomfort.

'*Alors, c'était comment hier soir?*' he enquired, eyes twinkling above his newspaper. My cheeks flamed. How was it last night? Could he really be quizzing me about his son's prowess in the bedroom? Surely, even in notoriously permissive France, that wasn't a normal thing for a parent to say? '*Le dîner, je veux dire, bien sûr,*' he added, as if to imply that, if I had jumped to the wrong conclusion, the mistake was mine entirely. But when I looked askance at Yann and saw his smirk, I knew his father's innuendo had been intentional.

'I had a very pleasant *soirée*, thank you,' I replied, still gazing at Yann as I spoke. Something in his eyes spurred me on, making me forget my bashfulness for a moment. 'A good time was most *definitely* had by all,' I added, with what I hoped was a suggestive smile.

Yann's father snorted with suppressed laughter. 'She gives as good as she gets, this *petite anglaise*,' he said, half to himself, in an approving tone.

I savoured the sound of my new name, and wore it, from that moment on, as a badge of pride.

Landing a posting, a year later, to the Sorbonne Nouvelle – the real Sorbonne University's poor relation, housed in a seventies building of dubious charm – was a piece of good fortune so unbelievable, it almost seemed fated. I'd got away with ploughing through the whole of my higher education with tunnel vision, eyes fixed on the Holy Grail – France – without pausing to give any thought to plotting an actual career path. The teaching job, which fell into my lap when no one else in my year even applied for it, was the perfect stalling mechanism. Not only would it take me to Paris, but it would buy me a whole year to consider my next move. And when my university failed to find a single willing graduate to send over the following year, a situation without precedent, my one-year contract stretched, with convenient elasticity, into two.

A Eurolines coach deposited me early one September morning in a nondescript car park somewhere near La Fourche, north of Place de Clichy, if I remember rightly, although at the time I had only a sketchy idea of the geography of the city. I didn't linger, hefting my rucksack on to my shoulders and diving straight into the nearest *métro* station, where I pored over my map. First things first: I needed to find a place to live. I had a room booked for a week in student halls near Denfert-Rochereau, but my first destination was the American Church on Quai d'Orsay, and the noticeboard filled with handwritten adverts for student accommodation I'd been told I would find there. Setting a course for Pont d'Alma, I crossed the city in a series of underground trains, seeing nothing but my own reflection in the windows, feeling a vein pulsing anxiously in my forehead. Arriving at my destination, I clambered up the concrete steps, blinking in the bright daylight.

The first thing I saw was the Eiffel Tower outlined against the sky, rising high above the residential buildings and offices which lined the *quais*. I was just as surprised as I had been the first time I'd seen it up close, with Yann by my side, never expecting it to be painted a rusty shade of brown. 'It's just a glorified pylon,' I'd said then, pretending to be unimpressed, and earning myself a good-humoured poke in the ribs. But now, as I dug around in my pocket for my map and tried to get my bearings, I felt a rising tide of excitement. I had arrived. This was it! I was about to make Paris my home.

The first number I noted down and dialled with shaking hands from a nearby payphone belonged to a woman renting a *chambre de bonne* a few minutes' walk from there, a narrow garret in former servants' quarters on the top floor of an imposing stone building with heavy double doors and a marble entrance hall. The room, accessible by a service stairwell, boasted views across the Champ de Mars to the glorified pylon itself. My enthusiasm was swiftly dampened, however, both by the prospect of shared toilet and shower facilities on the landing, and the fact that my landlady would be living on the floor below – too close for comfort – and I returned to the payphone, crestfallen, to try the next number on my list.

A *deux pièces* in the eleventh *arrondissement* was my second port of call, a short walk from the Place de la Bastille. The apartment buildings were of the same era as the bourgeois building I'd just visited, but there the resemblance ended. This neighbourhood was resolutely working class so, instead of elaborate stonework and ornate windows, the façade of 104 rue de la Roquette was painted white and without ornament. But once I stepped inside it was love at first sight, and I darted across the road to the nearest bank, cashing in every last traveller's cheque in my possession to pay the deposit and close the deal. There was something shifty about my landlady, a striking *divorcée*, chic but tousled, as if she had got out of bed seconds earlier and thrown on a designer outfit. There was no written lease, and she instructed me to pay the rent cash in hand when she dropped by at the beginning of every month. I wasn't about to let this unconventional arrangement worry me, though. Two rooms, with a bathroom and kitchen, for the same price as the garret I'd just visited by the Eiffel Tower. It was simply too good to turn down.

As I leaned against the back of what was now my front door and contemplated my surroundings, my landlady's footfalls receding in the stairwell behind me, my smile was almost too wide for my face to contain. My first ever *chez moi*, and it was in Paris. The shy schoolgirl clutching her *Tricolore* textbook, the carefree eighteen-year-old who ran wild in Florence's village, the starry-eyed student with her first French *amoureux*, all of my past selves looked over my shoulder now, rubbing their hands together with glee. This was the culmination of all our dreams. Let the Parisian chapter of *petite anglaise* begin.

2. *Parisienne*

Rue de la Roquette was a lively street, both by day and by night, lined with boutiques, bars and restaurants, leading from the overflowing bars of Bastille to the calm sanctuary of Père Lachaise cemetery and growing steadily shabbier along the way. Although I was new to living alone, I rarely felt lonely. My life was set to the music of the neighbourhood: the animated chatter of passers-by in the street below my window, the vibrations of the bass from the record shop downstairs, the drunken cries of revellers stumbling home in the early hours of the morning. And it wasn't just the street sounds which permeated my home: the green neon sign above the *pharmacie* across the road infused my bedroom with an eerie phosphorescent glow when the lights were out, while the living room was tinted pale orange by the street lights at the nearby crossroads.

Inside, all was quintessentially Parisian: an alcove with two electric hotplates above a mini-bar-sized refrigerator constituted the kitchen; the two main rooms were tiny; the bathtub so short that I had to draw my knees up to my chin. In one musty corner of the bedroom black mould began to advance across the cream wallpaper with its pattern of green foliage, and my bedclothes often felt damp to the touch. The apartment was inhospitable in winter: tiny electric wall heaters nestled under each draughty window, all the better for any warmth to escape into the street before it could make an impression on the room. Returning home after the Christmas break, I found a thick coating of ice on the inside of my bedroom window which took an eternity to thaw.

None of this mattered to me. Mostly I was to be found outdoors, roaming the city on foot, armed only with my *Plan de Paris* or a guidebook, a lone *petite anglaise* in her elegant adoptive city, soaking up every last drop of Frenchness like a sponge, marvelling at every detail. I breathed in the distinctive scents of Paris: baking dough from the *boulangeries* I passed every few hundred metres or so; the stench of ripe goat's cheese announcing the presence of a *fromagerie* ten paces ahead; sulphurous *métro* smells wafting up through metal grids to street level; the tang of urine in underground corridors. Paris on a shoestring was the taste of a bitter espresso as I discreetly warmed my toes by a café radiator in winter; the acidic sting of cheap red wine on my tongue; a buttery *pain au chocolat* melting in my mouth.

As an *assistante* I had a special teacher's pass which granted me free access to almost every museum in the city, and I visited each one in turn: the Pompidou – or Beaubourg, as true Parisians seemed to call it – where I rode the escalators to the top level and enjoyed the free view; the Picasso museum in the heart of the Marais with its tranquil walled garden; the Musée Rodin in the shadow of Les Invalides. I traipsed around the Louvre, starting with the Egyptian relics, but never made it as far as the *Mona Lisa*, treating myself to a coffee in the Café Marly instead, so I could rest my weary feet and admire the glass pyramid which guarded the main entrance.

My favourite places were further off the beaten track. I loved ducking off the university campus at Censier to drink mint tea in the mosaic-tiled courtyard of the Mosquée de Paris, or taking a snack to the Arènes de Lutèce in the spring-time. In the gaps between lessons I killed time in the tiny cinemas on the rue des Ecoles where I watched countless vintage Hollywood films in black and white.

But – as in Rouen – I found it frustrating that my circle of friends consisted mostly of expats like myself, fellow teachers from the university, or Brits and Americans met in bars. We would spend long evenings comparing notes about our experiences and, while it was undoubtedly fun, I hungered for something more. I had pinned my hopes on making friends with my students, but was bitterly disappointed to find that many of them lived with their parents and returned home to distant suburbs on the RER as soon as lectures were over.

A vital part of the experience I craved eluded me: I was living alongside the French, not among them. Observing French life, but never truly living it. A hair's breadth away from fulfilling my dreams. And yet sometimes this tiny gap seemed so unbridgeable.

With my second Parisian winter behind me – a freezing winter of discontent punctuated by general strikes which brought lessons to a standstill for weeks on end – I also began to fret about my future in France. There could be no further extension to my teaching contract, but that wasn't what I wanted, anyhow. Teaching would never be my vocation, it had simply been a convenient means to a French end. I'd have to find an alternative way of making a living as a matter of urgency, something more permanent which would equip me for the long haul. A chance meeting with a friend of a friend, an admin assistant for an American law firm, gave me the answer I had been seeking: I would take a bilingual secretarial course. Demand was high for English mother tongue assistants who were fluent in French. Here was the perfect job for this *petite anglaise*.

My plan had one drawback: the only diploma worth its salt was taught in England. The French have a neat little phrase for the situation in which I found myself: *devoir reculer pour mieux sauter*. I'd have to grit my teeth and take a few steps back before I could take a leap forward. Despite my misgivings, I had no choice but to return to England for a few months before I could kickstart the next phase of my Paris life.

A tight ball of dread formed in my stomach every time my thoughts turned to leaving Paris. Meandering through the fruit and vegetable market on boulevard Richard Lenoir, buffeted by the crowds, feet at the mercy of the wheels of the shopping trolleys to which Parisians of all ages seem so attached, I felt a lump in my throat. Alone at a showing of *Chacun Cherche Son Chat* playing at the Majestic Bastille, I watched, spellbound, as the events unfolded in my beloved neighbourhood: my red and white laundrette, my favourite café, the record shop where I collected flyers for nightclubs. The audience burst into enthusiastic applause as the final credits rolled – a phenomenon I have only ever witnessed in France – and my tears flowed freely in the semi-darkness. England seemed flat and two-dimensional to me now, compared with the richness, the texture of my Paris life, where I was constantly challenged by having to manipulate a language which was not my own, where every hurdle overcome represented a small private victory.

I became friendly with Sarah, a fellow *lectrice* at the university, around that time. A Scottish girl with a mop of dark curls and a penchant for sex with strangers, Sarah's behaviour both fascinated and repelled me. It certainly did nothing to dispel the preconceived ideas held by the French about *petites anglaises* and their loose morals, although it would be unfair to hold Sarah single-handedly responsible for the perpetuation of this myth, especially as, being Scottish, she was, strictly speaking, a *petite écossaise*.

One March evening, two or three months short of my impending departure, we sat cross-legged on the single bed that served as my sofa. As usual, the first-floor room with its paper-thin windows was under siege: an icy draught sliced under the ill-fitting front door and the grumble of traffic grew so loud at times, as motorbikes with sawn-off exhausts turned over their engines at the traffic lights, that we might as well have been sitting on the pavement outdoors. Senses dulled by the cheap Bordeaux in our tumblers, we were oblivious to the discomfort, our attention focused on the pile of letters Sarah had pulled from her leather satchel and strewn across the eiderdown.

A couple of weeks earlier Sarah had placed a personal ad in an Anglo-French classifieds magazine. '*Jeune fille anglaise ouverte cherche amis français*,' it read. She had been overwhelmed by the volume of enthusiastic responses, ranging from the filthiest of indecent proposals to earnest letters from men claiming they sought only to practise their English. Together we flicked idly through the applications Sarah had consigned to her B list, meaning she had no intention of taking things any further. Open-minded she might be, but there simply wasn't enough of her to go round.

'I can't believe how many people have replied!' I said incredulously. 'You've really got your money's worth here . . .'

'Absolutely,' replied Sarah, pouring another glass of wine. 'Especially given that the six I've met so far all bought me dinner . . .'

I dreaded to think what the sort of guy who replied to a personal ad would expect in return for dinner. Even though I was single myself, after a recent fling with an English guy – a fellow expat – had ended in tears, I couldn't imagine ever going on a blind date. There was something rather seedy about the whole enterprise, to my mind, and I was glad to remain a detached observer, living vicariously through Sarah.

One B-listed letter caught my attention, however. The exact text I have long forgotten, but what made it stand out from all the others was its playful tone and perfectly dosed irony. The author had taken the trouble to snip sublimely ridiculous pictures out of magazines to illustrate his words: a man with a Tom Selleck moustache wearing Speedos, white socks and plastic sandals was pasted above a handwritten caption which read 'I prefer casual footwear.'

'This guy seems really quite funny, for a Frenchman,' I exclaimed, waving the letter under Sarah's nose, wondering why this candidate had not made it to the A list. A sense of humour certainly scored highly on my list of desirable attributes. 'And look, he likes clubbing, electronic music, he used to work on a magazine . . . It might be cool to meet him . . .'

'Gimme the phone then.' Sarah grinned slyly. 'No time like the present, eh?'

'No, wait! You can't!' I protested, suddenly shy. 'What on earth will we say?' But it was too late. Sarah had reached across and grabbed the phone; she was already dialling.

Seated at a round table sipping unladylike glasses of *bière blanche*, Sarah and I were deep in conversation when he made his entrance. Somehow, despite our fits of giggles and Sarah's wine-slurred speech, she'd managed to persuade the bemused B list guy to meet us at one of my favourite haunts. We'd told him to bring a friend, male or female, if he wanted; this was emphatically not a date. I was busy marvelling at how the waitresses in the Café Charbon, as in so many 'in' places in Paris, always conformed to a particular type: wiry, effortlessly stunning and vaguely disdainful of their edgy, bohemian clientele. The acoustics of the high-ceilinged bar – which was either painted the exact shade of nicotine or had once been white and now bore the collective stain of a thousand cigarettes – reduced the animated conversations around us to an unobtrusive background hum.

My friend's posture changed, her eyes narrowing in a predatory fashion, and I wheeled around to see exactly who, or what, she had in her sights. A blue-eyed boy, swaddled in an oversized duffle coat, had just pushed open the heavy swing door and was clearly looking for someone. The description fitted: this was our guest. Slim-built, with short, dark-blond hair, he paused to unbutton his coat in the doorway, revealing a snugly fitting black jumper with a rainbow motif which made me wonder, initially, whether he might not be gay. Sarah caught his eye and waved. Mr B list looked relieved to see us. Maybe he shared my horror of entering crowded bars alone.

'*Bonsoir les filles*,' he said, stowing his coat over the back of his chair. 'I know you said I could bring a friend, but I'm pretty new in Paris – I've just moved here to look for a job – and I don't know a lot of people. So, I'm afraid you'll have to make do with just me.' Sarah and I stood for a moment, our chairs scraping on the mosaic-tiled floor so that he could plant the obligatory *bises* on our cheeks.

'Your English is really good,' I remarked shyly. 'Far better than any of my students', and very British-sounding . . .'

'Ah, well, I did a Masters in San Diego,' he explained, settling into the seat opposite me, 'but I had a lot of English friends there, exchange students like me, mostly. So I didn't catch an American accent.' I grinned at his comical choice of words: he made an American accent sound like some sort of disease.

'I'll bet there was an English girlfriend too . . .' Sarah said speculatively, leaning closer and touching him lightly on the arm. I couldn't believe how forward she could be sometimes, but I had to admit, grudgingly, that I was interested to hear what his answer would be.

'Well . . . not quite. There was a girl, but she was Welsh,' he explained with the tiniest of grimaces, as though the memory still smarted.

Over the course of the evening I took more and more of a fancy to our guest. He was quietly charming, with a dry sense of humour that struck me as unusual in a Frenchman. Physically, he was the exact opposite of the dark-haired, floppy-fringed types I had always been attracted to, with his fair hair and pale complexion. But attracted to him I was, there was no denying it, and although I could sense that Sarah was equally keen, the more we talked, the more I hoped he would spurn her advances and choose me instead.

'Some friends of mine are playing at the Rex club on Friday evening,' he said casually while Sarah was queuing for the Turkish toilet at the back of the café. 'Would you like to come along?' I wondered whether the timing of his invitation was intentional; whether 'you' was meant to be in the singular or the plural.

'I might just do that,' I replied, picking at the label on my bottle of beer with my fingernails. 'I love the Rex club. Although I'm not sure it's Sarah's cup of tea . . .' In actual fact, I had no intention of even mentioning it to Sarah. I justified this tiny betrayal to myself by saying it would be a terrible waste if this boy were to wind up as another notch on her belt when I sensed he might be rather special.

Years later, Mr Frog never fails to look bemused when I tell the story of how we met. A satisfactory explanation as to why he was responding to a small ad in the first place has never really been found. Perhaps unsurprisingly, his version of events tends to be somewhat abridged:

'Oh,' he says vaguely, 'we met in a bar.'

★

Mr Frog and I moved in together when my stint at the Sorbonne Nouvelle finally came to an end. With some reluctance I left my *deux pièces* on rue de la Roquette to share his tiny *chambre de bonne*, a couple of minutes on foot from the Luxembourg Gardens. It was a move born out of pure pragmatism, but we were deliriously happy in our little cocoon, and I rarely complained about the sloping floors, the dodgy wiring or the fact that I had to arm myself with a weighty, medieval key and pad up a flight of icy, tiled stairs to a shared toilet on the next landing.

That summer I sweated behind the bullet-proof glass of a foreign-exchange bureau, working as a cashier, squirrelling away money for my English sabbatical, while Mr Frog looked for a job. By night we ate at the cheapest *bistrots* we could find, or went to one of the cinemas at Odéon with discounted tickets I bought at work. On my days off we revisited my favourite haunts together. We wandered hand in hand through the Buttes Chaumont park; made a pilgrimage to Serge Gainsbourg's grave, strewn with green *métro* tickets, in the Montparnasse cemetery; we strolled along art nouveau passageways near the grands boulevards or cobbled backstreets atop the Butte Montmartre. Our discussions were punctuated by comfortable silences: we had a connection that seemed to transcend language barriers and cultural differences. Looking into his eyes, chameleon's eyes which appeared pale blue, green or grey according to his changing surroundings, it all quite simply felt right. A perfect fit.

In the company of my friends, Mr Frog held his own incredibly well. He was sufficiently at ease in my mother tongue to engage in word play or tell jokes – to my delight, and the admiration of my friends. But he also made endearing mistakes, some of which I adopted. We developed our own secret language, peppered with *franglais* and riddled with intentional grammatical blunders. 'I'm so hanged over,' I would groan after a heavy night. 'My hair hurts.' Mr Frog gently mocked what he called my 'disastrous English dress sense', teased me about my tendency to drink rather more than a French girl on a night out, but tactfully knew better than to dash my confidence by correcting my every gender mistake.

In turn, I met his friends. We ate leisurely, home-cooked meals with a couple he had known since childhood who had gravitated towards the capital to work but considered city living a necessary evil, their apartment an oasis of calm in the sleepy fifteenth *arrondissement*. Our names were on the guest list at nightclubs whenever DJs he knew from his university years in Grenoble made guest appearances. Wherever we went I was welcomed with open arms, complimented on my French and accepted as one of the crowd.

At long last I had found that elusive ingredient which had been lacking from my Paris experience. I was beginning to shrug off the uncomfortable sensation of being a perpetual outsider which had dogged me for so long, observing the Parisians from a distance, as if from behind a sheet of glass, unable to reach out and touch what I coveted. Mr Frog might not be a Parisian himself, but he took me by the hand and led me effortlessly inside.

The looming prospect of leaving for England no longer terrified me, because now I had not just some*where*, but some*one* to come back to. During what I jokingly referred to as my exile, we would spend long evenings on the phone, talking passionately in French. I would visit for weekends, and in end-of-term holidays. Firm ties bound me to Paris now. And in a few months' time, when I returned, I would finally be able to start living my new life to the full. With a new career, and with Mr Frog by my side, I would lay the foundations for my French life.

I was no longer just any *petite anglaise*. I was his.

3. Echoes

One of the best things about the bourgeois apartment building on the avenue Simon Bolivar where Mr Frog and I lived, seven years later, with Tadpole, our one-year-old daughter, was the shop downstairs – *Les Intondables*: a hairdresser's salon with a sense of humour. Everything about the bite-sized boutique smacked of playfulness: the name, which could mean anything from 'the un*shave*ables' to 'the un*shear*ables' or even 'the un*mow*ables' depending on your preferred translation of the verb '*tondre*'; the sign on the door advertising branches in Paris, Ouagadougou and Gif-sur-Yvette (the French equivalent of, say, Bognor Regis); the naïve swirls of psychedelic paint on the walls.

It was a far cry from the overpriced salons of the eighth *arrondissement*, where smug fortysomething *Parisiennes* parade their designer handbags while an army of uniformed colourists, stylists and head massagers pander to their every whim, circling like vultures, angling for generous tips. Designer fortysomething women and dogs in Chanel coats tended to be few and far between in our neighbourhood. And that was precisely why I liked it.

Les Intondables also boasted a CD jukebox packed with music I loved, both old and new. Pausing to tear up my junk mail in the dimly lit entrance hall, I would surprise myself by remembering every single word of a vintage New Order track, or find myself grinning as I recognized the opening chords of 'Smells Like Teen Spirit'. If a song was playing which I couldn't quite put a name to, I fought the temptation to pop an enquiring head around the salon door. The gregarious girl I once was, who bounded up to DJs in nightclubs, wouldn't have needed much encouragement. But the woman I'd become had little time for such frivolity, too busy dashing to the childminder's, to work, and back again, with a detour via the supermarket thrown in for good measure. I was a working mother now, and my life was set to the ticking of an invisible metronome. If I strayed off course, I was afraid I'd miss a beat.

Passing in front of the salon one Saturday morning in late June, Mr Frog, Tadpole and I returned home, shoulders sloping downwards in defeat, fresh from yet another disappointing apartment-viewing. Our hopes had been riding high when we'd set out: the photographs on the estate agent's website showed original wood floors and working fireplaces, and on the phone the agent had emphasized the desirable location, with views of the *mairie du 19ième* and the Buttes Chaumont park. But our enthusiasm began to fade the moment the front door swung open to reveal a series of former maid's rooms leading off one another with no connecting corridor or central heating, and was snuffed out completely when we spied a *sanibroyeur* instead of a real toilet in the bathroom, which made an infernal racket when flushed. True, if you leaned out of the bedroom window at a dangerous angle, it was just about possible to make out a sliver of the park and spy the slate roof of the town hall, but, all in all, that was scant consolation for all the apartment's shortcomings.

Back home, Mr Frog held open the heavy wooden door while I tilted Tadpole's pushchair up and over the stone doorstep into the sombre entrance hall with its peeling paintwork. Our apartment, on the fifth floor of a turn-of-the-century sandstone Haussmann building, was admittedly difficult to beat. The rooms were well proportioned, with oak floorboards and marble fireplaces, and walls so thick that our neighbours were seen but rarely heard. A balcony ran the full length of our floor and south-facing French windows flooded the rooms with sunlight. The only snag was that it didn't belong to us and, even if the owner could be persuaded to sell, it would be way beyond our means.

Owning a place had become my obsession, ever since Tadpole was but a glint in her father's grey-blue eyes. Mr Frog was at a loss to understand why I was so anxious to get a foot on the property ladder: the French – unlike the English – think nothing of renting until they are in their forties. But as property prices in the City of Light continued their dizzy upward spiral, I became more and more terrified that if we didn't hurry up, we'd miss the boat.

'I still can't quite believe anybody would be willing to pay that sort of money for a flat with a glorified Portaloo in it,' I railed, fumbling for my keys. 'I mean, if people like us are priced out of the market, who the hell actually can afford to buy anything in this city?'

Before I could launch into one of my familiar rants, an unmistakable guitar riff stopped me in my tracks. I glanced at Mr Frog, who was busy investigating the communal letterbox marked '*courrier volumineux*' while I freed Tadpole from her safety harness. I could see from the smile dawning on his lips that he recognized the song too: 'Bigmouth Strikes Again' by The Smiths. The English Channel may have lain between us but, in our teens, Mr Frog and I had sulked and skulked to much the same music.

No sooner had I set Tadpole down on the tiled floor than she began to wave short, chubby arms in the air, prompting me to wonder whether our combined musical tastes hadn't been woven into our daughter's very DNA. Without a moment's hesitation Mr Frog joined her, leading by example, encouraging her to move her legs by executing the kind of moves that would make you howl with shame if you saw your uncle doing something similar at a wedding. I've never been much of a dancer myself, especially when sober, but Mr Frog undoubtedly has a gift. From robotic dancing to gyrating like John Travolta in *Saturday Night Fever*, his repertoire is vast. Wiggling his hips in the most sublimely ridiculous fashion and swinging an imaginary microphone like a lasso, he urged Tadpole on. '*Danse! Pivote! Oui, comme ça!*'

Laughing so uncontrollably that tears streamed down my cheeks, I was nonetheless the first to notice a shadow fall across my daughter. The volume of the music and the carpeted stairs, which muffled every footfall, had conspired against us. Seeing my expression change, palms clapped over my mouth to stifle my laughter, Mr Frog stopped, mid-wiggle. Only Tadpole continued her dance, oblivious, as an unsmiling stranger – a man in his fifties with a deeply lined forehead and a mouth which turned down humourlessly at the corners – made his exit, giving our family a wide berth.

Once the front door had swung closed with a heavy clunk, Mr Frog and I burst out laughing, in the throes of what the French would refer to as a *fou rire*.

'Did you see his face?' I crowed, once I'd regained my composure. 'That was priceless!'

'Your face was a picture too!' Mr Frog picked up Tadpole and hoisted her on to his shoulders. 'Did you notice the way he kept his distance when he walked past?'

'He looked scared stiff that he might catch a sense of humour if he came too close! Oh, God, I nearly wet myself . . .' Thankfully this wasn't true in a literal sense and, for that, I had the French state and their free post-natal physiotherapy sessions to thank.

Mr Frog looked at me with a mirthful sparkle in his eyes and, as we filed into the lift together, I was reminded of one of the things that made me fall for him in the first place – the easy laughter we used to share.

How the years had scurried by, with accelerating speed, since first we met. We'd never married, so there was no seven-year itch to speak of, but the earth beneath us had shifted, almost imperceptibly at first, until hairline cracks began to appear and slowly widen. I hugged moments like this one – increasingly rare these days – to me tightly, storing up the good times and hoping against hope that they might be enough to keep us going.

'You likely to be finished in there any time soon?' I set down the plastic feeding spoon I had been holding for a moment, listening intently for any sound emanating from our tiny bathroom. There was no reply – none of the vigorous splashing noises that usually accompanied Mr Frog's weekday morning ritual – only the whine of the extractor fan as it laboured noisily to evacuate dense, steamy air from the windowless room. I contemplated Tadpole's porridge-coated cheek and sighed. It rather looked as though Mr Frog had fallen asleep in the bath again. It was Monday morning, two days after the dancing incident, and once more we had become slaves to our respective routines.

'Poor Daddy is very tired,' I remarked to Tadpole, torn between irritation and pity, then put a hand to my mouth, stifling a yawn of my own.

One unforeseen advantage of having a small child was that it gave me the excuse to talk to myself to my heart's content and pretend it was for my daughter's benefit; for the good of her English. Tadpole's repertoire of words was limited to a few animal sounds and two-syllable words like 'Mama',

'Daddy' and 'doggy', so our exchanges could not by any stretch of the imagination be called conversations. Yet in spite of this I had fallen into the habit of providing a running commentary whenever I was with her, a continuous narrative in which, for some reason, I always referred to myself in the third person.

'Mummy's not feeling great either,' I added, rubbing sleep from the corners of my eyes. It had been a rough night. Mr Frog, whipping the bedclothes into a frenzy and occasionally muttering incoherent phrases, had been dreaming about work. I knew this because his weary tone of resignation was unmistakable: it might have been 3 a.m., but what I'd heard was definitely one side of an imaginary telephone conversation with his boss at the advertising agency.

Tadpole, punishing me for letting my attention wander, grabbed her spoon and flung a dollop of porridge in a perfect arc. It landed on the dark-purple sofa, splattering copiously on impact, and she giggled at my horrified expression. Spurring myself into action, I dabbed at the viscous white blob with a bib, snatched a furtive gulp from my now lukewarm bowl of *café au lait* and prised the offending spoon from her grasp. If I was to arrive at work anything like on time, she and I would have to be fed, dressed and out of the front door in ten minutes' time. Our chances were not looking good: Tadpole wore pyjamas and a nappy, which, if my nostrils could be trusted, needed changing. I was still naked under my bathrobe.

Through the arched window to my left, the envy of every-one who visited our home, the rooftops of Paris were spread out before me, suffused with a warm, honey glow. Light bounced off metallic chimney stacks, the bold Legoland colours of Beaubourg stood out against the sea of slate and stone and, further away, the spires of Notre Dame and the dome of the Panthéon rose up majestically, appearing deceptively close to one another from this perspective. The Montparnasse tower, usually the most distant recognizable landmark, was temporarily invisible, shrouded in a haze of early morning pollution.

But the glorious view – the very reason I fell for our apartment when we'd hunted for a larger space to rent, an avocado-sized Tadpole ripening in my belly – merited only the most cursory glance that morning. I looked without really seeing, concerned only with second-guessing the weather, trying to gauge how we should dress.

The gurgle of water spiralling down the plug-hole signalled the end of Mr Frog's bath and, sure enough, he emerged from the bathroom seconds later, his compact frame enveloped in a towel. His face was drawn and tired; his jaw clenched tightly. It pained me to see how much he had aged in the last few years: long hours at his desk had leached the colour from his cheeks. The boy I'd fallen in love with had eyes that twinkled like the illuminations on the Eiffel Tower, he kidded around, and never failed to see the funny side. The man I lived with now was a pale, grey-scale shadow of his former self. We shared a home, slept side by side, and yet we were trapped in separate routines, a widening gulf between us. Just as I looked out of my window without seeing, I took Mr Frog's presence, or absence, for granted without really feeling. All that remained were echoes of how we used to be.

'*Daddy! Daddy!*' Tadpole clamoured as soon as she clapped eyes on him, raising her arms aloft, desperate to be released from her high chair. Mr Frog stooped to plant a kiss on her forehead as he walked past, studiously avoiding my gaze.

'*Finis ton petit-déjeuner, ma puce,*' he said, gently brushing porridge from her top lip with the back of his forefinger.

'So what is it today, remind me?' I aimed for an even,

neutral tone. It was a good job Mr Frog couldn't see my face, because I looked like I'd been sucking lemons, not drinking milky coffee. But there was no need to conceal my bitterness: he'd already disappeared into the bedroom.

'*Une nouvelle présentation* . . . the latest version of the storyboards . . . in London.'

There was a swoosh of legs sliding into trousers, a psshht of deodorant. 'I don't know at what time I'll be back. The presentation is in the late afternoon, so I might be taking the last Eurostar.' Mr Frog's English was almost word perfect these days, give or take a few misplaced prepositions. Eight years of living with a *petite anglaise* and working with international clients had all but eliminated the blunders I'd found so endearing when we first met.

I choked back sullen words which rose up like bile in my throat. 'Another late night?' I wanted to say. 'But we never see you!' Most nights Mr Frog returned home hours after Tadpole's bedtime; long after I had eaten, watched a film or retired to bed with my book. He would fix himself a sandwich and fall asleep alone on the sofa, bathed in the light cast by the flickering television. We'd lost count of the number of films he'd dozed through and, more often than not, I was called upon to fill in the blanks: an expert in the narration of closing scenes. In the mornings he either left before Tadpole awoke, or languished in the bath as he had today, struggling to gather the strength he needed to face the office while I scurried around getting myself and Tadpole ready.

On the worst days I would hear an ominous cough from behind the bathroom door, a telltale sound which meant that nerves had made his stomach heave.

Today I withheld my useless protests, too weary to pick another fight. Instead, I buttoned Tadpole's dress with resentful fingers, then threw on my own clothes, grabbing whatever happened to be clean in my haste. Ready, by chance, at the same time, we squeezed into the rectangular lift, a modern afterthought the size of a photo-booth wedged in the centre of the carpeted stairwell. As it lurched towards the ground floor, I hoisted Tadpole up to mirror level so she could gaze at her reflection. In the unforgiving fluorescent light, a family portrait was captured fleetingly in the glass before us. Three pale faces, framed by blond hair; mine a thick, unkempt mane which I pulled back off my face for work in as sleek a ponytail as I could manage, Mr Frog and Tadpole's sparse and downy. Three pairs of blue eyes: mine dark, distorted by the lenses in my glasses, father and daughter's pale and flecked with grey. Tadpole fizzed with energy; Mr Frog and I looked brittle and exhausted, eclipsed by our daughter.

The lift doors folded back, concertina-like, and Mr Frog held Tadpole while I retrieved her pushchair from the store room with its floral wallpaper and lingering smell of damp – the *gardienne*'s quarters in days gone by. Planting a perfunctory kiss on his smooth-shaven cheek, I mumbled '*bon courage*' and watched as he hurried off in the direction of his Vespa. The front door swung closed, and I remained in the quiet sanctuary of the hallway for a moment, fiddling with Tadpole's straps and stowing my handbag under the pushchair. It was too early for the hairdresser to crank the jukebox into action, so all was quiet. The weekend's dancing episode seemed like ancient history now, but conjuring it up for a moment, our peals of laughter echoed in my ears.

The morning walk through the Parc des Buttes Chaumont with Tadpole was the highlight of my day. We took the same route in reverse in the evenings, but by then I was invariably clammy and flustered from my brush with the rush-hour *métro*, and the return journey had the added disadvantage of being uphill. Bound for the childminder's, however, the pushchair rolled gently down the sloping paths. My hands guided rather than pushed, and the lightest of nudges was required to spare us an impromptu shower from a water sprinkler, or steer us out of an oncoming jogger's path. Lifting my head to inhale the scent of freshly cut grass, I tried to shrug off some of the resentment and worry that had descended over me like a dense fog that morning. Disillusionment with my daily routine tainted my view of Paris, if I let it. But I knew, deep down, that the city was not to blame: it was only guilty by association.

The Buttes Chaumont is my favourite park in Paris by far. Unlike the formal gardens of the Tuileries or the Jardins du Luxembourg, there are no manicured box hedges or signs beseeching visitors to refrain from walking on 'forbidden' patches of lawn; none of those sandy paths that I so detest which dust your shoes with a coating of white, floury powder.

Landscaped on the site of a disused quarry and rubbish dump, the sloping ground below our feet was a honeycomb, riddled with holes. A plaque in the nearby *métro* station cheerfully recalled an incident many decades ago when a mature tree had been swallowed whole by the park overnight, and I often wondered whether history wouldn't repeat itself one day, the ground engulfing a uniformed park keeper before my very eyes.

Although it looks more natural than many of its rather sterile, over-groomed peers, everything about the Buttes Chaumont is artificial. The lake, the waterfall which feeds into it, the caves with their stalactites, all are manmade. Fences, which at first glance seem to be fashioned from knotty branches, are actually sculpted in *trompe-l'œil* concrete.

Sometimes I felt as though I were walking across a film set made to look like a park, although if that were the case, the costume designers would have a lot to answer for. The uniform of the average Buttes Chaumont jogger could be a truly disturbing thing to behold.

Aside from the distant drone of traffic and the chorus of early morning birdsong, the park was peaceful. Creatures of habit, we slipped into our morning ritual: Tadpole pointed, I described. A spider's web glistened with morning dew on the wrought-iron park railings and, although its architect was nowhere to be seen, I launched into a current favourite, 'Incy Wincy Spider', while Tadpole mimed the actions with her fingers.

'Incy Wincy spider climbing up the spout . . .'

I was distracted by the sight of a jogger in figure-hugging Lycra shorts, 'spout' clearly visible as he bobbed past, and my song died in my throat. Tadpole froze, fingers aloft, waiting for the signal to make the rain fall down. Stifling a snigger, I resumed my song and reprised it not once but three more times as we passed the meandering stream, the boarded-up tearooms and the suspension bridge leading to the rocky island in the middle of the lake. Given my daughter's appetite for repetition, I didn't need a vast repertoire of nursery rhymes.

Exiting by the main gate, we crossed the rue Manin in front of the *mairie* – where, in happier times, I'd dreamed Mr Frog and I would be married one day – and turned into the side street leading to the childminder's flat.

In contrast to our own home, most of the *assistantes maternelles* I'd interviewed just after Tadpole was born lived in social housing, low-rent, state-owned apartments in tower blocks dating from the seventies which were often shabby but had the advantage of being spacious enough for several children to romp in. Our childminder was no exception and, as her children had now grown up and left home, she had two spare bedrooms in which her charges took their naps. To reach her building, I first had to circumnavigate the rubbish strewn across the driveway – a broken pushchair, the shell of a TV set – and there was a lingering odour of stale urine as we approached the entrance hall. The tenants might not show a great deal of respect for their environment, but they seemed to know one another well, and took the time to stop and chat. Everyone I came across greeted me with a polite '*Bonjour Madame!*' and today two teenaged boys gallantly held the doors open to let us pass. In stark contrast, the apartment building Mr Frog and I called home had all the warmth of a mortuary. One old dear generally spoke to me when our paths crossed but, as her memory was failing, we never got beyond her '*Comme il est beau votre petit garçon*' and my defensive 'Actually, *she*'s a girl.'

'*Tata*' was one of Tadpole's first words although, at first, admittedly, the sound was almost indistinguishable from '*Papa*'. French childminders always seemed to go by this name, a childish rendition of 'auntie'. *Tata* was a middle-aged Algerian lady with grey-brown curls falling to her shoulders, and her authoritative but caring demeanour had so impressed Mr Frog and me at our first meeting that we had quite literally begged her to work for us, Mr Frog conducting a gentle but persistent charm offensive by telephone until she caved in. Good childminders are a scarce commodity in Paris. They hold all the cards, hand-picking their charges.

A cloud of vegetable steam escaped into the hallway as *Tata* opened the front door, fogging my glasses and rendering me momentarily blind.

'*Bonjour! Comment va mon petit ange?*' she cooed, scooping a giggling Tadpole out of the pushchair for a hug, delighted, as always, to be reunited after a weekend apart.

'*Nous avons passé un très bon weekend,*' I replied, groaning inwardly as I noticed that in my haste I'd managed to dress Tadpole in non-matching socks. '*Elle a été adorable. Et vous,*

vous allez bien?' It was a loaded question, as ever. My greatest fear was always that *Tata* would get sick, and I'd have to use up all my holiday leave to care for Tadpole. Luckily, our childminder seemed to be invincible: so far she hadn't missed a single day's work.

'Any luck with the apartment hunting?' *Tata* enquired. *Her* greatest fear, now that she had grown so very attached to Tadpole, was that we would find a place to buy in a different neighbourhood and no longer require her services.

'No, another visit, but no good. A shame, because it was just around the corner. Anyway, I'm running late, I suppose I'd best be off . . .'

As the lift doors slid closed, a tiny hand waved from the other side of the glass pane, causing my heart to somersault in my ribcage. The cabin, and my spirits, plummeted: my favourite part of the day was officially over. I looked at my watch. 8.43 a.m. If a train pulled into the station as I arrived, I might just make it to the office on time. By 'on time' I meant 9.05, my current personal best.

Arms weightless and oddly redundant without the push-chair, I hurried along avenue de Laumière, pausing to snatch a free magazine from the rack in front of the estate agent's. Seeing there was no queue in the baker's shop, I darted in to fetch a *pain aux raisins*. At this rate, the remaining kilos I still hadn't quite managed to shift since Tadpole's birth would never leave me, but it was Monday morning, and I was in need of a high-cholesterol morale boost.

My violet *Navigo* pass made its satisfying 'drrriiinngg' as I swept my handbag across the scanner inside Laumière station. '*Je peux passer avec vous?*' muttered a man's voice behind me and I recoiled as I felt a stranger pressing up against my rear – far too close for comfort – as I reluctantly allowed him to pass through the metal turnstile with me, without paying.

Taking the stairs down to the platform two at a time, I prayed the first train wouldn't be crammed full, imploring the god of the RATP to spare me delays on *ligne* 5. As luck would have it, a sparsely populated train pulled into the station right on cue and I dived in, making a beeline for a fold-down *strapontin* seat by the door. Holding my breakfast away from my work clothes – its twisted paper wrapping already translucent in places as butter bled through – I scrutinized the small ads. Any new two-bedroom flats on the market? Apparently not. Of the five or six properties listed, we had seen three, and rejected two others on the grounds that they were on the wrong side of the Canal de l'Ourcq, out of range of the park. My eyes drifted across the page to the longer list of one-bedroom apartments, and I made a rapid set of calculations to see what I might be able to afford, just supposing I were to buy something on my own.

'If I'm going to live like a single mother, caring for our daughter and for this home on my own, even though *I* work too, then I might as well *be* a single mother,' I'd barked at Mr Frog in a heated moment, the previous week. 'At least that way I'd have one less person to take care of.' We'd had one of those arguments which started with me rebuking him for not washing up – or something ridiculously trivial like that – but escalated into a rant about every single thing that was wrong with our lives, according to me. Mr Frog took my protests with a pinch of salt, as he always did, filing them under 'hormones' or 'empty threats' and withdrawing into himself, refusing to argue back. It was intended as an empty threat, of course; an unexpected, brutal bolt out of the blue, calculated to provoke a reaction. He and I both knew my bark was worse than my bite: however fed up I was, I couldn't really imagine taking such a leap.

Whether Mr Frog took my outbursts seriously or not, my

discontent was nonetheless very real. Just how and when had my life in Paris turned from wine to vinegar, I wondered, oblivious to the throng of poker-faced commuters hemming me in. I was supposed to be living my dream, wasn't I? On the surface, all the ingredients for happiness were present: my Frenchman, our beautiful half-French daughter, our lovely home, our well-paid jobs. And yet I couldn't help feeling deeply disappointed with our day-to-day reality. As the years had passed by we had melted into the background, Mr Frog and I, focusing first on our jobs, then on Tadpole; welcome distractions from the uncomfortable truth that our feelings for each other had dimmed. And as if this wasn't enough, my dream Paris had also melted away, dissolving before my very eyes, replaced by a leaden routine of *métro-Tata*-work-*Tata*-sleep. Lately I'd become a bitter, resentful shadow of the breathless, enthusiastic *petite anglaise* I once was; a person I was far from sure I even liked.

At Gare du Nord, where commuters from the northern suburbs, fresh from the RER, elbowed their way inside, I released my folding seat with a reluctant clatter and pulled myself upright. Through the windowpane, opaque with grime, I gazed into dusky tunnels.

In my mind's eye I could see myself running alongside the train. Out of breath, not quite as fast as I used to be, but there, all the same.

4. Online

The clocking-in machine read 09.06 as I swiped my plastic card, its loud beep sounding uncannily like a reprimand. I hurried along the grey-carpeted corridor, past the portrait of QE2 wearing her blue sash – the embodiment of the quintessential Englishness of the small accountancy firm where I'd worked for the past two years – and up the stairs to the fifth floor. Our office straddled two levels of an imposing building on avenue de l'Opéra, a chic address halfway between the old opera house and the Louvre.

The two floors couldn't have been more different, mirroring the diametrically opposed styles of the managers who presided over them. My boss, whose fiefdom was on the upper floor, had opted for an open-plan layout, his own office separated from the shop floor by a glass pane. From my desk I often watched silent films play out inside, divining my boss's mood from his gesticulations, the colour of his cheeks and the cowed posture of whoever had been summoned inside. A balding Englishman in his early forties, he was technically brilliant but also incredibly demanding. The fact that only a window separated us left me feeling exposed: if he raised his head, my monitor was clearly visible from his desk.

The lower floor, in contrast, was divided into a series of smaller offices. George, the firm's other Paris partner, held court in the grandest of these, sitting behind an immense varnished desk that would have done a cabinet minister proud.

My first stop, once I reached the top of the stairs, was the communal kitchen. I wasn't much use to anyone without my second or third fix of caffeine so, as there was no sign of my boss yet, I planned to fetch a double espresso and enjoy a leisurely breakfast at my desk with an online newspaper open on my screen. I flicked on the photocopier as I passed, then the lights, which stuttered as they warmed up, as reluctant to be spurred into action as I was. Hanging my coat in the cupboard, I slipped into the kitchen and set my mug under the coffee machine, which whirred loudly, setting my teeth on edge, as it began to grind espresso beans. Monday morning tended to be a slow starter. The majority of the professional staff, who worked flexi-time, were unlikely to surface much before ten.

The metallic in-tray suspended above my desk was reassuringly empty, so once I'd skimmed through the contents of my boss's inbox I was free to browse the day's headlines with a clear conscience. My hand remained immobile on the mouse for a moment as I felt the familiar vibrations of the *métro* passing, making the foundations of the building shudder. Then, as I scrolled down the screen, an article about an internet diarist with a French pseudonym caught my attention.

Belle de Jour, I read, was a high-class call girl who had won awards for her writing. Some people believed she really was who she claimed to be, citing her insider knowledge of the oldest profession, but sceptics were convinced she was an aspiring author using salacious subject matter to snag a lucrative publishing deal. The very existence of 'blogs' – as these diaries were apparently called – had escaped me until that day, even though I considered myself internet-savvy. I was fascinated – both by Belle and by the blogging phenomenon. That day, whenever my boss strayed a safe distance from his desk and there were no dictations to type or phone calls to answer, I surreptitiously hopped from blog to blog. Call

Centre Confidential reminded me of an episode of *The Office* – a different register from Belle, but so dry and witty that some of the entries had me snorting coffee down my nose. Little Red Boat was whimsical, meandering and utterly hilarious and, after reading a handful of posts, along with the funny comments left by readers, I was hooked.

Anyone could create their own little outpost on the internet in a matter of clicks, according to the 'how to' articles I found. Maybe *I* could start a blog, I thought to myself. I'm often trapped in front of a computer screen with nothing much else to do. It might be fun. Why ever not?

The idea slowly took hold until, finally, at a loose end while my boss was in a late-afternoon video-conference meeting, I decided to take the plunge. Gnawing on a biro – a filthy habit I've never been able to kick – I stared out of the window above my desk, deep in thought. I needed an angle. 'The secret diary of a secretary' sounded less than riveting and, more to the point, I didn't much like discussing my job with other people, as a rule. It was well paid, granted, even reasonably challenging, due to the bilingual nature of my work, but I still cringed every time I was called upon to say what I did for a living. I was ashamed of it, when all was said and done. Somewhere along the line I couldn't help feeling I had squandered my potential, sacrificed any hope of having a career, as opposed to a job, to the greater goal of living in France. The logical thing to do, I decided, was to focus on where I lived instead, the sole aspect of my life of which people tended to be jealous; to write a 'fish out of water' account of life in Paris.

All I needed now was a title. I liked the idea of writing under a *nom de plume*, not because I had anything much to hide, but because it seemed to be an unwritten rule of the game. The name '*petite anglaise*' popped into my head immediately, along with an explanatory subtitle 'the diary of an English thirtysomething in Paris'.

Creating a blog was astonishingly simple: in a few short, sharp clicks I signed up for an account, named my blog and chose a rudimentary template. Seconds later, my alter ego was born. All that remained now was to dream up something to actually write about.

It would be a harmless hobby, I thought to myself; my *jardin secret*; my virtual playground. Little did I know I had just unleashed a force which, within less than a year, would turn my life, and the lives of those dearest to me, inside out.

'Have you ever heard of Belle de Jour?' I asked Amy a few days later, easing the filling back into my overstuffed sandwich with a teaspoon. I got on well enough with most people from the office, but as I'd had little social life to speak of since Tadpole was born, there were few colleagues I saw outside work. Amy, a fragile-looking brunette with a porcelain complexion, was the exception: we'd become friendly when she qualified as an accountant and moved up to the top floor, and we'd fallen into the habit of eating lunch together in the office kitchen.

We were seated on the stylish but singularly uncomfortable stools my boss had picked out when he refurbished the office, with our feast laid out on a smoked-glass table. I'd treated myself to an egg and bacon sandwich from Lina's, the closest thing to an English breakfast I was likely to find on the avenue de l'Opéra, although the egg was mashed with mayonnaise, and the bacon was in the form of crunchy little flakes, too small to be satisfying.

'*Belle de Jour* . . . Do you mean the film, with Catherine Deneuve?' Amy replied, frowning as I shook my head, my mouth full.

'No, it's the name of a blog as well,' I clarified, once I'd finished chewing. 'An internet diary thing. I was reading it the other day – it's addictive stuff, it really draws you in. There was an article about it in the *Guardian*.'

'Never heard of it . . . or of blogs for that matter,' Amy said. 'Although "blog" sounds like some sort of nasty disease to me . . .' Our conversation drifted away from my latest discovery, which didn't seem to interest Amy much, and on to more usual subjects: deconstructing the previous night's episode of *EastEnders*, moaning about work, comparing French boyfriend stories, or wishing we were outdoors catching a few rays instead of cooped up inside an air-conditioned office so chilly that a cardigan had to be worn at all times. Good, I thought, I'm not the only one around here who didn't know what a blog was. Keeping my new hobby a secret shouldn't pose too much of a problem.

I wrote my first entry a couple of days later, off work with a suffocating summer cold. I called it 'Calpol and Suppositories' and, though it was hardly a masterpiece, I managed both to be scathing about the French medical profession's tendency to prescribe pointless drugs for common ailments – many administered via the rectum – and to convey an unhealthy amount of disdain for my job. I read and re-read the four short paragraphs, took a deep breath, and clicked on 'publish'. I don't think a single person actually stumbled upon *petite anglaise* that day but seeing my sentences published online gave me a tiny thrill nonetheless.

I remember all the first times clearly. The first ever comment, on my ninth entry, a week later, in which I described seeing a cockroach scuttle into the recesses of the office coffee machine. ('That is nasty, and too much information,' said Cass, a faceless reader from America.) The first message I received on the *petite anglaise* email address set up for this purpose, was from a fellow blogger who called himself Tim. The first time another blogger added *petite anglaise* to their list of favourite reads.

A few weeks later, an email popped into my inbox informing me that the *Guardian* newsblog had elected to feature *petite anglaise* as Blog Pick of the Day. I navigated over to their site, nauseous with excitement, to read just exactly what had been said. It was short and sweet – 'a rather elegant new blog written by a woman who describes herself as a British thirtysomething in Paris' – but the brief mention brought readers in droves. That day I drifted around the office in a delighted daze, on my own private cloud. 'Rather elegant,' I repeated under my breath as I went to the kitchen to fetch a celebratory hot chocolate, smiling a secret smile. No longer 'just a secretary' or 'just a mother', I was now 'a blogger' too. *Petite anglaise* was a secret I hugged close, something to fortify me through mind-numbing hours of photocopying and typing, through long evenings trapped alone in the apartment while Mr Frog worked and Tadpole slept.

'I think it's great,' said Mr Frog that evening, wrestling with a particularly slippery piece of sushi while I sneaked the last of the moist pink flakes of ginger into my mouth. We were on a rare outing, to a Japanese restaurant in the shadow of the Saint Jean de Belleville church. Tadpole was staying with Mr Frog's parents – two whole hours away by train – while *Tata* holidayed with her family in Algeria. It was the first time we'd been separated for a whole week and, while I savoured the blissful calm and the opportunity to wrestle back some of my freedom, I also felt guilty for admitting, even to myself, that I was enjoying the break. 'I mean, you've only been writing this thing a month.' He reached for the missing ginger and frowned in puzzlement. 'And you've already had a thousand visitors. It's unbelievable. I'm sorry I don't get more chance to read it, but you know, things get so frantic at work . . .'

'It's okay. I know reading has never been your thing – especially in English.' That was something of an understatement. The most expensive piece of furniture in our apartment was a Habitat bookcase, stacked three layers deep with my paperback fiction. Mr Frog owned five, maybe six books, but to my knowledge had only actually read one of them.

I wasn't being entirely truthful, because I did mind, just a little. I'd found a hobby I loved; I'd created something of which I was beginning to feel justly proud. Was it too much to hope that he might share my enthusiasm; that he might care about what I was writing? Distracted, I dropped a piece of tuna into the soy sauce, and winced as brown droplets splattered all over my white T-shirt.

Petite anglaise wasn't really about me, at least not at first. For a month or two I filled the blog with what I hoped were witty, arch observations about life in Paris, describing how the local park keepers loved blowing their whistles, puffed up with their own self-importance, or lamenting the reluctance of the French to clean up after their canine friends. Mr Frog was first introduced in a post about how French women seem to be conditioned from an early age to accept adultery as a fact of married life, a subject prompted by a conversation with Amy about a surreal chat she'd once had with her boyfriend's stepmother. 'Mr Frog works late every night,' I wrote in my closing sentence, 'allegedly.'

His pseudonym wasn't particularly inspired, and coining it took only a moment's thought. But from there it was a small leap to begin referring to our daughter as Tadpole, and both names stuck. Slowly I began to flesh out my 'characters', describing amusing things they said or did, but I still stopped short of revealing much about myself, unwilling to open Pandora's box.

One day the following autumn I finally stuck a toe across the line, writing an entry which began with the words 'Mr Frog won't marry me . . .' I went on to list the pragmatic, unromantic arguments I had come up with in favour of tying the knot since Tadpole's birth, revolving around inheritances, pensions and house purchases, bemoaning the fact that my rational reasoning had left Mr Frog thoroughly unmoved.

'I just think it's depressing that all these scenarios are about providing for each other if one of us dies,' he'd said on more than one occasion. 'If I ever do get married – and I'm not sure I will ever want to – I'd like it to be for more positive reasons.'

I also admitted to feeling a twinge of jealousy whenever I was called upon to spell out my daughter's surname, which I did not share. There was nothing in the substance of what I wrote that I hadn't already discussed with Mr Frog a hundred times in private, but here I was suddenly inviting comments from strangers on our personal life. What on earth was I trying to achieve? Did I secretly hope to shame Mr Frog into popping the question? Did I think he would read the indignant comments left by my readers and suddenly see the error of his ways?

'If you go down on one knee and produce a ring and say "Please marry me because I can't live without you," would he say yes?' wondered Zinnia, a fellow blogger who'd become a regular commenter. 'Why don't you call his bluff?'

'We could always make him jealous?' suggested a commenter who called himself Watski, presumably in jest. 'How about it?'

'I hope you don't mind what I wrote today,' I said to Mr Frog when he arrived home that night, looking up warily from my computer screen where I was busy tweaking the new template I'd spent many a long evening designing in shades of dusky pink, cappuccino and chocolate. The banner picture across the top was a view from our balcony at sunset, on to which I'd superimposed the words *petite anglaise*. The letters were not quite evenly spaced, but I was childishly proud of my handiwork, all the same.

'Mind what? I haven't read it, I'm afraid. Work is so crazy at the moment.' He set down his keys and cigarettes with a clatter on top of the marble fireplace, and glanced at the screen over my shoulder. 'It's looking good though. It's really come along since I last looked.'

'I wrote about marriage today,' I said, my right hand gripping the mouse tightly, my left worrying away at the loose hem of my skirt. 'You know, about how we don't agree on whether it's necessary. It's a bit more personal than usual. Not that anyone actually knows who we are, of course . . .' The only people other than Mr Frog who knew about the blog were my parents: I hadn't been able to resist letting the cat out of the bag when my blog was mentioned in the newspaper.

'Oh, you go ahead and write whatever you want. It's your blog. I'm just glad you've found a hobby you enjoy,' said Mr Frog magnanimously, removing his suit and donning his pyjamas. He left the room in search of a late-night snack, and I heard the fridge door open, the hiss of a bottle of beer being opened. I returned to my tweaking, much relieved. Hadn't he pretty much given me *carte blanche* to do as I pleased?

Spurred on by Mr Frog's benevolent indifference and the supportive emails and comments I was receiving in ever-increasing numbers, I began pouring more of myself into *petite anglaise*. I found the experience unexpectedly cathartic, and this encouraged me to dig deeper inside myself, secure in the knowledge that no one actually knew who *petite anglaise* was. Unflinching honesty became my calling card. I documented my dissatisfaction with my job, the guilt I felt when I admitted that I had no desire to be a stay-at-home mum, and the feelings of jealousy which surfaced when Tadpole clamoured for her father, clearly her favourite parent. And when I sounded off about the long hours Mr Frog worked, or our dithering over whether or not to have another child, even my discontent with my relationship with Mr Frog occasionally escaped from its hiding place between the lines, however much I tried to hold myself in check. The blog was an outlet; writing a strangely liberating experience. Here was a way to process my thoughts and emotions; a safe place to get my frustrations out of my system without doing anyone any harm. My negative feelings often evaporated – albeit temporarily – as soon as I pressed 'publish'. It was easy to forget that every time I vented my spleen, my words appeared across thousands of computer screens in chocolate-brown font.

My online persona was wittier and sexier than I could ever hope to be. *Petite anglaise*'s words were scripted and edited, her every move choreographed, whereas in real life I often stumbled over my words, and my humour was as hit and miss as the next person's. My readers couldn't see whether my socks matched, or whether my highlights needed touching up, and they seemed to assume I was elegant and poised, as though some of the glamour they associated with Paris had rubbed off on me, too. I wasn't about to set anyone straight – I enjoyed projecting this new, improved version of myself; this person I longed to be. Being popular as *petite anglaise* online took some of the sting out of feeling so lonely and hollow, so taken for granted at home.

And, over time, it was as though *petite anglaise* really did begin to write a part of me back to life. The girl I used to be – who had reluctantly taken a back seat while I grappled with the realities of work and motherhood – grew stronger and more confident with every post. *Petite anglaise* leaped off the screen; she lived and breathed; she cast a shadow. Together we walked taller. The blog made me more attentive to my surroundings, gave my life added texture.

Mr Frog, although he readily admitted he was relieved I'd found a pastime which deflected my attention away from the long hours he was spending at work, seldom took the time to look through this virtual window on to my soul. If some of my entries were cries for help, pleas for attention or thinly veiled warnings, then they were futile, because no matter how many people read my words, no matter how many people commented on them, the one person they were intended for didn't appear to be paying attention.

'I teased Mr Frog the other day that I could be having a torrid extra-non-marital affair, writing about it in the public domain, and he would still be the last to know,' I wrote wryly in my comments box in December, six months after the blog's inception.

That evening I braced myself for an indignant reaction which never came. I don't believe Mr Frog ever read those words.

5. Contact

'Atishoo!' sneezed Tadpole as I held a spray of pale pink blossom under her nose for her to sniff. The petals were scattered by the blast; confetti drifted gently down to settle on her jeans. I felt perversely pleased that she had sneezed in English, rather than with a French '*Atchoum!*' France: *nul points*; *Angleterre*: *dix points*. Only the other day I'd lamented on my blog how thoroughly her father tongue had gained the upper hand since her most recent stay with Mr Frog's parents – or *Mamie* and *Papy* as she called them – so every syllable of English I could coax from her lips right now represented a small victory; music to my Anglo-Saxon ears.

It was March, and *petite anglaise* was now nine months old. Stripes of gentle sunlight filtering through the wooden shutters and the insistent cooing of pigeons had woken me earlier than usual that morning and, filled with spring optimism, I had slipped on my new, powder-blue mac, the fruit of a hasty lunch-time shopping expedition, for its inaugural outing. I'd fallen in love with its racy apple-green lining, regardless of the fact that it was invisible to everyone but me.

'Knees 'n toes?' pleaded Tadpole, referring to her new favourite song. Her second birthday was looming, and her speech had advanced in leaps and bounds since I first started writing about her on the blog. I often thought to myself how glad I would be one day that I'd documented her progress, preserving snippets of our conversations for posterity.

'Hmm,' I said, casting about for alternative entertainment, 'it's a bit tricky to do the actions to "knees and toes" while

I'm pushing your buggy . . . How about we count instead?'

We had been practising numbers over the past few days: counting toys in the bath, apples in the fruit bowl, fingers and toes. At first, Tadpole only smiled while I did all the work, although I knew she was recording everything, her eyes following every movement of my lips. Then, sure enough, one day when I was listening with half an ear, she counted all the way to ten unaided. The only sticking point seemed to be the number four, which she always said twice, for good measure.

'One,' I began, pointing out a parked car, its bonnet grazing the back bumper of the van in front in typically Parisian, too-close-for-comfort parking style.

'*Toe*, *free*, four . . .' continued Tadpole, pointing in a vaguely similar direction. 'Four, five, six, sefen . . .' She paused, running out of steam. There was no shortage of cars to count: scarred, nicked and splattered with the evidence of pigeons roosting overhead.

'After seven comes eight,' I prompted.

'*Ett* . . . nine, TEN!' Tadpole cried triumphantly. Bringing the pushchair to an abrupt halt, I leaned over, brought my upside-down head level with hers, and touched my lips to the tip of her nose.

As I raised myself upright again, I noticed Tadpole's finger still pointing at 'ten' and the truth finally dawned. While *I* had been counting promiscuously parked cars, my daughter had been diligently counting the dog messes of varying sizes and shapes which we swerved to avoid. Such were the joys of city living. At least I'd get a good blog post out of it, I thought, smiling to myself. Tadpole was arguably the most popular character on the blog these days, while Mr Frog was mostly conspicuous by his absence.

For a moment the dirty pavement faded from view as

I pictured a very different life: a ramshackle country cottage, an unkempt garden, a small family car. We'd recently toyed with the idea of a move to the countryside outside Lyons after Mr Frog spotted an interesting job opportunity in a trade magazine. I'd embraced the idea, surfing the web obsessively for house prices and secretarial work, getting ahead of myself as usual. Mr Frog's enthusiasm, on the other hand, had soon withered, and it wasn't long before he began back-pedalling.

'The thing is, if I accepted a job *en province*, I'd have to be prepared to shift my career down a gear,' he explained, taking a seat on the bed by my side, next to my desk, the night before. 'And I don't think I'm ready for that. Not for a few years, at least . . .'

'A few years?' I cried, turning from the computer screen to face him, tears of frustration prickling my eyes. 'Well, I really hope this *career* of yours turns out to be worth it. Because right now you're working all hours, and we don't seem to have an awful lot to show for it . . .' I looked back at my screen, which was filled with pictures of the bilingual school set in leafy parkland over which I'd been salivating for the past half-hour: mummy porn. 'You shouldn't have let me get my hopes up like that if you weren't serious. It wasn't fair!' I closed the window with an emphatic click of the mouse.

Mr Frog and I seemed to have reached an impasse: incapable of agreeing on whether to continue our long search for a flat, whether to try for another baby, whether to move away from the city. I kept pushing for change – any sort of change – pinning my hopes on the foolish, misguided notion that a new home or a new baby might be just what we needed, while Mr Frog dug in his heels, using his workload as an excuse to postpone any decisions. This charade was all very well, but I suspected we were both equally wary of further commitment. We shied away from saying so out loud, for fear of causing irreparable harm. Instead we stuck to our script – I pushed, he resisted – and we muddled on, uncomfortably, side by side.

Luckily, on this particular spring day I had other, more cheerful things on which to focus my mind. I had a lunch date. Today, I'd arranged to meet a fellow blogger in the flesh for the very first time. A virtual friend, an American girl who I knew only by her pseudonym, Coquette, was about to become a walking, talking, lunching person, as opposed to a collection of emails bounced back and forth. It was a blind date, of sorts, I supposed, something I hadn't experienced since I met Mr Frog eight years earlier, or Florence before him. And if I was honest with myself, I was wearing my new mac because I was dressing to impress.

That morning at work, as my fingers raced across the keyboard, my mind wandered, my mounting excitement tempered by twinges of shyness. 'Meeting someone who has previously been anonymous lends itself to an "I preferred the book to the movie" scenario,' Coquette had admitted in her last email, although she only had good things to say about the other bloggers she'd got to know since arriving in Paris. Was I worried I'd disappoint in real life; that I'd be less interesting than *petite anglaise*? Or could it be the fact that Coquette was in her early twenties, in the first flush of her romance with Paris, and I was afraid of seeming old and jaded in comparison, my Paris-weariness thrown into sharper relief by her boundless optimism? My foot jabbed at the pedal under my desk, spooling the tape back to the beginning. It was no good: my concentration was shot to pieces.

'Do you fancy grabbing some lunch and taking it to the Tuileries today, to catch some sun?' said Amy, appearing suddenly at my elbow. I plucked the headset from my ears and turned to face her, flustered, casting around for an alibi. Amy knew nothing about *petite anglaise*, and I was reluctant to admit that I was meeting someone I'd only spoken to on the internet. It had taken me months to get used to the idea of meeting strangers from cyberspace. How on earth could I expect her to understand?

'Actually, um, I'm meeting an old friend – from home – who's over for a couple of days with her job,' I replied, not quite meeting her eyes. 'I haven't seen her in years. She's taking me out to lunch on her expenses, otherwise I'd invite you along . . .'

'Oh, right.' Amy's face fell. 'Well, don't worry about me. I'm sure you have a lot to catch up on. I've got a book. I'll be fine on my own.' Things had come to a sticky end with Amy's long-term French boyfriend recently and she'd taken it hard. The weight had dropped off her already narrow frame, and the skin around her eyes looked bruised, as though she'd been crying in the toilets again. I'd invited Amy over for dinner a few times, and she'd even got to know Tadpole, who loved having visitors. Amy had become the closest thing to a best friend I'd had in years, and I hated lying to her. I was tempted, for a moment, to come clean and tell her about *petite anglaise*. But if I didn't get a move on I'd be late. I would tell her, I decided, but for now my revelation would have to wait.

Coquette and I had arranged to meet at La Ferme on the rue Saint Roch, an organic café where the sandwiches were admittedly overpriced, but much more innovative than the baguettes with cheese, or ham, or ham *with* cheese on offer pretty much everywhere else. As I drew closer – ears filled with the mournful sound of the emergency sirens which are tested without fail at noon on the first Wednesday of every month – I had to make a conscious effort to unclench my jaw and relax the quotation mark creases forming between my eyebrows. Rounding the corner and adjusting my course to avoid the queue snaking across the pavement from a nearby cashpoint, I spotted Coquette straight away, recognizing her auburn curls from a photo she'd posted on her blog. There were no photos of me on *petite anglaise*, but apparently the description I'd given her – long blonde hair and distinctive, dark-rimmed glasses – was enough.

'So you're *petite*!' she shrieked, as we both cracked open nervous smiles. 'You're not as, well, *petite* as I expected.'

'You can call me Catherine, if you want,' I mumbled, bemused to hear the name '*petite*' spoken aloud.

'And I'm Elisabeth,' Coquette replied. 'But you'll have to forgive me if I slip up and call you *petite*. I've gotten so used to that name; it won't be easy to reprogram my brain . . .' We kissed the air by one another's cheeks, awkwardly, as expats always do, and stepped inside the café. I was relieved to note that Elisabeth looked just as anxious as I felt, which was somewhat at odds with the confident voice Coquette adopted on her blog. Hastily I chose a quiche and salad, my fingers trembling as I fumbled for my purse. We scoured the room for a quiet nook with comfortable armchairs where we could talk as we ate.

'Isn't this weird?' I said, conscious that I was already shedding my accent, mimicking Elisabeth's American vowels and intonation. I've always been something of a linguistic chameleon: unconsciously adopting the speech patterns of the person I'm with. My French accent is almost pitch-perfect as a result, but I worry sometimes that people I imitate might entertain the suspicion that I could be mocking them.

'I suppose it is, but weird in a good way,' Elisabeth replied, pouring vinaigrette over her *mâche* and Roquefort salad. 'I feel like I know you already. I've been reading about you for months now, and my whole family read your blog, back in the States.'

'Well, do stop me if I start telling you something you've already read about . . .' I quipped, aware that of my stock anecdotes, many had already been used up before we even met. Would we still find things to say, or would lunch be punctuated by awkward silences? But in her next breath Elisabeth dispelled my fears. 'There are so many things I'm burning to ask you,' she said. 'Our blogs skim the surface, but there's a lot we hold back, or just hint at . . .'

Dispensing in one stroke with small talk, we dived straight into honest, searching questions, exclaiming over the common ground we quickly uncovered, laying the foundations for friendship. It felt natural: I'd known Elisabeth for only a matter of minutes but Coquette since long before we met.

'Of course, I don't talk about personal stuff in the way you do,' Elisabeth said thoughtfully, setting her fork to one side, having just finished demolishing a slice of cheesecake with a gusto that set her apart from the French girls around us savouring cigarettes with their espressos. 'I often wonder how your Mr Frog feels about what *you* write . . .'

'Well, not that he reads it very often, as far as I know,' I said cautiously, 'but my theory is that he sees the blog as somewhere I can let off steam, anonymously, without causing any real harm . . . He likes the fact that it keeps me busy, too, because I probably give him less stick about working late these days.' I paused, wondering whether I was speaking the truth, or just trying to convince myself. Mr Frog was a man of few words: how he really felt was anyone's guess. 'And yes, I do write personal things, but I hold plenty back too. I make the final cut. I decide what to show, and what not to show. All people really get are brief glimpses into our lives.

They pretty much join the dots themselves, and somehow seem to wind up feeling like they actually know the real me.'

'So, is the real *me* anything like you expected?' Elisabeth quizzed me as we parted. My lunch hour had flashed by in a blur; I couldn't remember the last time meeting someone new had been such fun. 'Do you think the voice on the blog fits my face?'

'Yes and no,' I replied evasively, struggling to remember whether I'd had any preconceived ideas of how she would talk or behave. If anything, I was relieved to find out just how normal she was. Coquette was articulate, witty, opinionated . . . but, in person, Elisabeth tripped over her words from time to time, or fiddled nervously with her hair. She was, in short, reassuringly human. I didn't quite dare ask how I measured up, but sneaking a peek at her blog later that day, I was delighted to read that she had described meeting *petite* as 'awesome'.

My confidence duly boosted, I signed myself up for a Parisian bloggers' *soirée* taking place later that month and persuaded Elisabeth to do the same. The time was ripe to drag myself out from behind my monitor and let *petite anglaise* kickstart my social life.

'I really, really need you to get home from work early next Tuesday.' I plonked down a tray of cheese and *charcuterie*, a pot of *cornichons* and a *demi-baguette* on the coffee table by the sofa where Mr Frog lay. The Paris skyline twinkled behind him, an orange haze of light pollution blotting out the stars which should have been visible above the rooftops. Kneeling by the table, I poured myself a glass of Bordeaux, waving the bottle at him questioningly. Mr Frog shook his head, easing himself into a sitting position, ready to eat.

'Remind me why again?' He took up a knife and began

paring thin slices from the block of Comté, arranging them across his bread.

'But I told you the other night.' I set down my glass sharply. 'Don't you ever listen to a word I say?'

'You never stop talking,' Mr Frog shot back, indignantly. 'How on earth am I supposed to remember it all?' I blame my parents for my verbal dysentery. They dangled me from the top of an Irish castle as a teenager so I could kiss the Blarney stone. In the evenings, when Mr Frog got home from work, I was invariably desperate for adult conversation, with a million things I wanted to share, many of them related to the blog. Unfortunately, his dearest wish was to unwind in peace, and more than once he'd begged me to be quiet, protesting that his 'head was too full'.

'Well, as I said last week,' I repeated, 'I've signed up for a Paris Bloggers' meet-up. *Paris blogue-t-il*, remember? It's all the way down in the fourteenth *arrondissement*, so it'll take ages to get there on the *métro*. I had hoped you could try and make it home by seven.' My wheedling tone made me cringe: I abhorred having to beg. Seven was hopelessly optimistic, but if I said that, there was an outside chance Mr Frog might just put in an appearance by eight, after which I could leap into a taxi and hopefully not arrive too late.

'Tuesday . . . I don't know, there's this meeting on Thursday to prepare for now, I'll have to see . . .' Mr Frog's sentence trailed off as he saw stormclouds gathering above my head.

'This is important to me,' I said, my tone now peevish. 'I haven't asked you to babysit since that mums' night out a month ago.' I didn't need to remind him how on that particular occasion he had arrived home so late I'd had to ask a friend to order my main course and arrived just as the pepper sauce was beginning to congeal on my steak.

'I've apologized for that. How many times are you going to throw it back in my face?'

'I'm sorry,' I said, feeling anything but apologetic, 'but I'm just fed up with feeling like I'm the one making all the sacrifices. If *you* want to see friends after work, all you have to do is jump on your Vespa and go. I've forgotten the meaning of the word spontaneous. I have to plan ahead, ask your permission and, even then, I can't be sure something won't come up at your office at the last minute and ruin my plans. And when I *do* go out, first I have to dash around getting myself ready in between the feeding, bathing and story-reading, and I'm so exhausted by the time I've finished, I'm in no fit state to be sociable . . .'

Mr Frog shrugged. He'd heard it all before. 'Look, I'm sorry,' he said quietly, not wishing to incense me further, 'but Tuesday is going to be tough. I'll have a better idea nearer the time . . .'

'Well, if I can't count on you, I suppose I'll have to call the babysitter,' I said, making it clear that it was the very last thing I'd wanted to do. 'She probably needs a new handbag.' Maryline, a student I'd recruited by pinning up an ad in the local *boulangerie*, always flounced into our apartment looking so impossibly glossy-haired that I felt frumpy in comparison. When we'd first met, she was never to be seen without her Dior handbag, a monstrosity with enormous dangling 'D's and a logo-print canvas. But last time we'd booked her, for one of our rare weekend outings to the cinema, she'd arrived brandishing a quilted white Chanel clutch in its place, which we had, no doubt, unwittingly co-financed. 'Of course, once I've paid her, plus a taxi there and back, it will be one hell of an expensive night . . .'

'I'll pay for the sitter and the taxis, *t'inquiètes pas*,' Mr Frog said wearily, seizing the opportunity to redeem himself and put an end to the conversation.

'Thanks,' I said grudgingly. 'I'll give her a call tomorrow. I hope, for your sake, that she's free.'

I withdrew to the bedroom, touched a random key and watched the computer screen flicker back to life. Hesitantly at first, I began writing a post about how frustrated our exchange had made me feel. 'Motherhood has clipped my wings,' I wrote, 'but fatherhood seems to have left Mr Frog's life essentially unaltered. Why are *liberté*, *égalité* and *fraternité* in such short supply when it comes to the business of raising a child together? Sometimes I feel as though Paris is constricting around me, as if the walls of my apartment are slowly closing in. Is it any wonder I long to crawl through my computer screen and escape along the information superhighway once my daughter is tucked up in bed?'

It was the first time I'd turned to writing while my emotions were still so fresh that I could almost taste the bitterness on my lips, and it was all I could do to staunch the flow of words which welled up, my fingers racing over the keys, finding it difficult to keep pace. Writing them was exhilarating, but when the river finally ran dry and the mouse hovered above 'publish', I had a sudden change of heart and pressed 'delete' instead. My inner censor had spoken: it would be too easy to write things, in the heat of the moment, which could never be unwritten. I was wary of overstepping an invisible line: the next thing I knew I'd be sharing feelings with my readers that I dared not voice aloud, even to my partner.

Turning off the computer, I undressed and turned out the light. By the time Mr Frog eased himself into bed beside me, I would be fast asleep, as usual. We might share an apartment, but often it felt as though we lived in different time zones.

6. Persona

'C'est un poisson, ça!'

Tadpole held up a bath toy, an orange plastic fish which could be used to squirt water, although thankfully she had not mastered the deployment of fish as weapon quite yet.

'Yes, my love, it's a fish.' I leaned towards the fogged-up bathroom mirror to apply mascara, a delicate operation for a near-sighted person at the best of times. I'd just had a hasty wash in Tadpole's bathwater – to her delight, she loved co-bathing – and was now putting the finishing touches to my make-up, although I had yet to pick out the clothes I would wear, despite the fact that Maryline was due any minute. The evening, so far, had been something of a struggle. Tadpole had daubed dinner all over her face, then hurled her dessert bowl on to the floor the moment I chose to leave the room to start her bath running, splattering the parquet and walls liberally with apple *compôte*. Once I'd sponged everything clean, I'd gathered up her protesting, squirming body and forcibly undressed her, plonking her unceremoniously into the bathwater where she had howled for a full five minutes until I joined her.

Looking at her now, calmly playing with her toys, her face framed by damp corkscrew curls, you'd never suspect her of such devilry. My hasty make-up job finished, I threw on a pair of trousers and a sleeveless top – both in forgiving, slimming black – then scooped Tadpole out of the water and cradled her in my arms, covering her warm skin with kisses. There was something so delicious, so edible about her. It

63

never ceased to amaze me that my daughter could exert such a physical power over me. All she had to do was snuggle up, or turn her smile on full beam and I was utterly disarmed, her tantrums forgotten.

When the doorbell rang, I didn't bother peering through the peephole: a familiar, cloying scent of perfume preceded Maryline, as always. '*Bonsoir!*' I said, trying to sound welcoming and friendly, when really I was cursing her lateness under my breath. Few things are more frustrating than running around like a headless chicken to get ready on time, then having to wait. '*Vous allez bien?*' It felt odd using the polite '*vous*' with a babysitter more than ten years my junior, but she intimidated me, so '*vous*' it was.

'*Bien, merci.*' Maryline stepped inside, towering over me in her heels, her face powdered and painted with far more skill than my own.

'*Merci d'être venue, en tout cas . . .*' My taxi would be clocking up extra euros in waiting time downstairs, but it would be indecent just to hand over Tadpole and run. A couple of minutes of insincere small talk were *de rigueur* first. But pyjama-clad Tadpole was so excited to see 'Ma-Leen' that she took her by the hand and began clamouring for a bedtime story before the poor girl even had a chance to take off her jacket. Seizing my opportunity to make a quick getaway, I hugged Tadpole, brushed my lips across her damp, shampoo-scented hair and slid my feet into my shoes. Secretly, I hoped my daughter wouldn't give Maryline too easy a time of it. Let the designer babysitter earn her handbag money, for once.

'Her daddy will be home before me,' I called over my shoulder, as I snatched my mac from its hook and slid my arms into the sleeves. 'Mobile numbers are on the notepad by the phone, as usual, and you can help yourself to drinks and biscuits . . . *Faites comme chez vous.*'

Employing Maryline took me back to my own babysitting days as a teenager in the Yorkshire village where I did most of my growing up. The internet was an unknown quantity then, but I surfed the bookshelf instead, foraging for forbidden titles. A well-thumbed paperback by Dr Alex Comfort here, some D. H. Lawrence there: most of my sex education probably came from other people's bookshelves. Given my own track record, I'd rather not imagine what Maryline got up to when I wasn't home. The computer was switched on, and I doubted she really was using it to do her homework. I suppose it wasn't inconceivable that she might have a blog of her own . . .

My *Taxi Bleu* was parked across the corner of rue Pradier and had clocked up ten euros on the meter before I'd even given my name and slipped inside. The driver, who smelled strongly of perspiration and cigarettes, wasn't chatty, which suited me fine. One of those interchangeable French women who sing Céline Dion-style ballads was warbling on the stereo and, fastening my seatbelt, I let the music wash over me, the knots in my stomach unravelling a little.

I wanted to savour the delicious taste of freedom, as unfamiliar as the lip gloss on my mouth, but the fact remained that, with the exception of Elisabeth/Coquette, the taxi was speeding towards a roomful of strangers. A hundred or more people had signed up for the event, and the idea of battling through the crowds to find my friend was intimidating, to say the least.

What would the evening hold in store, I wondered, fiddling nervously with the ring on the middle finger of my left hand. Given my readership was mostly made up of Brits and Americans, would anyone present at this very French gathering have a clue who *petite anglaise* was? Maybe not, in which case I wouldn't have to worry about fulfilling any preconceived notions people might have of how I should look or behave. But if they did, what then? Should I be myself, or try to be more like *petite*? I suspected I'd need a stiff drink – or two – on arrival to give me the confidence and poise which my alter ego seemed to have in spadefuls.

Our Paris by Night tour was scenic: the taxi plunged into an underground road tunnel north of Les Halles, one of those twisting, turning, high-speed shortcuts which always remind me of Diana and Dodi, then surfaced, suddenly, by the Samaritaine department store, pausing at the traffic lights, the Pont Neuf and its kissing alcoves stretching across the river ahead of us.

My eyes drank in the view: the series of floodlit bridges visible in both directions, the spires of Notre Dame to my left, the riverbanks lined with majestic buildings as far as the eye could see. The necklace of lights which illuminated them was duplicated; reflected in the murky darkness of the river. A *bateau-mouche* passed under the bridge below us, unseen, its presence betrayed by the whooping of teenaged tourists, delighting in the sound of their own echoes.

I've always found Paris to be at her most beguiling at dusk, her imperfections masked by shadows, her ageing beauty shown to its best advantage in the soft halo of flatteringly placed lights. My pulse quickening, I felt a sudden surge of affection for my home, this city I rarely had the leisure to appreciate.

When had I last crossed the river to the Left Bank, I wondered? A year ago? Two? Could it be that I hadn't crossed the Seine since Tadpole was born? Where once I'd seen Paris through a wide-angle lens, delighting in every detail, boasting that I had covered almost every street on foot, my City of Light was now reduced to a series of stock Polaroids: office, apartment, park, *métro*. Anything beyond a pushchair radius of my home, or a lunch-time dash of my office, was basically off limits, no longer existing in my everyday, circumscribed world. Paris had shrunk to fit my new lifestyle: it was possible to live here, and yet, at the same time, to miss her terribly.

My destination was almost as far from where I lived as it is possible to be in Paris without leaving the city limits, and the journey took twenty minutes or more. Following the rue de Rennes as far as the Montparnasse tower, the taxi left the main thoroughfare and tore through a network of smaller streets, deep into the fourteenth *arrondissement*, before pulling up, finally, in front of l'Entrepôt, near Pernety. The venue looked as though it must have once been a warehouse, as the name suggested and, according to the vertical red banners which hung above the entrance, it was now home to a cinema and a restaurant as well as a bar. I paid my taxi fare, slamming the car door closed more violently than I'd intended in my nervousness, and hesitated for a moment on the pavement outside, peering through the glass doors to the dimly lit, smoky main room inside. It was crowded – I was late, after all – but at first glance it was impossible to see whether Elisabeth was already there. I would have called, if it wasn't for the fact I'd read on her blog the previous day that she'd lost her phone. As it was, there was nothing for it but to steel myself and plunge inside.

Standing by the entrance, allowing my eyes a few seconds to adjust to the semi-darkness, I scanned the room, in vain. The space was vast, but there were few tables, so most of the people assembled – and there were at least a hundred, maybe more – were standing between me and the bar. Some were in tightly knit groups, and clearly knew one another; others stood alone, or in pairs, looking shy. Most seemed to be French, and the overwhelming majority were male. Jeans and black T-shirts seemed to be their unofficial uniform.

I was about to head for the bar when I spied a table which had been set up to the left of the entrance. A couple of guys – the organizers at a guess – were consulting some sort of list and passing out name stickers. I sidled over and mumbled an almost inaudible '*bonsoir*' to the most approachable-looking of the two, who was tall, with curly black hair and dark-framed glasses not unlike my own.

'*Bonsoir. C'est quoi le nom de ton blog?*'

'*Petite anglaise*,' I said hesitantly. 'You probably don't know it, it's in English . . .'

'*Ah, c'est toi la petite anglaise?*' he exclaimed, apparently very pleased to make my acquaintance. I shifted my weight from one foot to the other, tongue-tied. 'Guys,' he said, beckoning to a couple of friends hovering nearby with beer glasses in their hands, 'meet *petite anglaise*!' My surprised hand was shaken with energetic enthusiasm. 'My name's Nathan,' he added, 'and of course I know about your blog. When you mentioned this meet-up the other day, hundreds of people followed your link to our website to check it out. Your audience figures are staggering!' Nathan was grateful; but there was more to it than that. With a sudden rush of pride, I saw that he seemed to regard me as some sort of minor celebrity.

'Oh, um, thank you.' I blushed, uncomfortable under the gaze of several pairs of eyes, yet to master the art of accepting a compliment gracefully. 'I don't suppose you can tell from that list whether Coquette has arrived yet?' I stuck the proffered name sticker on to my T-shirt. There would be no hiding from my alter ego now. 'I'm supposed to be meeting her. She's the only person I actually know . . .'

'Oh yes, she's definitely here too. It's difficult to miss the girls tonight, they seem to be in the minority,' Nathan joked. 'Last time I saw her, she was at the bar.' That didn't narrow things down much, I thought to myself wryly, given that the bar was at least ten metres long. Promising to return for a chat later in the evening, I made my way laboriously through the crowds. Elisabeth, when I spied her at last, was deep in conversation with a tall, bearded guy at the far end. She had her back to me, and he saw me approaching before she did.

'So who's looking after Tadpole this evening?' he enquired, as though we'd known each other for years. I looked at him blankly for a moment, until he gestured at my name badge by way of explanation. At the mention of Tadpole, Elisabeth had spun round. 'Ah, there you are!' she said, relief clearly etched on her face. 'Am I glad to see you! Now, this is Mathieu,' she added, once she'd recovered her manners. 'He reads us both, leaves comments from time to time.'

'Okaay . . .' I said, recovering from my initial shock, and tendering my cheeks for the obligatory *bises*. 'Hi Mathieu. Pleased to meet you . . . I have a babysitter tonight. Mr Frog, er, my partner, you know, well, he's working late tonight.' Saying the words 'Mr Frog' out loud felt very odd indeed, but it didn't seem fair to reveal his real name to complete strangers either. Especially not strangers who didn't even know *my* name. But Mathieu didn't press for any more information, and I began to relax, accepting his offer of a drink. He was with a friend, Stephan, who lost no time in telling me that he didn't read my blog on principle because it had a pink background.

'It's not pink!' I said sharply. 'Not Barbie-doll pink, anyway. It's dirty pink with shades of cappuccino and whipped cream. I picked those colours to set off the sunset image across the top . . .'

'I was only joking,' said Stephan with a smile, 'no need to get all defensive. I can see you feel quite strongly about this blog of yours.'

'I suppose I must,' I said slowly, realizing as I spoke how deeply I did care. 'It sounds silly, but it felt a bit like you just insulted what I was wearing or something.'

By the end of the night I was swaying cheerfully and talking to anyone who would listen. I'd lost count of the number of drinks I'd put away, and also of the number of strangers I'd spoken to who already knew many obscure details of my life.

Once I'd shrugged off the eerie sensation that people knew me, or *petite* – or at least thought they did – it was exhilarating to find myself in such diverse company. When I saw work friends, we tended to discuss the office; when I went for dinner with fellow mothers, we talked about children, or stretch marks, or moaned about how our partners didn't pull their weight. All I had in common with the people assembled tonight was some form of internet presence. For once, I wasn't playing the role of secretary, mother or girlfriend. Normal rules had been suspended for the evening, and I felt reborn, reinvented. With a few drinks inside me, I did feel confident, witty, elegant. Tonight I really felt as though I were *petite anglaise*. Assuming her identity had been a lot easier than I'd thought.

'*Maryline, mais tu es toujours là?*' I exclaimed, looking from my watch to her face, and back to my watch again. It was 3 a.m. when the taxi finally deposited me back home, my head spinning from an ill-advised mixture of beer and wine, and I had fully expected to find Mr Frog gently snoring and Maryline long gone, save the lingering scent of her perfume. Trying to rearrange my features into some semblance of sobriety, I apologized, far too profusely, and realized, mid-apology, that I'd slipped from '*vous*' into an overfamiliar '*tu*'. I didn't even have enough cash on me to pay her; I'd given every last euro in my possession to the taxi driver. Mr Frog was supposed to be taking care of that, and it hadn't occurred to me that he would work *this* late. 'Would you mind taking a cheque, just this once,' I said anxiously, 'or shall I pop down to the cashpoint while you wait here for five more minutes?'

'*Ça ne m'arrange pas vraiment, mais bon, juste pour cette fois,*' Maryline said grudgingly. I scrabbled in my bag for my chequebook and wrote with exaggerated care, rounding up the figure to compensate her for the 'inconvenience'. Without so much as a nod of thanks, Maryline gathered up her handbag and coat and turned on her heel. Once the door had closed behind her, I kicked off my shoes and inched Tadpole's bedroom door open. Praying the hinges wouldn't whine, I stole inside to spy on my daughter in her sleep. A favourite rag doll nestled in the crook of her elbow, and she lay on her tummy, one leg cocked, the other straight, mimicking my own favourite sleeping position. Her nose was congested, and she made a snuffling sound as she breathed deeply. Bending closer, I discerned movement behind her eyelids and I wondered whether she was dreaming about her day, hoping she wasn't remembering the moments when I'd lashed out with impatient, angry words.

I padded through to my own bedroom, discarding my clothes in an untidy pile on the floor, and snapped the bedside light off. The room rolled and tilted as though it were at sea, which did not bode well for the morning, and my hair smelled like it had passively smoked its way through an entire packet of cigarettes. I hadn't seen the answering machine flashing, and wouldn't hear Mr Frog's tired excuses until the next morning. But as I slipped into a deep, dreamless sleep, a contented smile on my face, it didn't even occur to me to feel angry.

7. Half-life

'OK, *petite*, I know you didn't ask for this,' the email began, 'but where would you go with the following? Happily married for eleven years (at least I thought so – never take anything for granted). Two delightful daughters, dream farmhouse in Breton countryside. Wife announces she's leaving you. So far so normal, if a bombshell. Wife announces she and your best friend are together. Nothing "Our Tune" didn't cover. Accidentally find solace with distraught wife of (now ex-) best friend. Develop intense relationship. Spend three years of wildly contrasting highs and lows, before finally splitting up. Remain great friends as she goes back to boyfriend from before her marriage; present (along with baby's father) at birth of ex-girlfriend's daughter. Firm friends with both her and boyfriend. Take stock of what the hell happened!'

It wasn't unusual for me to strike up a correspondence with someone who left comments for *petite anglaise*. Sometimes I instigated contact when I felt like responding privately to a commenter, but more often than not a stranger would email out of the blue using the *petite anglaise* address I provided on the blog. A post I had written might strike a chord and move a reader to tell me their own story, in confidence. The more I divulged of my life, the more other people seemed to feel compelled to reciprocate.

I already had a soft spot for this particular reader, James, an English guy who had left forty or fifty intelligent, erudite comments over a period of several months as Jim in Rennes.

He'd made the transition from comments to email one day by asking me the quickest way to get from Montparnasse station to Charles de Gaulle airport, which was innocuous enough. Then, a few weeks later, he'd made a cheeky request, asking me to namedrop his friend's band in exchange for a ticket to see them play in Paris. I'd never done anything like that before, and it felt a bit like selling out, but I cast my reservations aside and decided to do what he asked. James would be in town with a few friends to see the same concert the following month, so it would be an opportunity to meet him. But this email, which popped into my inbox a few days later, marked a turning point in our budding virtual friendship. For the first time we had stepped beyond banter. Suddenly, for whatever reason, he had decided to open up his life to me.

Little snippets of that email, and of those which followed, lodged stubbornly in my head, and I re-read his words several times over the next few days, looking forward to meeting their author. He had lived through drama; he spoke of hard-won emotions and overpowering desire. His words thrilled me, but also unsettled me. When I delved into my own past, any moments of intensity or 'wildly contrasting highs and lows' I managed to excavate and dust down were so remote, they seemed to have happened to someone else. My relationship with Yann, my first French boyfriend, came closest. It had been passionate but short-lived, eroded by jealousy, torn to shreds by bitter rows. But that had all ended a decade ago: it was ancient history.

Mr Frog and I seemed tame in comparison. Ours had been a quiet storm. Things had just felt right from the moment we met. We fitted, like my favourite, most comfortable flat shoes. We made each other laugh. He listened – so well that everyone who knew him confided in him eventually – and understood me better than anyone I'd known before. I remember lying on his lumpy futon the night we became more than friends. It was our third, maybe fourth meeting. Portishead played quietly in the background, and Mr Frog wore a silky-soft velour top which had become so threadbare over the years that it had to be relegated to the back of the cupboard, although he still refused to throw it away.

Our first night together was gentle: I don't remember sparks, but I do remember feeling at peace, as though I'd known him half my lifetime. There were few dramatic peaks and troughs in our relationship, and I had convinced myself over the years that, far from being a bad thing, this was our unique strength, the reason we would go the distance, while other, more volatile relationships were doomed to fail.

But James's messages had sown the seeds of doubt. What tantalizing possibilities lay beyond my comfort zone? Could there, should there be more to life than this? Had Mr Frog and I grown too complacent, flatlining through our lives? James summed up the way he felt in a way that made me wonder whether I might have settled for less than I deserved. 'Would I turn back the clock?' he wrote. 'No. Don't think I would. Monochrome contentment or Technicolor roller-coaster? No contest, is it?'

My relationship suddenly reminded me of Mr Frog's velour top: faded, washed out, but occasionally comforting; languishing, half-forgotten at the back of the cupboard.

Bound for work a few mornings later, music from my new iPod setting my life to a dramatic soundtrack only I could hear, I leaped up from my seat just as the warning siren sounded, signalling that the doors were about to close. If I had come to my senses a few moments later I would have missed my stop. As it was, my escape route was barred by a young couple, locked in a passionate embrace. She was arty-looking – maybe *Beaux-Arts* – with dark, silky tresses of hair piled faux-carelessly on her head and secured with a pencil. He was clad in jeans and a blazer, his face obscured by an overgrown fringe. Something about his stance, his hair, reminded me of a former boyfriend from my university days. Positioned squarely in front of the doors, eyes closed, love's young dream seemed oblivious to the commuters around them.

I coughed to make my presence known, and when they moved aside as one, faces still pressed together, I lunged out on to the platform just before the doors slid closed. Later, describing the episode on my blog, I dwelled on the feeling of wistfulness the episode had left with me, lamenting the fact that I couldn't remember the last time I'd felt so wrapped up in someone that I saw only him, caring not a jot what onlookers might think. I ached with nostalgia for a younger, more responsive me, who seemed to feel things more intensely. Was this kind of passion impossible in a relationship that had lasted eight years, or could things be different? I composed the entry during the first half of my lunch break and called it 'Half-life', after the song I'd been listening to on my iPod at the time. It read like a coded response to James's emails, although I only admitted this to myself much later.

'I've been trying unsuccessfully for at least an hour to express how this post makes me feel,' Jim in Rennes commented later that day, quick off the mark as usual. 'It's a bittersweet thing and no mistake.'

A week before the concert, Joanne, a fellow Brit I'd met a couple of times with a Tadpole a few days older than my own, sent me an intriguing email, which I opened at work. 'In my capacity of internet cross-referencer and Sherlock Holmes,' she wrote, 'have I solved another whodunnit? Is

Expatica's Date of the Week none other than *petite anglaise*'s faithful Jim in Rennes?'

In my haste to click on the link she provided, eager to take a look for myself, I narrowly missed knocking over my plastic cup of lukewarm coffee and accidentally baptizing my keyboard. It certainly looked as though my friend – and just what was *she* doing looking at a dating site anyway? – had been right. The profile matched the information I had: age, marital status, profession. And there were photos. Three photos. I enlarged the first, aware that my palm, cupping the mouse, was clammy.

The face which stared back at me was that of a man who looked as if he had lived more than me: haunted by his past, yet defiant, determined. The lighting was stark and unforgiving; he'd made no concessions to vanity. His eyes, a deep shade of blue, contemplated the camera with steady gravity, his mouth unsmiling. A shadow of stubble across his cheeks and chin made him appear rough around the edges, which I liked. He had broad shoulders, and looked muscular but lean. My gaze kept returning to his eyes though, irresistibly drawn to them, wondering what he had been thinking when the picture was taken; wondering who had taken it.

'You were right!' I replied to Joanne once I had recovered my composure. 'It *is* him, I'm sure of it! We're going to see a band together next week when he's in Paris. Just as friends, of course. He even invited Mr Frog, although I never had any intention of taking him along and, anyway, he'll be babysitting, for once. I don't know why, but I have the strangest feeling that it's a date now, as though I'm being unfaithful to Mr Frog just by looking at these pictures . . .'

'Well,' shot back Joanne, 'some might say Mr Frog could do with a bit of competition. Shake things up a bit. Teach him how to appreciate you more.'

'He knows I'm going to the concert,' I replied hastily. 'And he knows I'm going with a male reader, too, so there's no subterfuge. He seemed mildly surprised that I was going to see a band he'd never heard of, but that was about the extent of his reaction. Mind you, I wasn't entirely honest: I did imply that James might be bringing a girlfriend . . . And I'm almost certain that he isn't.'

I heard my boss's footfalls on the stairs and quickly cut our conversation short, executing a deft ALT+TAB just in the nick of time. But when Tadpole was safely tucked up in bed that evening, I couldn't resist looking at the photographs again. Joanne's words, however carelessly chosen, echoed in my head. '*Petite anglaise*'s faithful Jim . . .'

On the night of the concert, I auditioned almost every item in my wardrobe. I wanted to look attractive, but casual. It wasn't a date, but it *was* a night out, and I liked to have the opportunity to make an effort, or so I told myself, a touch defensively. I agonized over lenses versus glasses; hair up or down; shoes, or my favourite Tiger trainers.

Standing back to survey the results in the mirror, I took a long, critical look at myself. I'd twisted my hair into an approximation of a chignon, which thinned my face and left my long neck exposed, and allowed a few tendrils to escape, so that the overall effect was soft, rather than severe. My make-up I'd applied with caution, mindful that these days foundation had a tendency to highlight flaws rather than hide them, collecting in the laughter lines around my mouth, or the tiny crinkles which fanned out from the edges of my eyes. Dressed in jeans and a favourite tailored jacket over a scoop-neck T-shirt in a sheer beige fabric, I felt sexy, but hopefully it didn't look like I was trying too hard.

Grabbing my bag and keys, I took one last look at myself,

sighed, and plunged down the stairs, too impatient to wait for the lift. Mr Frog would soon be home with Tadpole, and although I'd made no secret of where I was going, or with whom, I wasn't sure why, but I had no desire to cross his path on my way out.

8. Crossroads

Striding along avenue Simon Bolivar I made a swift set of calculations. My destination could be reached far more quickly on foot than by *métro*, I decided, as I'd have to change from line 11 to line 2. My route led me downhill, at first, and as I made my way along the rue de Belleville, pulse racing, I marvelled, as always, at the unexpected view of the Eiffel Tower in the distance.

At the bottom of the hill I hurried along boulevard de Belleville, where several continents rubbed up against one another in the space of a few hundred metres. At first the signs were written in Mandarin, with French translations underneath. I passed Chinese restaurants, supermarkets, hairdressing salons and bazaars selling cheap plastic tat. But walking briskly in the direction of Couronnes, glancing at my watch impatiently at regular intervals, these quickly gave way to Tunisian restaurants serving tajines and couscous, *épiceries orientales* with window displays of fragrant, sticky pyramids of dates and figs, and bakeries selling Jewish breads and pastries. The air was filled with a Babel-like chatter: it seemed as though I could hear every language but French.

I hadn't eaten – there had been no time, and even if there had been, nerves had chased away my appetite – but nonetheless my stomach gave an involuntary growl as I smelled kebab meat grilling slowly on a spit, glistening with fat. Further on, the scent was overtaken by a dozen roasting chickens in a metal *rôtissoire* outside a halal butcher's, their skins crisped and browned to perfection.

The streets were littered and dirty, hosed down less frequently than those in the *beaux quartiers* and no doubt treated with less respect by the residents. Unwanted items lay abandoned on street corners: the carcass of a slatted bed, several of its ribs broken, a stained mattress with protruding springs, a cheap sofa without its cushions. But I felt more at ease here than I ever would in one of the chic but sterile neighbourhoods in the Western *arrondissements*. I liked my Paris worn and grimy. Rough and ragged. Working class. Teeming with life.

Drawing level with the McDonald's on the corner of rue Oberkampf, I ground to a halt for a moment, pulling out my phone and a wrinkled piece of notepaper with trembling fingers. Opposite was Ménilmontant *métro* station, where pockets of people loitered, waiting for friends, before they hit the bars of rue Oberkampf. This was 'bobo' territory, home to the expensively dishevelled, where dressing down was an art form.

A car screeched to a standstill in front of me and, when I looked up, startled, the man in the passenger seat, his teeth astonishingly white against the mocha brown of his skin, shouted something at me through his open window. His words were drowned out by the impatient horn of the car behind, but his gesture was abundantly clear. Did I want to go for a ride? I shook my head and smiled, remembering the description on Expatica of James's ideal date: 'a girl with dazzling wit, a romantic heart, a keen sense of irony, and *looks to stop traffic*.'

James's phone rang and rang, but just as I was beginning to despair, I heard an unfamiliar voice over a loud backing track of music and chatter. 'Hello? Catherine? Where are you? We'll be going through to the back in a minute, I think.'

I liked the sound of his voice: self-assured, warm and

unmistakably English, although his accent wasn't strong enough to be identifiable. The image which had slowly ripened in my head, built first on words, then fleshed out with photographs, now had sound: I was discovering James gradually, from the inside out. How had he known it was me? A lucky guess? Or had he already programmed my number into his phone? And, if so, did the name on the display read 'Catherine', or '*petite*'?

'Hi,' I said, my voice sounding far calmer than I actually felt. 'I'm about two minutes away. Can you wait a bit longer? I'd rather meet you in the bar first. It can be pretty dark and smoky once you go through into the concert venue out the back. Not to mention loud.'

'We'll wait, no problem.'

'See you in a minute, then. Watch out for me, okay? I hate walking into places like that on my own . . .'

I strode along the road, and the sound of my heart pounding in my ears was louder than my footfalls on the pavement. The Café Charbon, which now had a concert venue called the Nouveau Casino tacked on to the back, where the band would be playing, wasn't exactly where I'd expected it to be, and I stopped and fretted for a moment. Surely it wasn't this far along the road? Could I have overshot it in my haste? Copycat bars had sprung up all along this stretch of rue Oberkampf, which didn't help, and I was more accustomed to arriving from Parmentier, at the other end of the street, as I had on the night of my first meeting with Mr Frog. But a few steps further I caught sight of a familiar claret-red awning ahead.

Self-conscious, I stalled in front of the shop next door, inspecting my face, mussing up my hair. My breaths came fast and shallow. I was poised to step out of my blog and into James's life, and it was time to face facts, to be honest with myself. This wasn't anything like my lunch with Coquette, or the bloggers' *soirée*, where all I'd hoped for was to make some new friends. This thing with James was different. For the past few weeks I had been entertaining the faintest glimmer of possibility that something might happen between us, if I liked him as much in the real world as I had warmed to him online. Was it just a harmless fantasy? A way of testing what was left of my feelings for Mr Frog; exploring my own boundaries? Or was there more to it than that? There was only one way to find out. I took a deep, ragged breath and brought my weight to bear on the heavy door.

The round, wooden table, second from the window, where Mr Frog and I had met eight years before, still occupied exactly the same spot. A couple in their twenties slouched on the chairs where we once sat, drinking wine and playing footsie under the table. I watched them for a second, my head filled with ghosts. We had left an imprint on this place that only I could see: an echo of Sarah, a younger me and Mr Frog, who had been standing where I stood now when I first looked up and made eye contact. With a shy smile he had approached our table, kissed us both on the cheek – did I imagine it, or did he linger on mine? – then hung his duffle coat on the back of his chair, where it trailed on the floor, almost tripping up our hipster waitress when she arrived with the next round of drinks.

But tonight was not supposed to be about nostalgia, so I tugged myself back into the here and now and wove purpose-fully through the crowds lining the long, copper-coloured bar. Straining to hear English spoken, I let my ears be my guide. The group of people at the far end, by the waiters' station, sounded promising. A broad-shouldered man stood with his back to me, and when the willowy blonde he was deep in conversation with caught sight of my hesitant approach she put a hand on his arm, smiling and saying something I could not hear.

James was tall – much taller than I expected – and his hair was shorter than on the pictures I had seen, but I felt sure it was him. He wore indigo jeans, a brown corduroy jacket, cut as though it were denim, and I caught a faint but pleasant hint of aftershave. When he turned to meet my questioning gaze with grave blue eyes and a cautious half-smile, I knew I had found him. He was every bit as attractive as the photographs had led me to believe, and as our eyes met, the air between us seemed to crackle. I stopped in my tracks, petrified, like a deer caught in the headlights of a car.

'You . . . Your hair is shorter than in the picture,' I blurted out, once I'd found my tongue, immediately regretting my clumsy words, wishing I could press 'stop' and 'rewind' then start again. In one short sentence I'd managed to refer to his dating profile and imply I'd spent hours poring over it. But James brushed aside my comment with a grin and took command of the situation.

'*Petite anglaise*. Catherine. I'm so glad you could make it – it's lovely finally to meet the girl behind the blog. Now, first things first, can I get you a drink?' After introducing me briefly to his friends – band members and their entourage whose names I instantly forgot – we broke away from the crowd to take up an ordering position at the bar. James dug deep into his jeans pocket and removed a handful of coins. 'What's your poison?'

'Oh, a beer would be great,' I said thankfully, 'it'll take the edge off my nerves. I find meeting strangers a whole lot easier with a drink in my hand.' I was trying to cover my tracks, to make him think my nervousness had nothing to do with him, and everything to do with the context in which we found ourselves.

'It's funny,' James said slowly, 'but I don't really feel like I *am* meeting a stranger tonight, not after everything I've read. It's only your face which isn't familiar.' I dipped my head, unable to bear the weight of his stare. I wanted desperately to know whether I lived up to whatever he'd imagined. But once the barman had taken our order, James shifted down a gear, back to small talk. 'Cool bar this. Amazing frescoes on the walls.'

'Frescoes?' I looked up to where he was pointing, high up on the wall opposite the bar. Above the immense mirrors and the oversized Anglepoise lamps which zigzagged out from the walls to overhang the tables, there were indeed frescoes. Painted men in top hats courted women with crinolines under their full skirts. 'Do you know,' I exclaimed incredulously, 'I don't think I've ever noticed those before! And I must have been here a dozen times or more . . .'

We talked about his drive to Paris, my day at work, and the band we were about to see, and I studiously avoided all mention of Mr Frog. While my mouth opened and closed mechanically, my body savoured the long-forgotten feeling of being physically drawn to someone. It was as if all my senses were amplified: the beer tasted crisper and colder on my tongue, and when the sleeve of James's corduroy jacket brushed my forearm, it gave me goosebumps, the tiny blonde hairs on my forearms standing to attention, straining to close the distance between us. I had no idea whether my excitement was reciprocated, but it was thrilling enough just then to be faced with concrete proof that I still had some capacity to feel so powerfully attracted to someone. This emotion had been lying dormant all along, bubbling unseen beneath the surface, ready to erupt when the time was ripe.

Drinks in hand, we drifted through to the Nouveau Casino, its entrance approximately where the Turkish toilet used to be. The room – a rectangular, warehouse-like space with a stage, a second bar and a mezzanine level accessible via a narrow spiral staircase – was slowly filling up. Eve, the blonde from earlier, was already standing near the right-hand wall, not far from the stage, and we weaved through the crowd to take up a position by her side. I put my glass to my lips, but was surprised to find it almost empty. In my nervousness, I'd polished off my drink too quickly. Draining the dregs of her own beer, Eve suggested we head back to the bar to fetch another round while James saved our spot. I nodded, and held out my hand to take James's glass, my fingers grazing his. As we walked away, my hand tingling, I wondered whether I was only imagining his eyes following me, burning into the back of my head.

'He was very excited about meeting you,' said Eve, confidentially, while we waited to be served, immediately establishing herself as an ally, whereas any new French female acquaintance would most likely have held herself aloof, eyeing me suspiciously until she had assessed whether or not I posed some sort of threat. 'It's funny this internet stuff, getting to know people back to front, writing to someone before you've even met. I don't think I could do it . . .'

'I suppose it is odd,' I agreed, 'but so far I've only met nice people, no one weird. And I felt sure me and James would get on. You just know sometimes, I think.'

She smiled slyly, and something told me she knew more than she was letting on. Had James said something about meeting me beforehand? I was burning to ask, but held myself in check, not wanting to sound like a fawning teenager.

'James tells me you have a daughter too?' said Eve, changing the subject. 'About the same age as mine?' Eve's daughter, Maisy, it transpired, was just a few months younger than Tadpole. We made mummy small talk for a few minutes, although all the while I longed to steer the conversation back on to the subject of James. But before I could do so, the lights were dimmed and the band slouched onstage to enthusiastic cheering. We took this as our cue to grab our drinks and hurry back to base camp.

The band was a trio from Manchester fronted by John, Eve's boyfriend. As Eve and I slotted ourselves back into position alongside James, the opening bars of an acoustic song hung delicately in the air. When John began softly to sing, his words described loving a woman, despite her many flaws, amazed by the strength of her feelings for him. I glanced at Eve, feeling like an eavesdropper listening in on a private conversation. She caught me looking, guessing my thoughts, and leaned closer.

'These songs are all right, but the old ones, about other girls before me, they're really hard to listen to,' she hollered in my ear. James shot us a questioning glance – wondering if he was the subject of our conversation? – and our eyes locked with such force that I almost flinched. Turning back to the stage, I was glad of the dry ice billowing out, mingling with the smoke from a hundred cigarettes. In the semi-darkness my flushed cheeks would escape undetected.

A few drinks later, the concert over, we moved back through into the bar, where I sat alone with James in a booth upholstered in worn brown leather. Eve and John were saying their goodbyes a few feet away at the bar: the band would shortly be heading off to Germany in their tour bus. I wondered aloud about how tough it must be for them both to spend so much time apart, Eve raising Maisy alone, while John spent weeks away on the road.

'It can be hard, of course,' James agreed, catching Eve's eye over John's shoulder and flashing her a smile. 'I see quite a lot of her and Maisy, she gets pretty lonely. But she knew what she was getting herself into when she went back to him. They're pretty solid these days. You can see just by looking at them how crazy they are about each other . . .'

The penny suddenly dropped. 'She's the one you wrote about, isn't she? The woman you were with after your wife left?'

'Yes,' James admitted, 'she is. I didn't want to tell you until you'd had a chance to meet her and form your own opinion. It's all ancient history now, but she's still a good friend.'

I nodded, remembering her hand on his arm when I arrived, trying to stifle a twinge of jealousy. I found myself staring at James's hands, which were resting on the table in front of me, long-fingered, elegant yet strong-looking. How would it feel if he were to cup my cheek in his palm, or run a finger lightly along my thigh? Maybe some hint of the longing I felt showed in my face, because it was that moment James chose to say the words that caused my world to tilt sideways.

'I've been trying to keep myself in check all evening, out of decency, out of respect for the fact that you're in a relationship,' he said in a strangled voice, as if every word cost him dearly, 'but I'm sorry, I can't *not* say this, I just can't.' I looked up from his hands, which had curled into fists, and my breath snagged in my throat.

'Go on,' I half whispered, wishing I had drunk less. I needed clarity. I wanted to commit this moment to memory, so I could play the footage back over and over again. Tuning out the music, the crowds of chattering people who surrounded us, I heard only his voice.

'Ever since I started reading *petite anglaise*, I've felt drawn to the girl who wrote it,' he confessed, selecting his words with apparent care. 'I was seeing a French girl for a while, but my heart just wasn't in it. I couldn't get *you* out of my head. Even though you were in Paris, and with someone. And even though I had no idea what you actually looked like . . .' He gave a short, nervous laugh, acknowledging how far-fetched all this must sound, but I said nothing, willing him to go on. 'And then you walked into the bar tonight,' he continued, 'and – well, this is going to sound corny, but to hell with that – any doubts I had just vanished when I saw you.' He stopped speaking and looked at me, questioningly, his monologue over, his words hanging in the air between us.

'I . . . I don't know what to say . . .' My brain struggled to process this new, unexpected information, and my eyes, unable to sustain his penetrating stare, fled, alighting on his hands once more. Had James really just said that he had started falling for *petite anglaise*, before we had even met? This was either utter madness, or the most romantic thing I'd ever heard. I hadn't been alone in secretly hoping there would be sparks when we met. Our email exchanges, innocent on the surface, suddenly began to look like an elaborate mating ritual, leading us slowly, inexorably to the dangerous place in which we now found ourselves. But the fact remained: he knew far more about me – or about *petite anglaise* – than I knew about him.

'Cat-reen?'

The bar suddenly snapped back into focus and I whipped round to identify the owner of the voice, cricking my neck with the sudden movement and grimacing with pain. Benoît, a close friend of Mr Frog's, was standing near the door, looking back as though he had been poised to leave when he caught sight of me across the room. How long had he been watching me? What had he seen? I'd told Mr Frog the truth about my whereabouts, even about the company I would be keeping, but I still felt as though Benoît had caught me red-handed, *en flagrant délit*. Rising to my feet, I smiled and gestured for him to come over, anxious to dispel any mis-understanding. 'I came to watch a band,' I explained, kissing him on both cheeks. 'I'm here with a few English friends . . .' I gestured at James, but also at the band members at the bar to emphasize that the two of us were not alone. Benoît nodded, his eyes flickering over James only for a moment.

'*Et est-ce que Monsieur travaille toujours autant?*' he said, enquiring after Mr Frog. 'I don't see him nearly as much as I'd like to these days.'

'You and me both,' I said, my voice tinged with a bitterness I was unable to conceal. 'You know how it is . . . But I'll let him know I ran into you. We should have you over for dinner some time.'

'*Avec grand plaisir*,' Benoît replied, kissing both my cheeks again, and taking his leave. As the door swung closed behind him, I fell back into my chair, kneading my neck with my fingertips.

'I'm sorry, I shouldn't have said what I did, and in a public place too,' James said ruefully. 'I've just made a complete idiot of myself, and I don't blame you if you're angry . . .'

'No, don't say that,' I said quickly. 'I'm not angry. I just got a bit of a shock, that's all. You really took me by surprise. I mean, what you said seemed to come out of nowhere, even if I hoped . . .' I left the sentence unfinished. What had I hoped for, exactly? Did I even know? 'But I am going to need some time to digest what you said . . . And I could have done without bumping into someone who knows my boyfriend, just then.'

'I'll go to the bar and give you some space.' James's eyes were still anxious. 'But please understand, the last thing I want to do is casually interfere with your life. Given my history, I find it hard to believe I'm even suggesting whatever it is I'm suggesting . . .'

'Maybe a soft drink would be a good idea?' I suggested as he stood up and began digging in his pockets once more for coins. 'We've both had a fair bit to drink, haven't we? It might be time to slow down.' It certainly couldn't hurt to keep what wits I still possessed about me. I closed my eyes for a moment, so I wouldn't be tempted to stare at the wisps of hair at the nape of James's retreating neck. I was exhilarated. Terrified. Thrilled that he wanted me as much as I now knew I wanted him. Panic-stricken at the thought of what could lie on the horizon.

For weeks his words had reeled me in, slowly but surely, and I had hoped, even fantasized that there would be a connection between us. But despite all that, nothing could have prepared me for the chemistry. The attraction had flared up the moment I saw him, and only intensified as the evening wore on. My whole body – from the tips of my toes to my hair follicles – was tense with anticipation; I was tightly coiled, ready to spring. The strength of those feelings unsettled me, and I sensed I was a hair's breadth away from caving in. How could I be expected to think calmly, rationally, when all my efforts were concentrated on simply keeping my body in check?

When I opened my eyes I found myself staring blankly at the wooden clock suspended from the ceiling, which must have ground to a halt years before, because there was no way it was 5 a.m. A glance at my watch revealed nonetheless that I'd missed the last *métro* by a good half-hour. How had it got so late?

James returned, bearing two glasses of Coke clinking with ice cubes, and I heard my voice saying that I should really go home, persuading him to walk me to the taxi rank. 'Of course. If that's what you want,' he said sadly, abandoning the untouched drinks and putting out a hand to help me to my feet.

'It was lovely to meet you both,' I said to Eve and John as we passed, 'but I'm going to call it a night now.' I saw a meaningful look pass between Eve and James and suddenly felt sure she'd known how he felt about me all along.

'Take care,' Eve said, kissing me on the cheek, 'and I hope we'll see you again some time . . .'

As we walked downhill towards the nearest busy junction I slipped an arm around James's waist, my hand creeping inside his T-shirt, his skin hot and smooth beneath my fingers. He shivered and looked at me questioningly. What could I say? I couldn't explain what I was doing or why. Receiving no reply, he rested his own arm gently around my shoulders.

At the corner of rue Oberkampf and avenue Parmentier we paused and he pulled me close. My hands inside his T-shirt gripped his back, and I clung to him as though I were drowning. Partly because I didn't want to let go, but also because I was using our proximity as a shield, pressing my face into his chest so that I could hide it from his.

'You're so lovely, there's something so vulnerable about you,' he said, his voice muffled by my hair. 'I want to protect you, look after you . . .'

'I have a feeling that's not all you'd like to do,' I replied, half jokingly, conscious of a telltale stiffening in his jeans.

'Can I kiss you?' He released me suddenly, tilting my chin upwards, forcing me to meet his eyes.

'No, I can't,' I protested. 'I'm too drunk, too confused . . .' My mouth was bone dry, my head spinning. I was suddenly afraid I'd forgotten how to kiss and be kissed.

Stepping back, I hailed a passing taxi and watched as it screeched to a halt on the opposite side of the road. For a few seconds I honestly didn't know whether I planned to clamber into it alone, or drag James inside with me. I didn't stop to ask myself whether James would go along with this, or how

I would justify my absence to Mr Frog the next day. These were mere details, wholly irrelevant: at that moment I was incapable of thinking beyond what *I* wanted.

The taxi driver sounded his horn, signalling his impatience, and I darted across the road. I tumbled into the back seat alone, pulling the door closed with a dull thud before I could possibly change my mind. Not like *this*, I remember thinking. Whatever this thing was between us, it could only be tainted and cheapened by a semi-drunken encounter on the night of our first meeting. As the car pulled away, I stared back at James's shadowy figure on the street corner, still standing where I'd left him, one hand raised in a silent wave. The thought that I might never see him again, that I might never know what it would feel like to be kissed by him, seemed unbearably cruel.

At the crossroads, I had been faced with a choice: two possible versions of my future mapped out ahead of me. But by jumping into the waiting taxi, I didn't feel like I had made any sort of decision. All I had done was run away, taking flight like a frightened child.

9. Guilt

I was in no state to work the next day, laid low by a potent cocktail of beer washed down with a guilt chaser. As Mr Frog crashed resentfully around the apartment, forfeiting his usual morning bath in order to feed Tadpole breakfast and ready her for the trip to *Tata*'s, I buried my treacherous face into the cool fabric of my pillowcase, praying that the bewildering mixture of terror and elation which had overwhelmed me from the moment I had awoken would be mistaken for nothing more than a common hangover.

When Mr Frog finally slammed the front door closed behind him and Tadpole, I tossed and turned for a few minutes, exhausted, but too wired to sleep. Before long, I was in front of my computer composing an email to James, letting some of the words which thrashed about in my head bleed out across the screen. I couldn't write them on my blog, but they needed an outlet.

'I have writer's block,' I wrote. 'The only things I want to write about are off limits. And today I just can't do frivolous. I have this horrible feeling that I am going to regret bundling myself into that taxi for the longest time. Anything has to be better than '"what if . . ."' Despite having behaved like a paragon of virtue, I felt like a monster when Tadpole stroked my cheek and pressed her face up close to mine this morning.'

Shortly after I pressed 'send', a text message arrived on my phone, announcing that James's car had broken down. He would be leaving it with a garage in Paris, then catching a train home to Rennes with Eve. His mobile-phone battery was dying. He was sorry, but he'd be incommunicado for many hours to come.

I paced the apartment in a state of nervous excitement, my body held hostage by adrenalin, although fight or flight were not solutions I could consider right now. My thoughts were splintered and incomplete, my hands twitched, my heartbeat was rapid and arrhythmic. It felt as though my whole body was locked on fast forward.

With nothing to do but wait, I re-read his emails, and my replies, and studied his photographs, over and over again. I ran through the conversations we'd had the previous night. Closing my eyes, I conjured up the smell of his aftershave, the feeling of his body pressed against mine, the warm smoothness of his back under my palm. I wrote a short post about the concert, leaving out all mention of meeting James, and focusing instead on my exchange with Eve about her being the subject of John's song.

James's reply didn't come until later, much later, when Tadpole was in bed, at long last. Seeming to sense my weakened state, she had exploited it relentlessly: every well-rehearsed gesture of our evening routine had become a bitter battle of wills. Her bath seemed to have a calming effect, however, and she snuggled up to me for her bedtime story, running gentle fingers through my hair. This show of affection was even harder to deal with. Tears welled up and I blinked them back, not wanting to alarm my little girl.

Willing James to get in touch felt like betraying Tadpole. This fire I seemed intent on playing with had the potential not just to sear Mr Frog, but to torch my daughter's world completely, reducing our family life to a heap of ash. By even contemplating such a thing I had become an impostor in our home; I was unfit to be her mother.

'I have enough things to say to you to last from here to the third Wednesday in October (give or take),' James wrote, late that night. 'But a lot of these are things you have to want to hear, and I need you to tell me that you do want to hear them . . . Regretting "what ifs . . ." is what they are all about. In this instance, there's a way of re-running time and seeing what if . . . But it needs a password to work. You are no monster. Life has a habit of making the easy desperately difficult, and the hardest choices so easy as to be no choice at all. You have asked yourself a question, that's all. Tell me what you're thinking.'

What was I thinking? Simply that it *couldn't* end here. All synapses led to James. If I could have dropped everything then and there and leaped on the next train bound for Brittany, I would have done. I needed to know whether this was infatuation, whether I was being swept away by James himself, or simply enticed by the idea of letting romance back into my life. James's car breaking down, sentencing him to an imminent return visit, felt unnervingly like fate. I would get my second chance: to re-run the scene from last night, to resist the urge to take flight, to explore 'what if . . .' And I knew that when I did, I would take it.

In the meantime, there was nothing I could do but go through the motions. And wait.

'There's something different about you today . . . I can't put my finger on quite what it is,' my boss remarked, standing over my desk with a pile of papers in his hand. I looked up at him, eyes narrowed, trying to gauge whether he meant good different, or bad different. I was a few kilos lighter already, thirty-six hours after meeting James. My cheeks were flushed, my whole body was burning up and my palms felt so damp that every so often I was obliged to wipe them discreetly on my trousers under cover of my desk. As for the quality of my work, my concentration span was hopelessly short. I kept starting one task, getting distracted midway through, beginning another, never finishing the first. Which of this array of symptoms had he noticed, I wondered?

'I think I may have a bit of a temperature, actually.' I hedged my bets, hoping to deflect any potential criticism by playing for sympathy. 'Not quite recovered from that, er, tummy bug I had yesterday. If you don't mind, I might just go and pop the kettle on. Would you like a cup of tea?'

'Yes, why not,' he replied, glancing at his watch. 'Ah, but first, would you mind setting up George's video-conference in the upstairs meeting room? We have no IT support today, and his secretary is out, so he'll be a bit lost . . .' On my blog, I called George 'Old School Boss'. A few years older than the partner I worked for, he belonged to a world of public schools and gentlemen's clubs and wasn't terribly comfortable with modern technology. The fact that he persisted in referring even to graduate secretaries as 'typists' summed him up pretty well, as far as I was concerned.

I made my way to the meeting room, heaved the monitor and webcam from the sideboard on to the table, taking care not to trip over the trailing wires, and dialled the extension of the IT desk in London using the speakerphone in the middle of the table. The equipment was fairly new, and I'd never set it up on my own before.

'Hi Pete, it's Catherine in Paris. Would you mind talking me through getting a video-conference link up and running? Everything seems to be plugged in and switched on, but my screen is blank.'

'Hang on a minute, I'll just pop through to the boardroom at this end, and we can test the connection,' Pete replied. I drummed my fingers on the table, itching to get back to my computer and see if there was anything new waiting in my inbox. 'Right,' he said, a couple of minutes later, sounding out of breath, 'let's get started. First of all, can you press the middle button on the front of the monitor, then find the remote control . . .'

I complied, and the screen shuddered into life. I could make out a balding man dressed in a T-shirt and jeans – presumably Pete – and a slice of boardroom. I'd never visited the London office, and I'd only ever spoken to Pete on the phone, so I studied both with genuine interest.

'I can see you all right,' I said, 'but can you see me?'

'No, I'm just getting a marble fireplace and a mirror, you'll have to adjust the webcam angle and focus it. If you press the split screen button on the remote, you'll be able to see what I can see too. That'll make it easier.'

I pointed the webcam vaguely in the direction of the chair where I imagined George would sit, tilted it downwards, then reached for the remote.

'That's more like it!' Pete exclaimed.

I looked at the screen, and gasped. I'd leaned forwards across the desk to make the adjustments, and the picture currently being broadcast to the London office was a shot of my cleavage. With a nervous giggle, I pulled myself upright and darted out of range of the camera. George arrived seconds later, and I was relieved he hadn't witnessed me making such a spectacle of myself.

I wrote about the episode on my blog later that day, elated at being handed such a juicy, blogworthy anecdote on a platter, and what was more, a safe subject, perfect for distracting me from agonizing over the rights and wrongs of my decision to see James again. The anecdote had such comic potential, such slapstick value, that I milked it for all it was worth, even if that did mean distorting the truth. Unrepentantly, I padded out what had really happened, adding some mild flirtation with the IT guy, George's presence in the room by my side throughout, and an audience of partners on the receiving end of my cleavage. My shoulders shook with silent laughter as I typed. I suspected my readers were going to like this one.

Once I'd finished, I fired off an email to James, letting him in on what had really happened, and exposing the liberties I'd seen fit to take in pursuit of the perfect blog post. He was no longer a faceless reader like all the others, and I wanted him to understand the difference between what *petite anglaise* wrote and the reality of my life, to grasp that a diary written for an audience cannot be entirely trustworthy. *Petite anglaise* might have brought James into my life, but reading my blog could be no substitute for actually knowing Catherine, the master puppeteer pulling the strings in the background, occasionally blurring the boundaries between reality and fiction.

A few days earlier that email would have been destined for Mr Frog, regardless of the fact that there was little chance he would have read the blog post in question. In a sense, with every text message, with every email James and I exchanged, I was silently transferring my loyalties elsewhere.

I was already being unfaithful to Mr Frog. Inside my head, where it counted the most.

10. Subterfuge

In all the years we'd lived together, I had never cheated on Mr Frog. The idea of sneaking around behind his back to plot a secret meeting with another man would have been inconceivable to me a few days earlier. And yet, suddenly, I seemed to be able to rationalize and justify the very behaviour I would have despised in another; telling myself that it would be wrong *not* to take things one step further, that I owed it to myself to explore 'what if . . .'

Not only had I never cheated, but I'd never been wooed – covertly or otherwise – in the electronic age. The rules of courtship had changed, and over the next two or three days I took a crash course in deception. My inbox was awash with James's messages, and I had to keep my wits about me, changing my password and signing out of email every time I left the computer unattended. My phone was set to silent mode, allowing a steady stream of incoming text messages to slip under the radar. I hadn't really had much use for my mobile before: it had hibernated at the bottom of my bag gathering dust, its battery flat, useless in an emergency. Now its memory was filled with staccato text messages: short, sharp and dripping with innuendo.

Just over a year earlier, when text exchanges between a famous footballer and his alleged mistress were splashed across the English tabloids, I had been torn between disgust and total incomprehension. Only now did I grasp the power of a few choice syllables, intimate words which could reach me any time, anywhere, and deliver an electrifying jolt. Wherever

I went, James's words followed. I felt a prickling at the nape of my neck and fought the urge to look over my shoulder. It was as though he were tracking my every move from an unseen vantage point. He was thinking about me, I was sure of it. I could feel the weight of his attention.

'You look a bit flustered, is everything all right?' said Amy, as I emerged from the ladies' toilets at work, my mobile phone clutched in my fist.

I'd been sitting on the floor, enjoying the smooth caress of the marble tiles against my bare legs, while I flirted with James. 'I woke up thinking about your eyes, your lips, your skin,' he'd written. 'I wish we could speak on the phone so I could hear your voice.' I'd closed my eyes, shivering as I imagined his hands inside my clothes, moving over my skin.

'I can't wait,' I replied. 'But phoning is too risky . . .' In the past forty-eight hours my texting speed had increased tenfold, although I still looked at my right thumb as I wrote. But when I re-read what I'd typed – or rather what the predictive text function had *decided* I must have intended to type – I cried out and dropped the phone as though scalded. 'But sinning is too risky,' it read. Hauling myself to my feet, my message unsent, I'd run straight into Amy, my cheeks ablaze.

'Oh! Yes . . . Bit stressed, you know, work stuff . . .' I gestured at the mug in her hand. 'I was about to fetch myself a cup of tea.'

'Kettle's just boiled,' she said. 'I think there's enough left in there for another cup. I've got to get back to work, otherwise I'll never get out of here tonight.'

There was a part of me that longed to tell Amy what was going on: it would be a profound relief to be able to unburden myself to someone other than James. But I was afraid she would burst my bubble or, worse still, succeed in talking me out of seeing him again. Only a week earlier she'd confided in me that she had reason to believe her ex-boyfriend had been unfaithful to her before they parted. She had railed about his dishonesty, condemned his use of subterfuge, and I had agreed with her wholeheartedly. If she knew what I was now plotting, I would be no better than he was, in her eyes. I decided I'd much rather deal with my guilt alone for now than risk disappointing my friend.

After work I tried to lose myself in the comfort of my routine with Tadpole – home, dinner, bath, stories, bed – functioning on autopilot if my mind wandered irresponsibly away from the task in hand. I refused to check my phone or email in my daughter's presence, but this just made me feel doubly guilty for willing the hours to go by quickly so that I could read James's words in peace, once she'd gone to bed. I was distracted, constantly on tenterhooks, and my patience was in dangerously short supply if, God forbid, Tadpole chose to do battle with me.

'*Non, pas fait caca dans la couche!*' Tadpole protested, wriggling free of my grasp and distancing herself from the plastic changing mat which lay on her bedroom floor. Her claim was patently untrue: my nostrils did not lie. I should have smiled, grabbed her by the midriff and tickled her into giggling submission, but instead I shouted harsh words and manoeuvred her roughly into position. Tadpole yelped with indignant surprise.

'You *have* done a poo and Mummy needs to change your nappy right now!' I bellowed.

My daughter looked at me oddly, as if she was trying to figure out who had taken possession of her mummy's body. I closed my eyes for a second and tried to get a grip on myself. I was an elastic band pulled taut. What would happen if I snapped? Would I raise a hand to her, leaving an angry red palm print on her milky thigh, or would I dissolve into hysterical tears? Even if I did manage to hold myself in check, Tadpole was so attuned to my moods, I felt sure she had already sensed that something was very wrong. The betrayal I was plotting hadn't even happened yet, but already she was suffering from the fall-out.

With Tadpole finally settled for the night, a swarm of guilty kisses scattered across her cheeks, I took evasive action, cowering behind my computer screen or soaking in long, scalding baths until the water cooled and the skin on my fingertips puckered. Mr Frog, once he got home, snoozed in front of the television, blithely oblivious to my turmoil. When proximity was unavoidable, eating dinner together or engaging in normal conversation taxed me to my very limits. It was all a sham, a mockery: I was a counterfeit girlfriend, going through the motions, my mind elsewhere, and I couldn't believe Mr Frog noticed nothing amiss. Was I really so invisible to him? Could he not feel the tension in every sinew of my body, my every movement a spasm? When guilt choked back the words in my throat, leaving me uncharacteristically quiet, did he think we were sharing a companionable silence?

As the weekend loomed, I was filled with dread. How would I manage to play happy families for two whole days – under the constant surveillance of Mr Frog and Tadpole – when my only desire was to curl up in a tight ball under the bedclothes, shut out the real world and lose myself in the scenes playing out across the inside of my eyelids?

'I really don't feel well,' I moaned in my most convincing sick person's voice as I administered Tadpole's breakfast on Saturday morning. It was the same voice I'd used as a teenager to fool my mother when I couldn't face school, for whatever reason. 'I think I'm going to have to go and lie down for a while. Sorry.' Mr Frog looked up from his magazine in alarm. He had been about to run one of his famously long baths; I was riding roughshod over his routine.

'What about me?' he said, indignantly. 'I'm really tired too, you know. It's been a tough week for me at work . . .'

'Put the TV on,' I retorted. In spite of my own hypocrisy I could feel self-righteous anger welling up. Wasn't I only asking him to pull his weight, after all? Wiping the corners of Tadpole's mouth on her bib, I heaved her out of the high chair and deposited her on his lap. 'How do you think I manage when you have to work at the weekend?' I shot over my shoulder. 'Or when you come home at 4 a.m. after a night out and feel too *hanged over* to get up the next day?' I pulled the bedroom door closed behind me with a bang before he could remind me that I had rolled in well after midnight on Tuesday, the night of the concert, and done just that.

From our bed – its headboard separated by a thin internal wall from the sofa where Tadpole sat and Mr Frog lay – I listened to my daughter babbling in French, delighted to have Daddy's undivided attention. I heard the sofa creak, Mr Frog cursing as he grappled with the baby-proof device which prevented Tadpole from posting crayons inside the video player, then the semi-coherent baby talk of the Teletubbies. At regular intervals my shaking hand reached for the phone in the bag I'd taken to keeping by my bedside, checking for messages which came few and far between. James was working on a cottage he had been renovating with Eve – as business partners – deep in the Breton countryside, where phone masts were scarce. I foundered: without his words to cling to, there was nothing to stop me sinking.

Feigning illness wasn't especially difficult. Charcoal smudges under my eyes testified to the fact that I had barely slept a wink over the past few nights. And yet a single cup of coffee was enough to make me shake like an alcoholic with the DTs. I was secretly pleased about the weight loss which seemed to be a by-product of my anxiety – my clothes were beginning to hang off me, and I'd managed to squeeze into a pair of pre-Tadpole trousers for the first time in almost three years the day before – but there were less attractive side effects too. Perspiration drew acrid circles under my arms; my stomach cramped and clenched. When the *Teletubbies* video ended and Mr Frog appeared, looking sheepish, an hour later, he was forced to admit I didn't look well.

'I've brought you a cup of tea,' he said, placing the mug on the corner of the desk nearest to my side of the bed. 'You feeling any better?'

'No, I'm sorry, I just feel really run down, like I'm coming down with something,' I said weakly, propping myself on one elbow, bringing the anaemic, milky tea to my lips. In the eight years we'd spent together Mr Frog had never quite got the hang of making a decent cup of tea for his *petite anglaise*.

'Okay, well, I suppose we could go to the park for a while, and leave you to rest, in peace,' Mr Frog said grudgingly. 'Hopefully you'll be feeling a bit better by the time we get back.'

'Oh, that would be lovely, if you don't mind,' I said, summoning up a wan smile. I almost wished he wouldn't be sympathetic: my conscience, dulled by my annoyance earlier, was now prickling uncomfortably. But at the same time my mind raced ahead, plotting and scheming. If I was going to have the house to myself, maybe I could try phoning James? I hadn't heard his voice since I'd jumped into the taxi and left him behind. I'd told him phoning was too risky – preferring to read his words – but suddenly the desire to hear his voice had become almost a physical need.

'I don't much like going to the park on my own,' Mr Frog confessed. 'People look at me strangely. I'm sure they think I'm a *papa du dimanche*.' I was probably guilty of giving that same pitying look to lone fathers myself, I realized, when really I had no proof whatsoever of their marital status. Why is it that a father and child can't go somewhere alone without people assuming he must be a part-timer? When *I* wandered through the park with Tadpole, or took her to Franprix to shop for food without Mr Frog, people didn't automatically brand me a single mother, did they?

'Oh, you should milk that,' I said, making a weak attempt at humour. 'I bet it makes you very popular with the ladies . . .' The irony of the situation, the fact that Mr Frog might well wind up being a weekend daddy, was not lost on me, and I was simultaneously amazed and horrified at my own ability to make light of it.

'We go to the park now?' said Tadpole bounding into the bedroom, still wearing her pyjamas.

'You're going to go to the park with Daddy. Mummy's not feeling very well, I'm afraid.'

Tucking her favourite rag doll under the duvet beside me, Tadpole touched a cool hand to my flushed cheek. I shrank away. Mr Frog's sympathy was difficult enough to deal with, but my daughter's was just plain unbearable. I didn't deserve to be fussed over. I was a wolf in her mother's bed, a monster plotting to betray her father as soon as his back was turned.

Once I heard the lift doors close behind Mr Frog and Tadpole and I'd let a few more breathless minutes elapse to allow for a return journey to collect a forgotten bucket or spade, I was out of bed like a shot, pacing the creaky floorboards, fingers busily dialling. A few moments of nerve-racking dead air were followed by a click, then a ringing sound and, finally, James picked up.

'Wow! You called.' James sounded cautiously pleased. His voice was balm to my soul: normal, reassuring, real. 'Everything okay?'

'Yes and no,' I replied, my voice unsteady. 'I'm all over the place. I had to pretend to be ill so that I could get some time alone. They've gone to the park without me. I just couldn't be around them, it was too difficult, pretending . . .'

James sighed. 'I wish this didn't have to be so underhanded. I feel awful for putting you through this, making you lie. I of all people should know how wretched these situations can be.' He was silent for a moment, and I guessed he was revisiting scenes from his own divorce in his head. He knew all about deceit, about being played for a fool, and yet here he was, looking on from the sidelines while I put Mr Frog in the same position, betraying his trust, throwing dust in his eyes.

'No,' I said, feeling calmer now, soothed by the sound of his voice. 'This is *my* mess. You're not forcing me to do anything. I'm in a relationship which isn't making me happy; which hasn't for a long time. I hate sneaking around behind his back, but it seems like the only way, until I'm sure. Or as sure as I can be.'

'You haven't changed your mind then? About next week?' James must have been half expecting me to call everything off, dreading those words from the moment he picked up the phone.

'No. I haven't changed my mind,' I said. 'I have to see you again. I can't keep on sleepwalking indefinitely. I'm afraid I'd be missing out on something, and that I'd end up regretting it for the rest of my life . . .'

'Thank God,' he said forcefully. 'Well, the guy at the garage reckons the car will be ready by Thursday at the latest. So I could come up on the train on Wednesday, book a hotel for the night, and go back on Thursday afternoon. I don't want to put pressure on you, but any time you can snatch away from home, or the office . . .'

I'd thought about this part a lot, turning over and over in my mind how it could be done. Infidelity was a complicated business, logistically, for a working mother whose day was mapped out in detail from dawn until dusk. A hotel would be perfect. We needed to meet in private, away from prying eyes and unexpected interruptions, but also on neutral ground. I tried not to dwell on the fact that there would be a bed, or to think about the seediness implicit in the arrangement.

'I'll pretend I'm ill,' I explained. 'My boss won't like me leaving, but there's not a great deal he can do about it. Then I'll get a babysitter lined up in the evening, say I'm invited to a party with some blog friend. I'll need to come and go – I'll still have to do the run to the nanny's and back as usual – but we should be able to spend a good few hours together . . .'

James whistled. 'You've got it all worked out, haven't you? Leave the hotel to me. If I aim for something near Bastille, would that be easy enough for you to get to, but far enough away not to be uncomfortably close to home?'

'That would be perfect.' Bastille was familiar territory: close to my very first apartment, and a direct *métro* from the nanny's. It couldn't be more convenient. What a profound relief to have something set in stone at last, to know exactly where and when we would meet.

'Sure you haven't done this before?' James's tone said he was joking. But I wondered then whether there could ever be trust in a relationship based from the outset upon deceiving other people.

'I must be a natural,' I said, with a brittle laugh, eager to change the subject. 'Let's talk about something a bit less dramatic, shall we? How about you tell me about the work you and Eve are doing on the house?' I lost track of time as we talked. It was so refreshing to hear his voice. Our carefully crafted emails were often things of beauty, but sometimes I worried that it would be easy to get ahead of ourselves, to fall in love with the way our words looked on the page. On the phone we talked of mundane things and that normality was soothing. The conversation was anything but stilted – in fact it felt as though we'd known each other for years. I liked the way his mind worked; the way he seemed to have a thoughtful, measured answer to every question.

'I'm really glad you phoned me, Cath,' said James emphatically. 'It's good to hear your voice. I'm so glad you didn't wake up the next day and decide to put the whole episode behind you.'

'I could never . . . Oh! God! They're back!' A key was turning in the lock. I'd been so wrapped up in James that I hadn't noticed the lift clanking to a halt or the footfalls on the landing. Now the front door was already swinging open. I froze, telephone in hand, wondering what to do. There was no time to regain the bedroom. I'd just have to remain where I was on the sofa and brazen it out.

'Got to go now, Mum, they're back,' I said brightly, cutting off the call before Tadpole, who clattered along the corridor ahead of Mr Frog, could beg to speak to her grandma. Her cheeks were flushed from exertion and her eyes shone as she rushed over for a hug. 'You weren't gone very long. What happened?' I asked, as Mr Frog appeared in her wake.

'Oh, her nappy needed changing . . . You're up then? *Ça va mieux?*' His tone was hopeful. 'Because if you are feeling better, there are a couple of errands I'd like to run on the scooter.'

The old me might have made a tart comment about shirking responsibilities, about leaving me, quite literally, holding the baby. Today I held my tongue. For once, the parental relay race – passing Tadpole back and forth like a baton – suited me just fine.

'Sure, you go out for a while,' I said, noting his surprised, pleased expression. 'Take as long as you want.'

I wondered afterwards whether my uncharacteristic *laissez-faire* attitude hadn't set alarm bells ringing in Mr Frog's head. But if he did suspect that something was amiss, he certainly wasn't letting on.

11. Alibis

When James's call came through on my mobile the following Wednesday, I almost blew everything.

According to my painstakingly concocted master plan, which I had refined somewhat since speaking to James on the phone the weekend before, I was supposed to answer my phone and pretend I was talking to *Tata*, sticking to a pre-arranged script. My tone would change from friendly to concerned: anyone within earshot would believe I had a genuine childcare emergency on my hands, giving me a reason to leave early, without having to pretend to be ill myself. What I hadn't counted on was the nervous giggle which welled up in my throat as soon as I heard James's voice. I sounded more overjoyed than panic-stricken; it was impossible to keep the smile out of my voice. Luckily, my boss's door was closed, and those colleagues who normally sat within earshot of my desk had gone for an early lunch, so I didn't actually have to play to an audience.

'I'm going to set off now,' I murmured. 'I'll probably get to the hotel before you do, so I'll just wait in reception.' I took a moment to compose myself, my phone still pressed to my ear. James had called from Montparnasse station. He was in Paris. This was really happening: it was time to throw myself into the fire.

My phone still in my hand, I stood and walked briskly over to my boss's office, knocked and poked my head around the door. He appeared to be reprimanding a junior, and the air inside smelled of frayed tempers. My boss turned his head, his expression mildly irritated. 'Sorry to interrupt,' I said hurriedly, 'but my nanny just called to say she's ill. I'm afraid I'm going to have to collect my daughter and look after her myself this afternoon.' The corners of my mouth were already beginning to twitch treacherously. I needed this to be over quickly, before my smile had time to reassert itself.

'Well, if there's really no other way, then I suppose I'll have to let you go,' my boss replied, taking no pains to conceal his annoyance. I felt my hackles rising. He had young children of his own, so he ought to be more sympathetic to my plight, fabricated or not.

'I'm sorry,' I said, sounding anything but. 'I don't have an alternative right now. My partner's in London for the next couple of days, which doesn't help matters.' Another white lie wouldn't hurt. 'I'll ring you in the morning and let you know whether she's any better. If not, I'll try and arrange for a sitter . . .'

My boss sighed and turned back to the task at hand: I had been dismissed. Pulling the door closed more violently than I'd intended, I heard the glass rattle in its frame. Speedily, I gathered my belongings and charged down the stairs. Unwittingly, my boss had played into my hands by provoking me. With his help, I had played the role of indignant mother to perfection.

A caged bird freed from the office, I flew down the steps to the *métro*, praying I wouldn't cross paths with anyone who knew Mr Frog. I'd told *Tata* she could only reach me on my mobile so that she couldn't take it into her head to call me at the office, inadvertently blowing my cover. But as far as Mr Frog was concerned, I hadn't worked out any sort of alibi. I'd just have to hope I didn't run into any of his friends. The likelihood was slim, but then I hadn't expected to see Benoît in Café Charbon either.

The sweaty mass of rush-hour commuters had given way to tourists, pensioners and pregnant women, and there were plenty of available seats. I sat down next to an elderly lady with thinning, dyed-black hair and fierce dots of rouge on her heavily powdered cheeks, taking out my own compact to retouch my – hopefully rather more subtle – make-up.

A couple of days earlier, shopping for cartons of soup and bread for lunch in the Monoprix supermarket near the office, I'd mumbled an excuse about needing to buy a pair of tights and urged Amy to go downstairs to the food section without me. Once she was out of sight, I'd made a covert detour towards the lingerie section. The only vaguely sexy under-wear I owned had been a Christmas present from Mr Frog, and was therefore off limits for my rendezvous with James. Fingering the gauzy fabrics hesitantly, wincing at the price tags, I finally tucked a navy-blue bra and French knickers with a simple light-blue ribbon detail into my shopping basket, before making awkwardly for the men's hygiene sec-tion, in search of a packet of condoms. I hadn't bought any in over eight years, and many of the brands were unfamiliar. 'Hansaplast?' I muttered to myself. 'Don't they make sticking plasters?'

The packet I'd eventually chosen now burned a guilty hole in my bag, and here I was, wearing matching underwear under my office clothes for the first time in months. Not that I felt like a goddess – far from it – I was too busy wishing I'd had the foresight to remove the itchy label from inside my bra.

The Hôtel Saint Louis Bastille wasn't as close to Bastille as its name implied, but nearer République, at *métro* Oberkampf. A narrow building nestling between two stately apartment blocks on the boulevard Richard Lenoir, its stonework was clean, no doubt from a recent *ravalement*, and it didn't look seedy at all. In the middle of the boulevard, above the Canal Saint Martin, which ran its furtive course underground, old men sat sunning themselves on benches, sparrows took dust baths at the foot of the plane trees and childminders propelled their charges along in double pushchairs. For all those people, it was business as usual today. As for me, I felt oddly detached from my surroundings. I saw myself pause at the zebra crossing opposite the hotel as if watching from a great height through the beady eyes of a bird perched in the trees above. While I struggled to play this role I'd only ever seen in films – the Parisian woman indulging in an illicit affair – *petite anglaise* was busy composing a blog post in my head, simultaneously noting all the details of my surroundings, thinking about how the scene should be written. Without her, I wouldn't be here. I'd never have met James, for a start. But was there more to it than that? Would I have even contemplated putting myself into a situation like this before she came along?

A fleeting image of my former landlady from rue de la Roquette popped into my mind, as I waited for the traffic to thin. She'd always looked sophisticated yet dishevelled when she materialized to collect the monthly rent in cash, as though she had arisen from the crumpled sheets of a nearby hotel bed moments earlier. I could do dishevelled, but sophisticated had always eluded me. It was all I could do right now to prevent myself from surreptitiously lifting my arm to check my shirt for signs of nervous perspiration as I waited for the traffic lights to change.

The hotel reception was a spacious, stone-paved room, a desk set across one corner, behind which an immaculate and rather effeminate man was sitting.

'*Bonjour Mademoiselle,*' he said as I hesitated on the threshold. '*Je peux vous aider?*'

'Er, yes, well, no, I'm just waiting for my boyfriend – he

has the check-in paperwork. I'll just take a seat over here, if that's all right . . .' I lowered myself into a Louis-somethingth chair with patterned upholstery, which looked more comfortable than it felt. Studying my shoes self-consciously, worrying at the already ravaged cuticles around my thumbnails with my index fingers, I wondered if it was obvious that I had skipped work for an afternoon tryst with a lover. Hotel staff must see this sort of thing all the time, I reasoned. It might seem earth-shatteringly momentous to me, but infidelity was banal, commonplace. Hundreds of people were probably moaning and sighing in hotels all over the city at this very moment.

Registering a movement on the periphery of my vision, I glanced up from my shoes, and there he was, broad frame silhouetted in the doorway, a ragged-looking travel bag slung over his shoulder. Flushed from the heat of the *métro*, beads of sweat glistened in the cleft above his upper lip. He was cleanshaven and smooth – I'd never seen him this way – and for a long moment I hesitated, wondering what I was doing there, why I was meeting this stranger. Then he smiled, and I recognized the corduroy jacket he clutched in his right hand from the week before, and all at once he was familiar again.

'Hey,' I said. 'You made it.' Unsure how I should greet him – especially in front of an audience – I stood up stiffly and moved to stand by his side at the check-in desk.

'I'll say hello properly in a minute,' James said, fumbling in the inside pocket of his jacket for his passport and credit card, while I swayed by his side, feeling light-headed, wishing I'd managed some lunch before I set off. Then suddenly we were free, we were stepping into a mirrored lift; we were alone, at last.

Much of that afternoon remains an intense blur when I try to recall it: my memory is like a heat-damaged reel of film;

only a few selected frames subsist. Maybe extremes of pleasure and pain are just too much for the memory to handle? The images which do remain are out of focus, as though I were standing too close to one of Monet's vast water-lily canvases at the Orangerie, unable to see the big picture clearly, lost in the individual brushstrokes.

I know we lay face to face, fully clothed, on the white bedspread, talking in hushed voices for an hour, or maybe two. The queen-sized bed occupied three-quarters of the carpeted room, leaving only a narrow sliver of space around it: there was nowhere else to sit. I know I was overwhelmed with relief to feel my body finally slowing, relaxing, until I was limp in his arms, the exhaustion of a week of sleepless nights catching up with me at last. The guilt I'd been carrying around with me, even while I daydreamed about our meeting, I left outside the hotel-room door, for now.

'You can sleep, if you want,' James whispered. 'I'm happy just holding you.'

'There'll be plenty of time for sleep when you've gone,' I murmured, shaking my head. 'I don't want to waste even a second.'

I know that we didn't kiss until the afternoon was almost over, minutes before I left to pick up Tadpole. Propped up on one elbow, looking down on me from above, I saw a question in James's eyes which, this time, he didn't have to voice. I loved his patience; the fact that he presumed nothing. Here we were, stretched out on a hotel bed, and yet still he sought my permission, handling me with care, understanding my need to dictate the pace.

I smiled, nodded almost imperceptibly and put a hand to the back of his neck, my fingers stroking the wisps of hair I'd ached to reach out and touch in the bar a week before. I was ready. It was time. I pulled him closer.

So much excitement and anticipation were distilled into that kiss: a week of waiting, wondering and fantasizing. The kiss I had declined on the street corner after the concert would have tasted of beer and recklessness. It could all too easily have been clumsy, toothy, disappointing. Deferred, it was charged with emotional significance. There was no alcohol haze to hide behind. It was neither throwaway, nor impulsive; it felt measured, binding. Breathless, shaking, lips tingling, I had to acknowledge that it had been worth the wait.

'I can't believe it's time for me to go,' I groaned when my watch started to beep a few minutes later, wishing I'd kissed him sooner.

'Hey, we've got plenty of time,' James replied, putting a finger to my lips. 'There's no hurry. I'll have a glass of wine waiting when you get back, and we can pick up exactly where we left off.'

I took the lift down to reception alone, my heart pounding. Soon I would return. But first I had to collect Tadpole, get her fed and bathed and ready for Maryline to take over. Thank goodness Mr Frog hadn't been free to babysit, I thought to myself. How on earth could I have faced him with James's kiss still warm on my lips? The next few hours would feel like the longest of my life – the waiting exquisite and excruciating in equal measures – but my reward, when I returned, was that I would stay with James until the small hours.

When Maryline arrived, maddeningly late, I found something about the way she looked me up and down unnerving. Could it be that, as a woman, she was able to sense what Mr Frog had failed to pick up on? Was she noting the unusual amount of care I had put into my appearance, for once, on a night when Mr Frog would not be accompanying me? Or was the guilt I was struggling to fight back, now that I was alone, clouding my judgement and making me paranoid? Whatever the truth of the matter, I was glad to close the front door behind me and rest my burning cheeks against the cool mirror of the lift as it plunged downwards.

The man on the desk recognized me immediately when I strode into the hotel reception for the second time that day, despite the fact that I'd changed out of my work clothes and applied fresh make-up, in keeping with the alibi I'd given Mr Frog, that I was going to a party. He waved me straight upstairs, and I knocked quietly on James's door, anxiety flaring up when he didn't answer immediately. What if he had got cold feet and left? But no, there he was, hair damp from the shower, a tumbler of red wine in his hand.

'I'm a bit late,' I smiled shyly, 'but here I am.' Stepping inside, I pulled the door softly closed behind me.

Midnight came before we lay naked between starched white sheets and I felt the full weight of him, smooth and hot against my skin. 'Are you sure you want to do this?' James whispered. 'Because we don't have to, today. I can wait . . .' Putting my finger to his lips this time, I shook my head, my other hand moving lower, leaving the impurity of my intentions in no doubt.

'You're crying!' he said, afterwards, touching my cheek with his finger, brushing away silent tears. I didn't speak at first. I wanted to focus every ounce of concentration on savouring the half-forgotten sensation of being at one with my body; aware of its power; desirable. The thin film of sweat covering my skin, mine and his. The aftershocks rippling through me.

'I'm not sad,' I said at last. My voice sounded languid; so different as to be barely recognizable. 'I'd just forgotten, what this, what any of this, could be like.' Our timing had been faultless; every single movement had been delicious. All the excitement of discovering new terrain was mingled with an unexpected feeling of familiarity, of rightness.

'Forgotten? What do you mean, forgotten?' He looked puzzled. 'How long has it been?'

I buried my face in his shoulder, seeing the perfect crescent of my teeth marks, suddenly embarrassed. 'Too long. So long I'd forgotten what my body was *for*.'

'I don't understand,' said James incredulously. 'Why?'

How could I explain? Whatever it is that makes it possible to touch another person in a sexual way, Mr Frog and I had lost somewhere along the way. On the rare occasions when he or I had tried to initiate something, instead of arousing me, his touch irritated, or tickled, and I had to suppress the urge to swat him away like a fly. He protested he was too tired; I claimed I wasn't in the mood; eventually we both gave up trying. Talking about it seriously meant acknowledging deeper problems, so instead it had become a sort of feeble joke between us. I even remember raising a glass to toast a year of celibacy. There didn't seem to be any way back for us. It was nobody's fault. But something vital had been irretrievably lost.

In the company of good friends, I would poke and prod, in vain, for signs that other people's sex life had burned down low, wondering if it was normal for every relationship to dim to friendship over time. But now that my slumbering needs had been awakened, I suspected I would no longer be able to settle for chaste hugs and the occasional lingering peck on the lips.

The sound of my mobile phone pealing in my bag caused me to flinch as though I'd been electrocuted. Maryline? I leaped off the bed and crouched naked on the floor, upending my handbag in my haste and tipping its contents on to the carpet. But the name on the display was Mr Frog's: his ears must have been burning. I would have to take his call with another man's sweat drying on my skin. I could hardly ignore it. It could be some sort of emergency. 'Hey, is there a problem?' I said as evenly as I could manage. My cheeks were on fire, my hands shaking. Please don't let Tadpole be ill, I prayed. Please don't make me have to leave now. Mr Frog's voice was crystal clear, as though he were right beside me in the hotel room. It felt as though by rights he should be able to sense that I was naked; he must know instinctively what I was up to.

'No. Maryline just left, and I was wondering how long you'd be, that's all.'

'Oh. Right,' I said, my voice filled with relief. 'I'm not sure. A couple of hours at least.'

'Where are you?' Mr Frog said, his voice suddenly sharp. 'It sounds a bit quiet for a party . . .'

I faltered, my knuckles white around the telephone. 'Oh, it's more like a group of friends eating and drinking, really,' I replied, hoping my lie wasn't detectable. 'But I moved into the bedroom when I picked up the phone.'

'I see,' he said. Was it my imagination, or did he sound unconvinced? 'Well, I suppose I'll see you later . . .'

'No need to wait up, though,' I said hurriedly. 'I might be quite late. Bye for now.' Dropping the phone on to the carpet, I sat still for a moment, my head buried in my hands.

'Was that who I think it was?' James asked cautiously. I raised my head and nodded silently. 'What rotten timing!' He gestured for me to join him on the bed. 'Are you okay?' I crawled into his arms, my shoulders quivering.

'I hate doing this lying thing,' I sobbed. 'I'm not cut out for this at all.'

'I wish you didn't have to,' James murmured. 'You need time and space to get your head around all of this. Take as long as you need. If you decide this isn't what you want, I'll disappear, and you'll never have to hear from me again if you don't want to. I really, really hope you don't feel that way. But I'll respect whatever decision you make.'

In the early hours of the morning I tore myself out of James's arms, showered, ran out into the night and flagged down a taxi. As I slid into bed by Mr Frog's side, saying a silent prayer of thanks when I realized that he was sleeping deeply, I was conscious of the fact that my skin was still tingling, my breaths still fast and shallow. Wide-eyed, my body rigid, I relived the past twelve hours over and over again. When the alarm sounded, I felt sure I had only slipped in and out of sleep for a matter of minutes.

'Good party last night?' murmured Mr Frog sleepily as he heaved himself reluctantly into a sitting position.

'It was cool.' I stifled a yawn and shifted my position so that he couldn't see my face. For once I was glad of his morning routine: the longer he languished in his bath, the less I would have to face him. Tadpole woke in unusually high spirits, and our morning preparations went relatively smoothly. As soon as Mr Frog left for work, I called the office to speak to my boss. 'I'll be in at lunch-time,' I said, picturing his irritated expression, and struggling to keep the smile out of my voice. 'I'm waiting for an agency babysitter to arrive, but she wasn't free until midday.'

'Well, I suppose that's better than nothing,' he said with an exaggerated sigh.

'If you need to speak to me, best use the mobile number,' I added, amazed at my own foresight. 'I'll probably pop to the park in the meantime.'

Once I'd dropped Tadpole off at the childminder's, only a couple of hours remained before James had to check out of the Hôtel Saint Louis. When midday came, not wanting to part, not yet, I suggested we grab some lunch together near by. With me clinging to his hand like a love-struck teenager, my caution now cast aside, we meandered aimlessly for a while, unable to focus on the mundane task of choosing a restaurant. Eventually we stepped inside an unassuming café on boulevard Beaumarchais and ordered two *croques madames*. It was early, and there were few customers. As we waited for the toasted sandwiches to arrive, I gripped James's hand tightly across the Formica tabletop with its garish paper place-mats, reluctant to let go.

Eating in front of James for the first time almost felt more intimate than removing my clothes. My mouth was dry, and I found it difficult to swallow. Cutting my food into tiny pieces, I pushed them self-consciously into my mouth, which felt bruised and swollen from all his kisses. We said little, and I concentrated hard on fighting back the waves of despair which had begun to well up. Soon I would be alone, with only my guilt for company. I pushed my plate away, half-full. 'I don't think I can prolong the agony any longer,' I said. 'I ought to go.'

At the top of the concrete steps leading down into the *métro*, James cupped my face in his hands and I let him kiss me, in full view of anyone passing by. 'I know this is much harder for you than it is for me,' he said, brushing my hair from my eyes, 'but be strong. I'll call you when I get home, if the coast's clear.' I nodded, and gave him a long, hungry look before I turned and walked down the steps, clutching the hand-rail tightly. Some superstitious notion prevented me from looking back, as though one backward glance from me would turn him to stone.

In the *métro* carriage, I withdrew my iPod from my bag and selected a song big enough to contain my emotions: 'Gorecki', by Lamb. The words suddenly seemed to resonate with more meaning than ever before, and tears – happy tears – began to slide down my cheeks. I stared at my reflection in the glass doors as the train rattled along, wishing I could run back along the dark tunnels to where he stood. Words thrashed around in my head and I ached to turn them loose.

As I stepped into the brightly lit, mirrored lift which would deliver me to the office, my phone stirred in my pocket.

'Can see every detail of your face in my mind. Makes opening eyes pointless.'

I tapped my reply as the lift bore me upwards, hitting 'send' just as the doors slid silently open. 'Drive carefully, preferably with eyes wide open.'

12. Confidences

Amy found me in the kitchen a few minutes later. My boss wasn't yet back from lunch, and I was too agitated to sit still at my desk, regardless of the vertiginous pile of documents waiting in my in-tray. Shunning the coffee machine – because caffeine would only make me even twitchier – I had set the kettle to boil and was digging through the contents of the cupboard searching for herbal tea.

'Catherine!' she exclaimed. 'I didn't see you arrive – I take it your nanny's better now if you're back here again?' I withdrew my head from the cupboard, my cheeks reddening. Now was probably time to come clean and face the music. If I kept all this to myself a moment longer I was afraid I would burst.

'It wasn't the nanny,' I confessed. 'I've met a man, and I'm really, *really* into him. He was visiting Paris and I had to make up the nanny story to give me a chance to spend time with him . . .'

'Met a man? How? Where?' Amy looked astonished, and clearly what perplexed her most was how I'd found the time. Whenever she'd seen me outside work, it had invariably been at my place, while Tadpole slept. She knew nothing of my blog, nothing of my budding parallel social life. A lengthy explanation would now be required.

'Gosh, I don't know where to begin,' I replied, unable to meet her eyes at first. 'It's a really long story . . .' A familiar voice floated up the stairwell, and I knew the rest of my confession would have to wait: any minute now my boss would materialize in the kitchen to fetch coffee. 'Damn, I'd better go,' I said, gesturing towards the doorway. 'He's been saving up all my work while I've been out. You'd think I was the only secretary in this office capable of typing a letter.'

'Okay, well, why don't we go out for lunch together tomorrow, just the two of us?' Amy suggested. 'You can tell me everything then. And in the meantime, get a good night's sleep. You look like you could really do with some rest.'

Back at my desk I grabbed my headset and got started on a dictation tape, glad of a mechanical task which allowed me to daydream and shut the world out while I worked on autopilot. My boss made no reference to my absence, nor did he make any allowances for all the catching up I had to do, but at four o'clock, when he disappeared into a meeting room for a video-conference, I was finally able to come up for air. I sat, half in a trance, eyes not really seeing the building opposite through my window, and traced the outline of my collarbone with my fingertips. My skin felt softer, smoother, more sensitive; no longer an envelope I barely noticed. Since James first touched me, I'd become aware of this body of mine pulsing with life under my clothes, every nerve ending reawakened. I felt like an instrument which had been tuned after long months of disuse.

Re-reading the letters I'd hammered out after lunch, I found them peppered with typos and transposition errors which I hastily corrected before printing them on to company headed paper for my boss to sign. The most glaring mistake – in a letter to a client – was also the most revealing. 'Please sign and date the documents and return them to me in the *usual* way,' my boss's voice must have said on the tape, a pretty standard closing paragraph for a letter to accompany a client's tax return. But with my mind elsewhere, my fingers moving across the keyboard as if of their own volition had typed 'in the *sensual* way'.

'So, let me get this straight. You know James through this internet site of yours, but you only actually *met* him last week?' Amy's eyes were wide with disbelief.

Amy had made a reservation in an Italian restaurant called Barlotti, one of the many which lined Place du Marché Saint Honoré, catering primarily for the suits from the transparent office building in the centre of the cobbled square. As we'd walked past, I'd marvelled, as I always did, at the way the glass structure reflected the older buildings around it and complemented them: it was good to see old and new Paris peacefully coexisting. 'Oh my goodness, there's a salad bar called *Cuisine et Confidences*,' I'd cried out as we'd passed it by. 'I never noticed that place before! How apt it would have been if we were eating there . . .'

I'd never set foot in Barlotti either, and when the waiter led us through to our table and the space suddenly opened up to reveal a huge, high-ceilinged room bathed in natural light, I was pleasantly surprised. But once we'd taken our seats, I no longer paid much heed to my surroundings. A plate of tomato and mozzarella salad before me, I began to recount the events of the past few months.

'I know it sounds odd,' I explained, 'but I've made a lot of friends through this internet diary of mine since I started writing it. Girls mostly, other expats who write about what it's like to live in Paris.' I picked up a piece of bread and raised it to my lips, then changed my mind and set it down again. 'I never intended to make anything other than virtual friends, never imagined for a second that I would meet any men, but there was something about James all along. He left these really articulate comments for months . . . Then he emailed. When we met the other night it was supposed to be as friends – although maybe we were kidding ourselves about that – but there was this undeniably powerful chemistry between us. It was one of those rare *coup de foudre* moments, you know . . .' I blushed and paused for a few seconds, images from the previous day in the hotel crowding into my mind.

'It's weird,' Amy said slowly. 'I don't know you all that well – although I've got to know you a lot better over the past few months – and I barely know your boyfriend, but I always got the impression, from things you said, that you were quite lonely. Especially when you came back to work after your maternity leave. And that evening when you both came to my flat for drinks – the one and only time I ever even laid eyes on him – I remember thinking you two just didn't seem like a couple . . .'

'It doesn't really feel like we are a couple any more.' I shook my head sadly. 'For a long time we've been more like flatmates, or good friends. I think I'd convinced myself that every long-term relationship ends up that way; I really thought I had no right to expect more. And, to be honest, the warning bells had been ringing for ages, since before we decided to have a baby. I could never regret that decision – I wanted to have his baby, I always thought he'd make a great father, and our daughter is so perfect, she means everything to me – but often I think she's the only cement binding us together. We don't ever, well, you know . . .'

'Never?' Amy looked as shocked as James had. I shook my head again.

'And that's exactly why I'm scared I'm letting this new thing get out of hand. I've been so starved physically; it's left me feeling so needy. It's wonderful to feel special and wanted and desired after all this time, but it must be clouding my judgement. How can I know if it's James I want, and not just to be wanted like this by *someone*?'

Amy's eyes glazed over for a moment. I suspected I had said something that triggered a memory of her ex-boyfriend; the speeches he had made when he tried to explain his reasons for leaving after six years of living together. I suddenly felt very selfish for making her, of all people, my confidante. None of this could be easy for her to hear.

'It is risky,' she agreed, 'if you're going to jump in with both feet when you're so vulnerable, when it's so long since you've had someone being attentive to you . . . What if the whole thing turns out to have been a terrible mistake? Can you bear the idea of actually moving out, and separating your girl from her daddy?'

'I don't think I can bear the idea of staying with him solely for our daughter's sake,' I said, surprising myself by how sure I sounded, how final. 'I know it sounds horribly selfish of me but, in the long run, I don't believe that staying can be for the best, for any of us. I can't know yet whether James and I have some sort of future, but I'm almost sure that I can't carry on this farce. I'll have to come clean. I won't sneak around any more. Once was hard enough.'

I let the waiter, who had appeared silently at my elbow, clear my untouched plate away. There was no point pretending I was going to eat anything: lunch had just been a pretext for our talk. I'd existed on mint tea and adrenalin for the past week and I hadn't keeled over yet.

'Well, if that's what you decide, it might be an idea to leave James out of the equation, at least for the time being,' suggested Amy. 'Maybe you could say you'd like a trial separation?'

'Without mentioning the fact that there's someone else,

you mean?' I twisted my napkin in my hands, almost wishing I smoked, so that my nervous fingers would have something to do. 'God. I can't believe I'm saying this. How am I going to tell him? I love him, but just not in *that* way any more.'

'Well, maybe he feels the same way, deep down. Maybe it won't be as hard as you think . . .'

I hadn't the faintest idea how Mr Frog would react. He could be amazingly inscrutable when it came to emotions. Whereas I'd been quietly letting off steam on my blog for months, Mr Frog was a man of few words, more of a listener than a talker. Might he actually be relieved? My gut instinct was telling me he'd be sideswiped, but maybe Amy would be proved right, after all? Obviously, there was only one way to find out.

'I'm going to do it tonight,' I said, suddenly resolute, catching the waiter's eye and gesturing for the bill. 'It's Friday night, I'll have the weekend to deal with the fall-out. I can't put this off any longer, however horrible it is.'

'Think on it some more this afternoon,' cautioned Amy, as she pushed back her chair and gathered up her handbag. 'I still can't believe that this has all come about because of a website. I'm itching to get back to the office and take a look at this blog of yours . . .'

'You won't find anything about what's going on right now,' I said hastily. 'I've written very little this past week. The last post was about seeing someone in the *métro* kissing his girlfriend's hand as she gripped the pole near the doors, and then realizing he'd singled out the wrong hand . . . I made it sound like it happened only this week, but actually it was something I saw years ago.' As we made our way back to the office, I wondered whether there wasn't a deeper significance to my unearthing that particular anecdote.

I seemed to be asking myself a lot of uncomfortable questions about my motivations just now – as a blogger, navel-gazing was becoming second nature to me – but seldom did I find any satisfactory answers.

13. Shellshock

I was sitting on Tadpole's bed, pulling her Miffy pyjama top over her head, when I heard the sound of a key turning in the lock. Tadpole heard it too and, wriggling out of my grasp, she ran towards the front door to intercept Mr Frog, shrieking, 'Daddydaddydaddy!' My ears ringing, the blood draining out of my face, I gripped the chest of drawers and pulled myself to my feet.

'Just in time for bedtime stories!' I said, forcing my lips into a smile as I stepped into the hallway. 'How come you're home so early?'

'I had a meeting outside the office and, when it finished, I couldn't face going back,' Mr Frog explained, as he swung Tadpole up into his arms. 'Mind you,' he added, 'I might have to do a bit of work later, if you don't need the computer . . .'

Mr Frog's early appearance was a mixed blessing. I would be spared the agony of waiting, which would surely have got steadily more unbearable as the hours ticked by. But I was also desperate to call James. I'd resisted the urge to phone while I walked home with Tadpole, while I prepared her dinner, while she splashed in the bathtub, but I'd been planning to speak to him as soon as she was in bed. I needed to hear his voice telling me that I was strong, that I could do this, that I was doing the right thing. Now I'd left it too late; I was on my own.

While Mr Frog read to Tadpole, I prowled around the apartment like a caged beast, my nerves jangling. I threw Lego blocks back into their plastic chest with a clatter, snapped the folding high chair closed, plumped the cushions on the sofa with my fists with more force than was necessary. Coming to a standstill in front of the fireplace in the bedroom, I stared at my reflection in the mirror. I looked as nauseous as I felt, sick to my stomach at the thought of what I was about to say.

Silently, I'd rehearsed my speech that afternoon in the office, and once again in a packed *métro* carriage on the way home. I'd even run through it one last time while Tadpole played in the bath by my side, blithely unaware of the treason I was plotting. All of this was futile, of course: I knew I would forget my lines once we were face to face. The most important moments of our lives are rarely scripted to perfection.

If I couldn't *speak* to James, maybe there was a message waiting in my inbox? I opened up my email and, sure enough, there was a new message. 'I miss you so much,' he had written while I must have been walking home through the park with Tadpole. 'It's like a huge earthquake has torn a hole in the path my life was taking, and I can't get around it and carry on unless you're with me. If you decide to do this, tonight, then I'll understand if you can't phone, but please, please, please find a way to tell me that you're okay.'

'Time for a cuddle, Mummy!' shouted Tadpole, before I could type any reply.

'Coming!' I hollered, closing my email. I paused for a moment in the doorway of her room, watching my daughter as she hung around Mr Frog's neck, showering his face, his neck, with kisses. My heart was a stone in my chest, heavy with the terrible knowledge that this would be the last time we would say goodnight to our daughter as a couple.

Leaving a sleepy Tadpole chattering to the assortment of soft toys that shared her bed, I left her door ajar, just how she liked it, and followed Mr Frog through to our bedroom, the furthest point in the apartment from where Tadpole lay. He stood by the fireplace, on the spot where I'd been standing only moments before, his cigarette packet in his hand, patting his pockets for his lighter. When I pulled the door closed behind me, he turned and looked at me apprehensively. The closed door could signal only one thing: no doubt he was bracing himself for a fight.

Moving past the computer desk, I sat on my side of our double bed, my back propped against the headboard for support, knees drawn defensively up to my chest. I studied a section of the mottled purple quilt cover for a moment, unable to raise my eyes to meet his. The bed creaked as Mr Frog took a seat at the opposite end, his knees on the duvet, his shoes, which he hadn't yet removed, hanging over the edge.

'I . . . I don't know how to say this,' I said, my voice unsteady, my eyes downcast. 'But I don't think being together is making either of us happy any more. We don't want the same things. We have the same fights over and over again. We never touch . . . When we're not arguing, we barely speak. I've thought about this a lot, and I want to try living apart.' My eyes were filling with tears, distorting my vision, and I blinked them away, forcing myself to lift my head, even though it felt heavy as a newborn's. I needed to see him, to see the effect my words were having.

Mr Frog's features were frozen in a mask of shock. Despite everything that was so obviously wrong, he clearly hadn't seen this coming at all. Too stunned to speak, he stared at me uncomprehendingly, as though I were speaking a language he didn't understand, instead of my mother tongue. 'We're not in love any more, are we?' I continued, my eyes begging him to agree. 'And I thought I could live with that but, now, well, I don't think I can any more. Being together for the sake of our daughter isn't a good enough reason.'

My monologue exhausted, I fell silent, waiting for Mr Frog to speak. However fastidiously I'd chosen my words, I couldn't shake off the feeling that I was trapped inside a scene from a badly written soap opera, serving up one spent cliché after another.

Mr Frog's mask finally slipped. His mouth trembled, almost imperceptibly, and his eyes, hard as flint, suddenly narrowed. 'You've met someone, haven't you?' he said flatly. It was a statement, not a question. What a fool I'd been to think I could leave James out of my explanation. It didn't take a genius to work out that something, or someone, must have brought things to a head. There had to be a trigger, a catalyst and, unerringly, Mr Frog had put his finger on the truth.

'There is someone,' I confessed, wincing as Mr Frog's face contorted into an ugly smile. 'And that's why I'm saying this now, you're right.' I bit my lip. 'But I think we both know this has been brewing for a long time.'

'So, that's it. You've given up on us.' Mr Frog shrank away from me, as though I were contaminated, almost losing his balance as he teetered on the edge of the bed. He put his face in his hands for a moment, and I stared at his thinning hair, his exposed scalp, horrified at how vulnerable he looked. Was I about to see him cry for the very first time, I wondered, curious to hear what noise he would make, if he did. But when he looked up, his cheeks were dry. 'How can I live apart from my little girl?' His voice was dazed and disbelieving, he spoke as though he were talking to himself. 'How can this be happening to me?' He pulled himself upright, grabbed his cigarettes, and backed away from me, towards the door. 'I'm going out. I have to be alone. I have to get away from here. From you.' Staring at the indentation he had left on the bedclothes, I made no move to stop him. I heard the creak of the door, the soft thudding of his feet crossing the living-room floor, then returning as he retraced his steps and paused in the doorway to deliver his parting shot. 'You can call your new boyfriend now,' he said bitterly. 'Tell him the good news.'

I flinched then as though I'd been struck. I had been planning to call James, of course I had, but now I wasn't so sure. Not that we would have gloated, or celebrated as though this were some kind of victory, but giving James a blow-by-blow account didn't feel right. Tonight was between Mr Frog and me, I said to myself, as the front door slammed closed behind him. James would keep.

Tadpole was still awake. With the bedroom door open, I could hear her now, softly singing. I glanced at my watch in disbelief: less than ten minutes had elapsed since we'd put her to bed. In the time it would take to nip to the baker's for a baguette, or for Mr Frog to smoke a cigarette on the balcony, I had laid to rest eight years of our lives and sentenced our daughter to a childhood spent flitting between separated parents. Rooted to the bed, I listened to my daughter's sweet voice. My limbs felt leaden, anaesthetized. I was numb. Now that the deed was done, I didn't know how I was supposed to behave.

If Mr Frog had cried or shouted, lost his temper, lashed out at the furniture – or even me – it might have been easier. I think I'd hoped for fireworks; I felt I deserved them somehow. There I was, announcing I had finally found the strength to walk away from the empty husk of our relationship, confessing that I hadn't come to take this decision without outside help, that there was another person involved, and the scene had been played out with scarcely a raised voice. Seeing Mr Frog's anguish as he grappled with the idea of having to live apart from our daughter had brought home to me, all the more forcefully, that there hadn't been a single moan or whimper on *my* account.

Uncoiling like a spring, I suddenly leaped up from the bed and stepped through the open doors on to the balcony, trying to catch a glimpse of Mr Frog's receding back. 'What about me?' I wanted to yell down melodramatically into the street. 'You're losing *me* too!' But there was no sign of Mr Frog. The park gates were closed; most of the nearby shop windows were shuttered. Only the kosher sushi and bagel shop across the road – a black and red eyesore which had sprung up overnight where my dry cleaner's used to be – was still open for business. I rested my arms on the wrought-iron balustrade for a moment, massaging my aching temples with my forefingers. A vein pulsed in my forehead and, when I pressed it, hard, it seemed to alleviate the pain. The sun was dipping slowly behind the buildings opposite, glinting off the metal covers on the chimney pots, the sky almost identical to the picture on my blog.

I had long suspected Mr Frog and I were together by default; that we were carrying on for Tadpole's sake, or out of inertia. It shouldn't have come as a surprise to see that where jagged emotions should have been there was only a gaping void. But a part of me felt sorely cheated. Our break-up had been a resounding anti-climax. I wanted to be wept over, bitterly. I wanted to be fought for. Mourned, or regretted just a little.

I wanted to feel like I was someone who'd been worth having in the first place.

Mr Frog was gone for hours. For a while I was incapable of doing anything, slumping back on to the bed and burying my face in my pillow. I didn't feel like talking to anyone – although I knew that I would need to call my mother and break the news to her soon – but the urge to write something slowly overtook me, and I surrendered to the feeling willingly. So while Mr Frog roamed around outside, I wrote a post. In essence, it was a letter to him: an apology, and an obituary to our relationship.

When you walked into the bar, wearing your cuddly blue duffle coat, I found you irresistibly cute. I remember you kissing me gently on the cheek after our second meeting and bundling me into a taxi. I remember going to watch some obscure film at a cinema near where you lived, so I had a pretext to stop by. I remember listening to Portishead, lying on the bed in your tiny *chambre de bonne*, with its sloping floor, seeing only your grey-blue eyes.

I remember the joy written all over your face when I told you we were having a baby. I remember holding on to you for dear life while I retreated far inside myself to deal with the pain of labour. I remember you giving Tadpole her first bath by my side, while I looked on, helpless, unable to move. I remember standing by her bed, by your side, many times, marvelling at our beautiful daughter as she slept, wondering how we came to create such a perfect creature.

I feel dazed yet strangely calm inside. Tearful at times, but mostly just numb. I am profoundly sad and sorry that it has come to this. But I know, without the merest shadow of a doubt, that it is what is right.

Emptying my head on to the blog, plucking the *mots justes* from the air which would do justice to something so earth-shattering was exhausting, yet satisfying. But going public with news so raw, so 'hot off the press' was a huge step, and not something I wanted to rush into on the spur of the moment. That I'd felt compelled to write the post at all brought home to me forcefully to what extent blogging had become almost a necessity. The more dramatic the events I lived through, the more keenly I felt the need to make sense of everything by distilling my tangled thoughts and emotions into neat sentences. Not that my audience was incidental of course: I wasn't *only* writing for myself. I might not be ready to admit it yet – even to myself – but an unsavoury part of me secretly longed to see the ripples my cryptic announcement would send out across the internet.

I would call my mother first, I decided, then re-read my words calmly one more time before I decided whether or not I should press 'publish'.

When Mr Frog finally returned from his prowl, deathly pale and smelling strongly of nicotine, a blanket of stunned calm fell over our household. We found ourselves discussing the practicalities of our separation in shell-shocked, subdued tones. We would do our utmost to make the transition as smooth as possible, for Tadpole's sake, we agreed. Maybe she would never remember a time when Mummy and Daddy lived together under one roof but, if she did, neither of us wanted her last memories of family life to be of animosity, fighting and upheaval.

'I suppose I ought to start looking for a place to live,' said Mr Frog. 'Somewhere near by. You should stay here, even if it's a bit expensive for you on your own. We need to give our daughter some continuity.'

I nodded, doing the mental arithmetic in my head. Things would be tight, but I would manage, I'd have to. It was comforting to focus on practicalities, and I was relieved that Mr Frog was not pressing me for details about the new man in my life, or indeed about how we met. When the time came to go to bed, Mr Frog disappeared into Tadpole's bedroom and emerged clutching a spare duvet and pillows. He began to make a bed up for himself on the *chaise longue* in front of the arched window.

'You really don't have to do that,' I said, gesturing at the sofa. 'Not unless you really want to. There are no curtains in here, the window's not double glazed . . . and how would we explain it in the morning?' I was picturing Tadpole, who often padded through to join us for cuddles when she awoke.

'I suppose you're right.' Mr Frog tore the sheet off the sofa and cast it aside, leaving the bedding in an untidy bundle on the floor. He disappeared outside, ostensibly to smoke a last cigarette, and I quickly undressed and cleaned my teeth so that I would be out of his way by the time he returned. When finally he eased himself into bed beside me, I kept my eyes tightly closed and slowed my breathing, pretending to sleep. I'd positioned myself as close to the edge of the bed as I could without falling out, and Mr Frog instinctively did the same.

Neither of us slept a great deal that night, and there was much tossing and turning. But as though there were a tacit agreement between us, we did not speak, and not once did we lie face to face.

14. Judgement

'Cath, I'm so relieved to hear from you this morning,' wrote James. 'I'm sure you feel partly numb and partly in a lot of pain. I imagine you can't quite believe it's really happening. What an utterly bewildering thing to have happened in ten short days. But I don't think I've ever felt so certain about anything as when I saw you for the first time. And the second . . .'

Mr Frog got up before me the next day, his face drawn. He took a long bath while Tadpole watched a video and I surfed the internet in my pyjamas. In addition to James's message there was a long email from my mother – offering to pay for a flight to England if I needed to get away with Tadpole for a few days – and a shorter message from Amy, wondering whether I'd gone through with it. But what stopped me in my tracks when I opened my inbox was the number of emails awaiting me from complete strangers.

I'd turned off the comment function the previous evening when I'd finished speaking to my mother and returned to the computer to press 'publish'; the first time I'd ever done so. Putting the dramatic news out there was one thing; allowing strangers to react to it publicly quite another. But many people had been so saddened to read my words that they'd sent supportive messages by email instead, often prefacing their messages with shy disclaimers.

'I'm not the sort of person who writes comments on blogs and I feel slightly odd emailing you . . .' began one. 'It is the first time in my life I have ever felt empathy with another *internaute*, someone I don't know and am unlikely ever to know . . .' began another. 'Although I don't know you,' wrote a third, 'it is almost as if you have become a friend.'

Some messages were from fellow bloggers I felt close to, even though we'd never met. 'Just read it . . . and don't know what to say. But . . . y'know. xx,' wrote Jonny Billericay, awkwardly. 'That sounds like an ominous post,' said Lucy Pepper. 'You ok? Hope so.' There was even a message from Anna of Little Red Boat, whose blog I had so admired before I decided to set up my own. 'Hope you are okay, poppet,' she wrote. 'You write so awfully well when you are feeling sad.'

Readers offered advice, a place to stay if I fancied getting away from it all, and one girl even offered to send me a care package of English food I'd written about missing on my blog. People genuinely seemed to care about our well-being: over time they'd grown fond of Tadpole, Mr Frog and *petite anglaise*. But although the messages touched me deeply, I felt twinges of shame as I read. I didn't deserve these outpourings of cyber-sympathy. The victim here was Mr Frog, and since I hadn't yet alluded to the reasons our time together had come to an end, my readers were making assumptions based on a woefully incomplete picture. How would they react, I fretted, when they knew the whole truth?

I was sneaking a look at the visitor traffic graphs when Mr Frog walked into the bedroom. He was dressed now and wearing his jacket, his Vespa helmet swinging from his right hand. 'What on earth is that?' he said, gesturing at the jagged peaks of green and purple, leaning closer to get a better look at the graph. '*Quoi?* You've had all those extra visitors since last night?'

I felt the colour rising to my cheeks. 'Not extra visitors, no. I think it's the usual suspects, but they're checking in a few times a day to see if there's any news.'

'Any news? You mean they already know . . . about us?' He sat on the edge of the bed for a moment, his face incredulous. 'What the hell have you written?'

'Don't worry,' I said hastily, realizing how incomprehensible my decision must appear to him, suddenly seeing it through his eyes. 'It's very dignified. In fact, I hope you'll like it, when you can bear to read it. I wrote it for you . . .'

'You're repackaging our life into some sort of soap opera, and you expect me to approve?' Mr Frog shook his head in disbelief. 'I'm going out to see a friend,' he said, pulling himself to his feet, seemingly keen to put as much distance between himself and my computer as possible. 'I don't know when I'll be back. But please think long and hard before you write anything else.'

Although Mr Frog and I strove to behave normally in Tadpole's presence over the next few days, on some unconscious level our daughter seemed to sense there was something going on.

I knew, from what the childminder had told me, that Tadpole was going through a maternal phase – mothering *Tata*'s youngest charges and obsessed with pushing baby dolls around in miniature pushchairs – but was there more to it than that? Was she picking up on the invisible undercurrents at home, divining intuitively that Mummy and Daddy were both in need of extra cuddles and kisses?

'*Mon petit canard*,' she said tenderly as I changed her nappy, reaching up and pinching my right cheek until my eyes watered, in what was supposed to be an affectionate gesture, and would have been, if only her fingernails hadn't been in such desperate need of a good clipping. '*Allez, mange!*' she urged as I listlessly pushed breakfast cereal around my bowl, unable to work up any enthusiasm for eating. The bran flakes

141

felt like cardboard in my mouth, but I forced myself to eat a mouthful, mindful of the importance of leading by example.

One morning, about to leave for work, I bent low to fasten the buckles on Tadpole's scuffed T-bar shoes. Mr Frog was on his knees in the hallway, busy cramming papers into his bulging briefcase. When I'd finished buckling, Tadpole grabbed me by the arm, and tugged me closer to Mr Frog. '*Donne bisou à* Daddy!' she commanded, looking at me with wide, serious eyes. I stared helplessly at Mr Frog for a moment, wondering what to do. We'd had no physical contact at all since I'd asked him to leave. When I'd brushed against him in the kitchen that morning with the sleeve of my dressing gown, I'd gone so far as to apologize. But now, under Tadpole's watchful gaze, I obediently grazed his cheek with my lips. Thankfully, Mr Frog did not flinch.

Tadpole's timing couldn't have been more ironic, her attempts at reconciliation more futile. I'd booked Maryline that evening and, although I hadn't spelled it out to Mr Frog, I knew he suspected I was going out to meet the mysterious new man in my life, whoever he might be. 'I'm afraid it doesn't look as though I'm going to be coming home tonight,' I said as we parted ways in front of our apartment building. I'd left my announcement until the last possible second: an act of pure cowardice.

'I see,' said Mr Frog evenly. 'Well, I don't suppose I have any choice in the matter.' I'd deliberated long and hard over which was worse: staying out all night, or snatching a few stolen hours with James before slipping into bed by Mr Frog's side, the invisible imprint of another man's kisses on my skin. If I'd come clean, it was precisely so I could put an end to the skulking around behind Mr Frog's back, wasn't it? And yet I didn't want to flaunt my new relationship either.

'I'm sorry,' I mumbled. 'I know this is horrible for you.' But Mr Frog had already turned on his heel.

This time I had insisted on taking charge of booking the hotel. Our plans had been hatched at short notice, in the midst of the Roland Garros tennis tournament, so we were forced to settle for a downmarket hotel near Strasbourg Saint Denis, close enough to the Indian restaurants of the Passage Brady for a faint whiff of curry to permeate the air. The shabby room with its cheap grey carpet didn't have a great deal to recommend it aside from a sixth-floor rooftop view, but James and I couldn't have cared less. When he answered the door, wrapped in a towel, his torso glistening with droplets of water, I could find no compelling arguments for him to bother getting dressed.

'Oh God, I missed you so much,' he groaned, as I burrowed deep into his arms, inhaling the scent of soap and deodorant on his skin.

I put a finger to my lips. Words were not what I craved. I wanted to be taken outside of myself. To silence the turmoil inside my head and concentrate on just *feeling* instead. Standing back, I unbuttoned my dress, and let it fall to the floor.

Later we whispered in the semi-darkness while James traced the contours of my face as though he were memorizing my appearance with his fingertips. I told him intimate things about myself I'd never shared before. Something about being in his presence made me want to shed every last inhibition, to hold nothing back. I desperately wanted to give him insights that went far beyond what *petite anglaise* revealed on the blog; to step deliberately into unknown, unwritten territory.

'I've never felt like this about anyone before,' he murmured, drawing circles around my nipple with his index finger. 'I want to build you a house with my bare hands and carry you over the threshold. I want to cook for you every evening and bring you tea in bed in the mornings. I want to read with you in front of an open fire, sipping a glass of wine. I want to drive you to the beach and lie next to you in the sun. I may not be a man of means, but I want to take care of you as best I can . . .'

If I were a cat, I would have purred. There was something so seductive about the combination of our explosive sexual connection and this desire to take care of me, pamper me. James seemed to embody everything I craved. He was everything Mr Frog was not.

'You do realize,' said Mr Frog as he ate his usual evening meal of *charcuterie*, cheese and bread, the contents of the fridge laid out on a tray on the coffee table, 'that there's nothing easier for this new boyfriend of yours – this guy who has been reading about everything you reckon is wrong with your life for however many months – than to say everything he knows you want to hear.' He fished a *cornichon* out of the jar and stabbed the pickle on to his fork, with excessive violence. 'He can exploit every weakness, every *faille* in our relationship and turn it to his advantage . . .'

'I don't think that's what's happening here,' I said defensively, standing over him with a mug of tea in my hand, on my way to the bedroom. 'He is who he is, and just happens to be very different from you . . .'

At first Mr Frog hadn't wanted to know a single detail, but then slowly, surely, the questions had welled up, and now he was beginning to slot the pieces of the jigsaw together. He knew James was a few years my senior, English, divorced, with children of his own. He knew we had met through *petite anglaise*. He knew he lived in Brittany, and had no desire to move to Paris. I'd taken pains to reassure Mr Frog that there was no question of Tadpole and me leaving Paris in the near future, and to impress upon him that James would never try to usurp Mr Frog's rightful role as Tadpole's father. After all, James had watched another man move into his home to live with his wife and children, looking on, helplessly, from a distance. No one else could possibly understand the implications of our situation better than he. James couldn't fail to be sensitive to what Mr Frog was going through.

'Well, don't say I didn't warn you,' Mr Frog retorted. He scooped the soft centre from his baguette and discarded it on the tray before popping the crust into his mouth. His jaw creaked as he chewed, a sound which set my teeth on edge. 'And once the honeymoon period is over,' he added, 'who's to say that things are going to be so much better than they were between you and me?'

I turned to leave, but not before I'd grabbed the abandoned tufts of bread and popped them into my mouth, through sheer force of habit. Mr Frog was trying to sow the seeds of doubt, to blight my happiness. I understood his reasons for doing so, but he was the last person I should be talking to about my new relationship, and I wasn't about to allow myself to get drawn further into the discussion.

Closing the bedroom door pointedly behind me, I positioned myself in front of the computer and took a look at the latest comments on my last post. I'd begun to hint at the sequence of events leading to the break-up, revealing that I had met the new man in my life via my blog, without divulging his identity.

'Hmm, you dump Mr Frog,' wrote Dan, 'deprive your daughter of her father and vice versa, and you expect not only sympathy from him, but from all your blog readers as well . . . who duly give it to you, amazingly enough. No doubt you are getting lots of attention from the new man in your life too. Well, give my deepest sympathies to Mr Frog. He might be feeling a tad(pole) lonely.'

'My god, Petite you cheated on Mr Frog?' exclaimed Fleur in disgust. 'I've enjoyed your blog, but right now my esteem of you has dipped to an all-time low.'

I felt tears prickling my eyes as I read those words. However vehemently I disagreed with Dan or Fleur's point of view, I couldn't help feeling that there was a germ of truth in what they wrote. And as vulnerable as I felt right now, such words passed through the skin barrier and penetrated deep inside. I fought the urge to defend myself, however, seeing that other commenters had already hastened to my rescue.

'Infidelity becomes an option,' wrote Susan, in the most measured comment, 'when your current relationship no longer meets your needs, whether you acknowledge it or not, and you therefore become open to a kind of contact with potential replacement partners that is instinctively avoided by the happily paired.'

Reading on, I was heartened to see another kind message from Anna Red Boat, who had also met her partner through her blog.

'All sounds a bit familiar,' she wrote. 'The internet is quite far and away the most civilized place to meet a suitor these days, I think. I wish you half my happiness, which should be enough in itself to make you explode, when combined with your quite palpable own.'

Other friends in blogging did their best to inject some humour, lessening the sting of the negative comments, something for which I was profoundly grateful. 'I just think it's shocking,' wrote Tim, his tongue firmly in his cheek, 'that you could even contemplate moving into a new phase of your life without so much as consulting us first. I know my rights.'

That was only the tip of the iceberg. Emails – from the supportive to the damning to the unambiguously insulting – clogged up my inbox. Everyone who read about my situation seemed to view it through the prism of their own experiences. Those who had never been tempted to be unfaithful were self-righteous and quick to criticize; those who had been cuckolded themselves saw me as evil through and through. Those who had been through something similar urged me to follow my heart.

It wasn't only online that I witnessed such mixed reactions. A male work colleague squirmed visibly in his seat as I poured my heart out to him over lunch one day. Was he casting an anxious eye over his own situation, wondering whether his own relationship was entirely sound? Perhaps he thought my behaviour might be *contagious* in some way, I surmised, as though one relationship collapsing could have some sort of domino effect.

'My, those commenters of yours are getting het up, aren't they?' my mother said incredulously on the phone later that evening. I'd taken the handset out on to the balcony, although I was pretty sure Mr Frog was listening to music with his headphones on.

My parents' reaction had surprised me. I'd always confided in my mother, and she knew better than anyone that I'd been unhappy for some time, but I'd still been worried that she would think I should have worked harder at fixing things with Mr Frog rather than bailing out. But when push came to shove, she hadn't questioned the wisdom of my actions at all. Her only fear was that I was diving in at the deep end with James; that things were moving too fast. She fretted that I might be setting myself up for a crushing disappointment further down the line.

'He *sounds* lovely,' she kept repeating, as I enthused about

147

James down the telephone, 'and I can't wait to meet him. But do be careful. He seems almost too good to be true, the way you tell it, but his wife must have divorced him for a reason, nobody's perfect . . .'

'Not for her, he wasn't,' I snapped, 'but that doesn't mean he can't be right for me.' Her pessimism infuriated me, as it always did, even if I knew full well that she was just being a mother, wishing she could protect me from harm.

'Don't get me wrong,' she said hurriedly, 'I'm happy for you, really I am, but it won't be easy, him living in Brittany, you in Paris, both with children of your own. And I doubt he'll be able to support you. You've said yourself that translating doesn't exactly allow him to live comfortably . . .'

'I know, Mum, I know. Being self-employed in France is really hard, there are so many taxes to pay, it's hard to stay afloat. And he has child support to pay to his ex-wife, too. But money isn't everything, is it? I want to give us a try. And after living with a workaholic who was never home, I think I'd rather manage with less money and more of my partner's time.'

Returning to the bedroom, I could hear my phone vibrating in my handbag. No doubt my goodnight message from James. I sat on the edge of the bed and pressed 'read'.

'I think I'm in love with you.'

My breath caught in my throat. James and I had known each other for barely three weeks. We'd written hundreds of emails, talked for hours on the phone, but spent less than twenty-four hours in one another's company. The words didn't surprise me – his eyes had told their own story the last time we were together, in the second hotel – but although my embryonic feelings were growing and ripening with every passing day, deepening into something beyond infatuation and physical desire, I couldn't respond in kind, not yet.

'Love' was a word I had cheapened with overuse over the years, bleeding it dry of meaning by saying it purely from force of habit, or to convince myself of something of which I was far from sure. I wanted to wait until the words started to feel meaningful again. And when I said them, I would say them to his face.

Wide awake hours later, Mr Frog fast asleep beside me, an unwelcome thought flickered across my mind, not for the first time. I'd seen with my own eyes that in James's phone, my number was programmed as that of *petite anglaise*. Was it really *me* James had fallen for, or was it my blog persona?

I wasn't even sure I knew any longer where one ended and the other began, so what chance did he have?

15. Parenthesis

Three whole weeks crawled by before I saw James again.

In the meantime, although we bounced emails and text messages back and forth all day long and spent hours on the phone in the evenings whenever Mr Frog stayed late in the office, or went out, it simply wasn't enough for me. I needed time in James's presence; I needed to be sure it was *me* he wanted.

'Listen, I'm a bit strapped for cash just now, but if you need me to come to Paris, if we have to do the hotel thing again, I will,' he said on the phone one evening.

'It's tempting,' I replied, shivering involuntarily at the memory of the last night we'd spent together. Undeniably, there was something about meeting in a hotel – a whiff of something illicit, forbidden – that was thrilling in itself. 'But what I really want is to do normal things. Take a walk in the park. Cook a meal together. Snuggle up on the sofa in front of the television. Fall asleep with your arms around me. I want to see where you live, so that when we're apart I can picture you there . . .'

'I want those things too,' James said earnestly. 'And we'll do them all when you come to visit. We just have to be patient. Enjoy your weekend in England with your parents. Make the most of your time with your daughter. When the time comes, I know you'll be worth the wait.'

But now that I'd met James, life in Paris seemed even more sterile and barren; my *métro–boulot–dodo* routine unbearably suffocating. Work was a tiresome obligation; the apartment I still shared with Mr Frog a prison with a view. His face was the first thing I saw every morning, a tangible reminder of the pain I had inflicted when I made my decision. My pause button jammed down, I waited, my feelings of guilt and frustration mounting, until I thought I would explode.

'You know, when I first told you about all this, I was convinced you were going to try to dissuade me from taking things any further,' I said to Amy as we set down our brown-paper lunch bags in the office kitchen and pulled out two stools at a table by the window. 'Given, well, your history and everything.'

'I suppose,' said Amy thoughtfully, 'that I did disapprove a bit at first. And I *was* worried about you.' I smiled, liking the 'at first' and sensing an imminent 'but'. I wasn't wrong. 'But you've got such a glow about you these days,' she continued, 'you look so different. It's impossible to feel anything other than happy for you. And I know you're not taking any of it lightly, it's clear from what you say – and what you write – that you feel guilty about all the upheaval, that you're trying to make the transition as painless as possible. But I will say one thing.' She gestured at the cake I was unwrapping, which was all I'd bought for lunch. 'You've really got to start looking after yourself properly . . .'

'I wish my body would just calm down,' I said, watching as she transferred her carton of salad on to a porcelain plate. 'Honestly, you'd think I'd had amphetamines for breakfast, the way I've been grinding my teeth all morning. Hopefully things will improve when I've got all this waiting out the way.'

'I think it's good that you're waiting.' Amy crossed the

room to the dishwasher and took out a clean fork, wiping it on a tea-towel. 'It's healthier this way. Maybe it's a good thing James doesn't actually live in Paris.'

'So the two men in my life never meet, you mean?' I bit into my lemon tart. It was tangy but sweet, and the pastry melted on my tongue. But however delicious it was, my dry, nervous throat had trouble swallowing it, and I had to force myself to take another bite. This was how I'd come to lose over a stone in the past few weeks.

'Well, yes, there's that, but I was thinking more of the fact that distance stops us from getting in too deep, too soon. Which can be a good thing . . .' Amy slid on to the stool beside me. It was then that I noticed she was blushing.

'Hang on,' I said, looking at her intently. 'Have I missed something here? Have *you* met someone new? You have, haven't you? Why on earth didn't you tell me?'

'Oh, well, it's all very recent.' Amy looked coy. 'But I have high hopes. There must be something in the air at the moment. I met someone this weekend. A friend of a friend. He lives in London, though.'

'That's fantastic!' Now that she'd told me, I wondered how on earth I'd missed the signs. The colour in her cheeks. Her unusually buoyant mood. 'I want details! Who is he? What does he do? When are you seeing him next?'

'Actually,' she said, clearly pausing for more dramatic effect, 'I'm seeing him the very same weekend you go to visit James.'

'No way! This calls for a celebration.' I looked at my watch. 'How about we nip out to the shops when we've finished eating? You, my friend, are going to need some new underwear.'

Tutting in unison at the price tags on the Princesse Tam Tam underwear in Monoprix half an hour later, I felt more relaxed, more carefree than I had in weeks. The feelings of guilt which had dogged me as persistently as my own shadow ever since I'd delivered my news to Mr Frog, had lifted, albeit temporarily. For a few minutes I pretended my life was as uncomplicated as Amy's; my decisions as free of repercussions as hers.

When the longed-for day finally came, I raced along the endless, white-tiled corridors of Montparnasse *métro* station, glancing anxiously at my watch. If I hurried, I might just make the main station in time to catch an earlier train, a prize worth breaking into a sweat for. But even as I wove through the crowds, I couldn't help thinking about Mr Frog. He must be collecting Tadpole in the park right about now, making small talk with *Tata*, daunted at the prospect of his first weekend as a single parent, alone. It was impossible to forget that my happiness – this intoxicating feeling of freedom and weightlessness, elation at being able to shrug off my parental responsibilities for a day or two – came at a high price. Balancing my right to happiness against Tadpole's and Mr Frog's was like walking a tightrope.

Pounding up the stairs which delivered me into the pulsing heart of the station, I paused for a moment to take my bearings. I hadn't been here in years. More familiar to me was Gare de Lyon, where I used to catch the train to visit Mr Frog's parents. Montparnasse, the gateway to the west, teemed with rucksack-wearing weekenders and commuters with laptops. Snubbing the crowded escalators, I took the stairs two at a time, then navigated around the queues of travellers waiting to retrieve tickets from the yellow SNCF dispensers. A clock suspended from the ceiling high above read 18.45. With some judicious elbowing I thought I should be able to battle my way to the platform just in time. Pausing only to stamp my ticket in a machine mounted on the wall as I passed, I adjusted my rucksack on my shoulders and lunged forward purposefully.

As the TGV eased itself out of the station, I sat back and closed my eyes, face flushed, still short of breath. I pictured James pacing around his newly cleaned flat, picking out a freshly ironed shirt, uncorking a bottle of wine to let it breathe. He'd been spring-cleaning all day, or so his emails led me to believe, and seemed anxious to impress. If only I could hold that thought, focusing on James and me, our first weekend together; anything to stop me dwelling on those I was leaving behind. It was futile, though: I couldn't chase away sorry images of Mr Frog. I imagined him wondering what to make Tadpole for dinner; forgetting to clean her teeth before bedtime; collapsing in a limp, defeated heap on the sofa. Rightly or wrongly, I suspected it would be some time before I could take my pleasure without a side order of guilt.

Three hours later the train began to slow, approaching Rennes station. I peered through the square pane of glass in the door, but saw only my own pale reflection staring, wide-eyed, back at me. Closing my nostrils to the stench of the chemical toilet, I'd changed out of my work clothes and applied make-up, steadying myself against the metallic sink as the train swayed drunkenly from side to side. I wanted to look picture perfect when I stepped off that train and fell into his arms. But now I was so giddy, so light-headed, that I was half afraid I would fall down the steps as soon as the train doors opened, striking my head on the platform before James could spring forward to catch me.

With a high-pitched shriek of the brakes, the train finally drew to a standstill and, seconds later, the hydraulic mechanism let out a hiss and the door swung aside. Stepping down on to the platform without mishap, I scanned the crowds anxiously for James's face, my heart thudding violently in my chest. At first glance, Rennes was no different from countless other French railway stations I had seen: neither pretty nor ugly, simply concrete and functional. James was nowhere to be seen, and I began to drift towards the exit, letting the crowds propel me forwards while I fumbled in my pocket for my phone. Suddenly I spied a familiar corduroy jacket. Seconds later, arms closed around me, and a familiar smell of aftershave and warm skin filled my nostrils. My bag dropped to the floor, forgotten.

'Let's get you home,' said James urgently when we came up for air. Home, I thought to myself, realizing that the tension of the past three weeks had fallen away the moment we touched, I like the sound of that.

James's apartment, although modestly furnished, was indeed spotless. A duplex under the roof of a fairly modern block of flats, its lower floor was open plan, the bedroom separated from the living room only by a thick curtain. The kitchen consisted of a row of white appliances ranged along one wall next to a sink, divided from the main room by a breakfast bar, upon which a vase of fresh flowers stood. A steep staircase – really more of a ladder – led from the other end of the living room to the upper level, which James used as his office. Two single mattresses lay on the floor of this room, under wooden rafters. This was where his girls slept when they stayed with him on alternate weekends. It was about the same size as my apartment in Paris, when all was said and done, only the layout was very different.

As I reversed down the ladder, I wondered where Tadpole would sleep if I decided to bring her with me one day for a visit. As though he'd read my mind, James opened the door to a tiny room which I had assumed was a cupboard. 'I've been using this for storage,' he explained, 'but, actually, the girls used to sleep in here when they were small. I was thinking of borrowing a travel cot of Eve's. It even has a little window, see, it's not too claustrophobic.'

'You really have thought of everything, haven't you?' I slipped my arms around his waist, inquisitive fingers creeping inside the waistband of his jeans. 'Although,' I added, raising one eyebrow, 'I'm not sure the tour of your bedroom was quite, well, thorough enough. I didn't get a proper look at that bed of yours . . .'

Hours later, we lay tangled in the sheets, our clothes abandoned on the floor, eyes locked, skin touching. James had lit dozens of tea lights and set them on every available surface. They flickered in the draught from the open window, and a cool breeze lapped at our exposed skin. As he moved, I felt as though our edges were blurring; and I clung to him, digging in my fingernails, pulling him deeper, closer, welding us together. I fought the urge to close my eyes, wanting to see his expression, to see my face reflected in his pupils. But when the pleasure broke over me, making me shudder violently, even though my eyes were open, my vision flickered, leaving blanks between every frame.

'Hang on, I just need to find my sunglasses.' I rummaged inside the cotton bag slung over my shoulder, blinking in the sun's glare.

It was Sunday morning – the first time we had ventured out of James's flat all weekend – and I had that dazed, disorientated feeling you get when you leave a cinema after a matinee performance and emerge, surprised to see daylight outdoors. The world was still out there. People were going about their chores as though this were any normal day: buying bread, going to church in their Sunday best, taking their dogs for a walk. And yet I felt anything but normal. My legs were made of cotton wool; there was a high-pitched ringing in my ears. James and I had spent much of the past thirty-six hours in bed and, for the first time in my life, I could relate to the stories I'd read about celebrity lovers who holed up in hotels for days at a time.

James held out his hand. 'Come on, I want to show you something other than the four walls of my flat. We could both do with some fresh air.'

'If you say so . . .' I took his proffered hand and squeezed it, tightly, and we set our course for the main shopping streets.

Rennes reminded me of Rouen, in many ways. A provincial town an hour or so from the coast, it was roughly the same size, and the architecture was very similar. The old town was a maze of narrow streets and paved squares; whole rows of medieval houses with timbered fronts. Letting James guide me, I soon lost my bearings. The shops we passed – Jacadi, Roche Bobois, a boutique selling educational toys made of wood – suggested the inhabitants were pretty well-heeled. We stopped in a *crêperie* on the rue Saint Georges for a snack and I wolfed down a buckwheat *complète* filled with mushrooms, ham and cheese and topped with an egg, its yolk still liquid. It was the closest thing to an English breakfast I was likely to find and, after the weekend's workout, I needed to keep my strength up. My appetite was slowly returning, and I noted I seemed to have got over my initial shyness about eating in front of James.

'I'm really glad I'd never been to Rennes before,' I remarked as we left the restaurant. 'It's healthier to start a new chapter on a clean page, isn't it?'

Unlike Paris, where everyone – including me – always seemed to be frowning at their watches, running late for something, in Rennes people strolled, and shops flipped the signs on their doors from *ouvert* to *fermé* at lunch-time. The very air I drew into my lungs felt cleaner. Paris had been tainted by everything that had soured there, by the negative emotions which hung over my apartment like menacing clouds, moments before a torrential downpour. For me, this weekend in Rennes was a *parenthèse enchantée*, a sidestep into an unsullied, idyllic parallel universe.

'So, you like it then?' asked James, cautiously. Between the lines I could hear his unspoken question. Did I think I might be able to picture myself living in Rennes, with him, one day?

'It's lovely,' I replied wholeheartedly. 'I feel so relaxed. It's so peaceful. I wish I could stay . . .' My lower lip wobbled as I suddenly found myself on the brink of tears. The thought of clambering into the TGV which would propel me back to Paris – to work, to Mr Frog – made my stomach lurch. Must I really close the brackets and go back to all that? Only the thought of seeing Tadpole made returning home bearable. 'Can we go back to your place for a while?' I begged. 'I just want to be held, I want you to distract me until it's time to leave for the station.'

'You, my dear, are insatiable,' replied James, raising an eyebrow. I silently thanked him for making light of my apprehension. He had been perfect all weekend, in every way.

A summer cold crept up on me by stealth as the TGV sped back in the direction of Paris. I sneezed and shivered, nursing a lukewarm paper cup of Lipton yellow with UHT milk, the SNCF's weak apology for tea. The weekend already seemed like a dream, receding further with every passing kilometre. By the time the train pulled into Montparnasse station, my head throbbed. I'd been seated in the last carriage, and it seemed to take an eternity to walk the full length of the train and leave the platform. Unable to face the prospect of public transport, I took the corridor leading to the underground taxi rank, but when I saw the length of the queue I beat a hasty retreat to the *métro*.

Before I turned my key in the lock half an hour later, I hesitated in the doorway for a moment. Tonight, in a bizarre reversal of our usual roles, it was Mr Frog who had given our daughter dinner, bathed her, and read bedtime stories. Tadpole was sleeping, and I was the one arriving home too late for a goodnight kiss. My nose was beginning to drip in earnest and, once inside, I went to grab a tissue from the box in the bathroom. Catching sight of myself in the mirror, I studied my reflection. You'd never guess I'd spent most of the weekend on cloud nine, I thought wryly, looking at my pale face, and my glassy, feverish eyes.

Mr Frog lay on the sofa, pretty much as I'd pictured him. He was wearing his threadbare velour top, which he must have exhumed from the back of the cupboard, and looked wan and exhausted. 'So, how did you two get on this weekend?' I enquired, trying to inject a brightness into my voice which I did not feel. 'I bet she loved having you to herself.'

'It was good,' he replied, stifling a yawn, not deigning to tear his eyes away from the TV screen, 'but really hard too. All that time to fill. She can be so demanding . . .' He didn't ask me about my trip, and I volunteered no information. Taking my rucksack into the bedroom so I could unpack out of sight, I pressed the 'power' button on the front of my computer as I went past. Kicking off my shoes, I sat down on the bed and rested my throbbing head in my hands for a moment.

'The good news is, I've found a flat across the road,' Mr Frog added, still speaking to me from the sofa, the partition wall between us. 'A really nice one. It's a bit expensive, but never mind.'

'And the bad news?'

'It won't be free for another month or so, until the beginning of July.' My face fell, and I was glad Mr Frog couldn't see me. Another month of limbo? Another month of this uneasy truce? My silence must have spoken volumes, even if my face was hidden. 'I'm sorry,' he added. 'I know you can't wait to be rid of me. But that's the best I could do.'

In the early hours of the morning I awoke to the sound of coughing in the bathroom and an empty space in the bed where Mr Frog should have been. This time, I doubted that work was the culprit. He would be signing the new lease later in the day; the fact of his leaving would suddenly become real. Hearing those sorry noises brought tears of remorse to my eyes. It was easy to trot out glib phrases like 'We can't move on until we no longer live under the same roof,' but I kept losing sight of how hard it was, this thing I was forcing him to do.

I'd been focusing on practicalities so I didn't have to think about the horror Mr Frog must feel at the idea of waking up alone in a place where his daughter would only be an occasional visitor. I busied myself making lists instead, or doing inventories in my head. Soon, I would have a bed, but no mattress. Cable TV, but no television set. I was pathetically relieved, with hindsight, that the computer was mine; likewise the stereo and the bookcase. There would soon be gaps, where pieces of furniture had once stood, and the flat would seem too big, at least at first. Which of the two sofas would I sit on, I wondered? Which side of the bed would I favour, when I finally began sleeping alone?

The only item whose fate we'd failed to agree on was the exercise bike which had long stood unused in a corner of our bedroom. After Tadpole's birth, I'd twisted Mr Frog's arm for weeks, begging him to help me find a way to lose the baby fat which clung stubbornly to my hips and stomach, until eventually he caved in. The bike hadn't seen much use, of course. The ironing pile had taken up residence on its saddle and, when I glanced at it, more often than not it was simply to read the temperature displayed on its console. As for Mr Frog, he'd never used it; not even once.

Neither of us was especially attached to the bike, but it had become our battleground, the focus of our anger and resentment. A more perfect, textbook example of displacement would be hard to find. It was safer by far to cross swords over the future of an inanimate object than it was to examine the things which were really eating away at us.

16. Families

Just as I tiptoed around Mr Frog in the home we still shared, throughout the period of limbo, I skirted around the subject of my new relationship on *petite anglaise*. While I hinted at my budding romance, I revealed little in the way of detail, for Mr Frog's sake, and the identity of the man I referred to only as 'Lover' still remained a secret.

But there was something else at play too: rationing the story kept my readers panting for more. The urge to tease them, to draw out the suspense for as long as possible, was irresistible. When finally one day I revealed that I'd met 'Lover' in my comments box, the race was on to unmask my suitor. Several commenters – including Jim in Rennes – fell under suspicion over the next few weeks. As the debate raged on, resurfacing every time I dropped another tiny clue into a post, James remained conspicuously silent, occasionally piping up only to deflect suspicion away from himself. Commenters who had been wrongfully accused entered into the spirit of the game and, on more than one occasion, I caught myself smirking, or even laughing out loud as I peeped at my comments while my boss's back was turned.

'(Heart)breaking news: a visibly shaken, broken-hearted and tearfully bitter Parkin Pig today sadly issued a formal denial of any romance with the mysterious *petite anglaise*. He was quoted as saying "Chance'd be a fine thing."'

'Is it me?' wondered Andre. 'Was I good?'

I had no qualms about toying with my readers in this way, but I did worry that I wasn't being as sensitive as I ought to

Mr Frog's feelings, when I allowed such comments through. I drew some comfort from the fact that he'd never followed the blog religiously in the past and had given me no reason to believe this was no longer the case. In truth, though, how Mr Frog felt about *petite anglaise*, or about me, was a mystery he guarded even more closely than I guarded James's identity.

Offline, I had another set of worries to deal with, too sensitive to air on my blog. 'I'm really nervous about this weekend,' I confessed to James on the telephone a few days before I was next due to visit, while I paced up and down the balcony, trying to tune out the sound of the traffic below. 'Not about you meeting my daughter. She likes everyone she meets, and you'll just be "Mummy's friend" to her, she won't understand. But with *your* daughters, it's different.'

James's girls – Amanda and Carrie – were eight and ten years old respectively. Pre-teens: an unknown quantity as far as I was concerned. I wanted to like them. I wanted to be liked by them. If things were to work out between James and me, we needed to get along. Not that I saw myself as some sort of stepmother in waiting. I was a few years younger than the girls' own mother, and doubted I'd be seen as an authority figure. The ideal situation, I felt, would be to be seen as a friend, a female ally. But what if they didn't warm to me? What would that mean for James and me?

'You worry too much, honey,' James reassured me. 'It's all going to be fine. Amanda said she was really looking forward to meeting you. They can both see how much happier I've been these past few weeks, and they're thrilled for me. Honestly.'

'Well, if you say so,' I sighed, 'but I don't think I'll be able to stop feeling nervous until we've got this out of the way. You know me – or at least you're beginning to – I always worry. That's what I do best.'

'I do say so,' he said firmly. 'And I'm not trying to make light of the situation. It is important – and you're right to care deeply about it – but I don't think getting all wound up is going to help anyone. You'll be fine. We'll be fine. Just wait and see.'

I turned, conscious of a movement on the periphery of my vision, and saw Mr Frog standing just inside the kitchen, lighting a cigarette at the gas hob. Had he been listening to our conversation, I wondered? Stepping inside, I pressed the mute button on the phone. 'We can swap places if you like,' I said. 'You go outside with your cigarette, and I'll take this call in the bedroom.' Mr Frog nodded, poker-faced, as usual.

'Sorry,' I said, once I'd closed the bedroom door behind me, 'just had an awkward moment. I think I'd better go. It feels too cruel talking to you when he's around. I'll email you from work, tomorrow, instead.'

Setting down the phone on the bed, I silently stepped out on to the bedroom balcony. I couldn't see Mr Frog from here – the arched window of our living room jutted out and broke the line of the building – but I could smell his cigarette smoke, and if I leaned forward a few centimetres, I could see his forearm resting on the balustrade. Was he looking to the right, towards the park, towards the building where he would soon live, as he drew the smoke down into his lungs? Sometimes I wished it were possible to see inside his head, to read his thoughts, just as thousands of strangers read mine.

The next morning, Mr Frog and I crept into Tadpole's room to wake her earlier than usual. Stroking her forehead with the back of my forefinger, enjoying the feel of her silky skin, I began to sing. Mr Frog stood by my side, his expression difficult to fathom.

'Happy birthday to you . . .' Tadpole pursed her lips, eyes

still closed, and rolled over to hide her face against the bedroom wall. I wasn't fooled. I'd seen the telltale twitch of a smile dawning on her lips: she was only pretending to sleep. 'Happy birthday to you,' I continued, and this time Mr Frog's voice mingled hesitantly with my own.

'*Non!*' Tadpole mumbled. 'I busy sleeping!' I shot an amused glance at Mr Frog.

'That's a shame,' I said with a sly smile. 'If you're busy sleeping, who shall we give all these presents to?' Tadpole shot bolt upright at the mention of presents, as I'd suspected she would, and I moved my face out of the way in the nick of time, narrowly avoiding a blow to the chin.

'To me!' she cried. 'My presents! Because I two years old!' She made an L-shaped two with the thumb and forefinger of her right hand, something which *Tata* must have taught her.

'*Joyeux anniversaire, ma puce,*' said Mr Frog. I stepped aside and let him scoop our birthday girl from her bed. The first hug of the day was always the best. Tadpole was warm, groggy and at her most malleable.

Mr Frog and I had filled the living room with scores of pastel-coloured balloons of all shapes and sizes the previous evening, after my phone call ended, just as we had on her first birthday. Tadpole clapped her hands in delight as soon as she saw them, wriggling out of Mr Frog's arms and scattering balloons in her wake as she ran to unveil her main present, a red and yellow tricycle which we had covered with a blanket. By its side a stack of smaller presents lay ready to be unwrapped – gifts which had arrived from family members by post. That evening, after work, I would bring out the Noddy cake I'd bought in England a couple of weeks earlier and transported home gingerly in my hand luggage, and there would be candles to be blown out, wishes to be wished. Amidst the popping of balloons under bicycle tyres, my camera would flash away, recording the bittersweet day for posterity.

I made a print of the photo Mr Frog took of the three of us that day, his arm outstretched to take a surprisingly well-framed self-portrait. There we were, sitting on the sofa: Tadpole beaming in the middle, Mr Frog and I doing our utmost, smiling with our mouths, but not our eyes. In the photo album I'd been compiling since our daughter's birth, I added her birthday photos one by one until I reached the very last page of the album. There I stuck the picture of the three of us, the very last picture taken of us together living under the same roof.

When I'd finished, I flipped through the pages back to the beginning and my eyes snagged on a picture I'd taken of a week-old Tadpole nestling against her father's shoulder, fast asleep on our bed; their faces, in repose, almost identical. They looked so innocent, so peaceful. None of us had suspected then what lay in store, two years down the line. Closing the album with an ache of regret, I hugged it to myself for a moment, then replaced it on the bookshelf.

'I playing with this!' cried Tadpole, as I tried, and failed, to swipe my lipstick from her stubborn paw. Luckily it still had its cap tightly in place. I removed my glasses, placing them out of Tadpole's reach, as a precaution, and endeavoured to apply mascara, holding a tiny mirror in one hand, and bracing my other elbow against the fold-out table to steady myself. Our belongings – my make-up and Tadpole's various forms of entertainment – were strewn across a table for four, and an elderly French lady was seated opposite us, reading a magazine. The last two hours had been spent spotting sheep and cows through the train window, reading Maisy books and drawing pictures. Despite my rising tide of panic at the prospect of meeting Amanda and Carrie, I had found reserves of maternal patience to draw on which I hadn't even known I possessed. That was the beauty of parenting with an audience, performing the role of 'perfect mother' for a complete stranger.

It wasn't that I thought I was usually a bad parent. But I knew for a fact that I was a better one if there was someone else within earshot. Regardless of whether or not my audience was actually paying attention, I engaged more with my daughter, was far more likely to try to teach her a new word or invest some energy in eliciting a giggle if someone just might be observing us.

I was proud of Tadpole's drawings, her burgeoning bilingualism, her soft blonde curls and the peachy perfection of her skin. When I bent double under the table every few minutes to retrieve yet another errant crayon, I didn't even grumble. We were a perfect double act. Every time the old lady looked up from her magazine and smiled at Tadpole, I basked in her reflected glory.

But now I really did need that lipstick she was holding. Our train would arrive in Rennes station in just a few short minutes. Hopefully she would consider a finger of Kitkat to be an appropriate trade.

Disembarking from the train gracefully was more difficult this time with a heavy weekend bag slung over one shoulder, a Maclaren buggy over the other, simultaneously trying to hold Tadpole's hand and help her down the step on to the platform. My hair fell into my eyes; my excitement at the prospect of seeing James was tempered by the apprehension I felt about meeting his daughters.

I spied him immediately, waiting further along the platform, flanked by two fair-haired girls who, at first glance, bore a striking resemblance to their father. I suppressed the urge to throw myself into his arms, contenting myself with a shy smile and an affectionate yet restrained peck on the cheek. Three young pairs of eyes would be trained on us all weekend. We would have to behave accordingly.

'Good trip?' enquired James, taking the holdall from my shoulder while I shook the pushchair open and pushed down on the locking mechanism with my right foot. 'And who's this little girl you've brought with you?'

'Say hello, sweetie,' I prompted, as Tadpole clung to my legs, doing a very convincing impression of shyness. 'This is Mummy's friend James.'

'And these are *my* girls, Amanda and Carrie,' said James, addressing his words to Tadpole. I was grateful to him for making the introductions – I hadn't been sure which was which, and didn't want to get off on the wrong foot by inverting their names. What if the tallest had also been the youngest? In fact, the tall, long-limbed girl wearing fine metal-rimmed glasses was Carrie, the older of the two; Amanda was shorter, curvier and looked more approachable. Both girls had been born in France, and spent their whole lives in Brittany, but to me they looked unmistakably English.

'Hi,' I said, kissing each on the cheek in turn. 'It's lovely to meet you both.' We stood smiling nervously for a moment, sizing one another up until, flustered, I turned back to Tadpole, trying to coax her into the pushchair. 'Are you going to hop in? It's quite a long walk to James's house.' Tadpole shook her head, and I could see from her mutinous expression that if I insisted, a tantrum would surely follow. What a start to the weekend, I thought to myself, grimly, and after she'd been so well behaved on the train, too.

It was Amanda who saved the day. As though it were the most natural thing in the world, she grasped Tadpole's hand in hers and led the way along the platform, bending her head low and whispering something in her ear. I caught James's eye and smiled, and we followed their lead, Carrie holding James's free hand, while I brought up the rear pushing the empty buggy. Any stranger who had seen us traipsing along the platform that evening must surely have thought we were a family like any other.

I would have blanched a few weeks earlier if someone had told me I was about to plunge into a serious relationship with a divorced older man, with children of his own and emotional baggage far heavier than the weekend bag which now dangled from his shoulder. On paper, it seemed like folly. But in practice? Well, maybe I had a bad case of the rose-tinted spectacles but, at that moment, on the platform of Rennes station, anything seemed possible.

The next day, the girls and I loaded up the boot of James's car with bathing suits, beach umbrellas and a picnic hamper, while he fiddled with the spare car seat he'd borrowed from Eve, fastening it in place in the middle of the back seat. Our destination was Saint Briac sur Mer, a small coastal town not far from Saint Malo, just over an hour's drive north-west of Rennes. Setting out for the beach, it felt as though we were on holiday. But if Tadpole and I moved to Brittany one day, I thought to myself, there would be nothing to stop us doing this every other weekend, if we so desired. I could even get behind the wheel again – something I hadn't done since I passed my test back in England, more years ago than I cared to remember – and learn how to drive on the French side of the road, a prospect which filled me with a mixture of excitement and trepidation.

There was something about sitting in the passenger seat, racing along the motorway, my hair ruffled by the breeze blowing in through the sliver of open window, which made me feel more like an adult. It had often struck me that Mr

Frog and I seemed like children playing at being grown-ups, whereas James seemed like the real thing. A half-smile on my lips, I listened to how his tone changed when he spoke to Amanda and Carrie, hearing the gentle authority in his voice. It was obvious that the two girls doted on their father. The previous night I'd noted with amusement how the girls fought bitterly over who would get to sit on the tiny sofa by his side. And I'd been surprised, but impressed, to see that he still disappeared up into the attic to read to them before bedtime. First I had known James as a lover, then as a friend. Now I was discovering another facet of his character, and I liked what I saw very much. The more three-dimensional he became, the more attractive I found him. I hoped that seeing me as a mother – as opposed to *petite anglaise*, or a lover – made him feel the same way.

Through narrowed eyes I watched him covertly as he drove: his assurance behind the wheel; the smooth brown legs protruding from his blue shorts which I longed to reach out and touch. Not in front of the children, we'd decided. After all, to all intents and purposes I was still sharing a bed with Tadpole's father. Nonetheless it would be excruciating having to wait until nightfall before we could finally spend some precious time alone, and even then I knew I would never be able to give myself over to pleasure in the same way, biting into the pillow, mindful of the children sleeping close by, the bedroom shielded from the living room only by a curtain.

It was a scorching day, unseasonably hot even for June, and by the time we reached our destination, the sun beat mercilessly down on the sand. Walking barefoot burned the soles of my feet and I moved as quickly as I could, Tadpole in my arms, yelping from time to time as though I were jogging over hot coals. Once we'd set up camp, shielding our possessions under a large parasol, we headed into the sea to cool off. But although it looked inviting, the water was brutally, icily cold.

'Jesus! It's freezing,' I protested, my teeth chattering, holding tightly on to Tadpole's hand as the waves lapped around her knees.

'What did you expect?' James yelled back to me, striding much further in, following his daughters, who were up to their necks already, and swimming. 'We're in the English Channel, not the Mediterranean!'

Tadpole loved to paddle, but there were sharp stones underfoot, and I hadn't thought to buy her any beach shoes. To her dismay I soon dragged her, protesting, back under the parasol, where I reapplied sunscreen and half-heartedly built her a sandcastle, while James and his daughters frolicked in the waves.

Under cover of my sunglasses I frowned as I watched them play, James pretending to be some sort of sea monster and diving under the waves to grab his daughters' limbs, making them shriek with delight. All of a sudden I felt more like a petulant child than an adult. Coming to the beach had seemed like such a lovely idea, in theory, but now I wasn't so sure. The age gap dividing our children was so great that we'd never be able to do the same things. A day spent sitting wistfully on the sidelines didn't appeal to me at all. I'd come here to be with James and his children, not to be a spectator.

'I'd forgotten how much work the beach can be with a toddler,' I said wryly as James flopped down beside us on a towel, smiling widely and sprinkling us with a shower of welcome droplets. Carrie and Amanda had turned their attention to the contents of a rock pool some distance away. Tadpole, bored with building sandcastles, was busy bulldozing them instead. Rolling around on the ground before her sun cream had penetrated her skin, she was coated in a thick layer of sticky sand.

'Aren't you enjoying yourself?' he said, genuinely surprised. 'I've been so wrapped up in the girls, I didn't stop to think . . .'

'Oh. No. I mean, yes. We're fine. Really.' I spoke with more conviction than I actually felt. 'It's a gorgeous beach, and the outing was a really lovely idea.' I swiped a mussel shell out of Tadpole's hand, just as she was about to put it in her mouth, and braced myself for her howls of protest. 'But I'd like to come here sometime just with you. Relax, eat some seafood . . .'

'We will,' he said with a smile. 'Alone would be good. And definitely wear that bikini.' I blushed. With all the weight I'd lost I'd managed to squeeze into a pre-Tadpole bikini I hadn't worn in years. But James was no longer looking at me, his eyes were riveted on the distant forms of his daughters pottering at the foot of the cliffs. Carrie appeared to have caught something and was brandishing her bucket proudly. James was on duty; we both were. Half his attention was the best I could hope for right now.

We braved the heat for as long as we could, munching our sandwiches under the parasol in a companionable silence and inspecting the small but feisty crab Carrie had caught before she released it back into a rock pool. But by the time our picnic was over, the heat had become unbearable, and we decided to head back to the car. James helped me rinse Tadpole – wailing and doing everything she could to squirm out of our grasp – under the cold tap set into a stone wall by the entrance to the beach, removing as much of the sand as we possibly could. To mollify her, I promised ice cream. We set off in the direction of a beachfront kiosk and I peered anxiously into my purse, wondering if I had enough money to treat the five of us.

Amanda and Carrie walked with a spring in their step, chattering nineteen to the dozen, their arms linked through James's, staking their claim with casual ease. Tadpole and I followed, the distance between us widening as she refused to walk at anything but a snail's pace, my face growing longer with every step as we fell behind. It was irksome having to share James so soon after we'd met; frustrating having to melt into the background. I couldn't help wishing we were alone, just like on that first weekend. I understood why he was lavishing attention on his daughters – it was their fortnightly weekend with him, every minute was precious – just as I appreciated that he was being careful not to crowd Tadpole and me. But there was no escaping the fact that I felt left out.

As if James could read my thoughts, he turned and looked back. 'How about you come for a ride on my shoulders,' he called out to Tadpole. 'Would that be okay with Mummy?'

'Oh, I think she'd love that!' I replied, suddenly ashamed of my selfish thoughts. James hoisted Tadpole on to his shoulders and she cried out in delight, thrilled to see how different the world looked from her new vantage point. Quickening my pace, I fell into step with Amanda and Carrie, determined to make more of an effort.

On the way back to Rennes the children were quiet, exhausted from the heady combination of heat and exertion. I tapped James lightly on the arm and pointed at his rear mirror. Tadpole's head rested on the side of her car seat, a thin strand of dribble extending from her chin, while Amanda and Carrie dozed uncomfortably, their heads lolling against the windowpanes. Above the sound of the engine I thought I could make out gentle snoring, although it was impossible to spot the culprit.

James caught my eye and smiled. 'I told you there was nothing to worry about, didn't I?' he said in a stage whisper. I nodded and put a hesitant hand on his thigh and, since there were no witnesses, I let it rest there for a while.

I knew that the blog post I was composing in my head would dwell on moments like this one, leaving out the petty feelings of jealousy I'd experienced on the beach, or the moments when I'd uncharitably wished our children away. If my glass were half empty, *petite anglaise*'s would be half full. It hadn't lasted very long, I thought to myself ruefully, this desire for James to know the real me, warts and all.

Not even two months into our relationship and I was censoring our story already.

17. *Canicule*

I've never been a fan of summertime in Paris.

Bathed in spring sunlight, the sandstone buildings which line the River Seine take on the hue of clotted cream. Bare branches give way to delicate leaves and bursts of colour: the candyfloss pink of cherry blossom, the buttery yellow of laburnum. The skies are capricious: deep azure blues pale to washed-out watercolour greys; flighty, inconsistent clouds are chased away by brooding, purposeful cousins. The spring sun plays hide and seek. It caresses but rarely burns; it bears no malice.

But in the summer months, when temperatures begin to soar, my spirits sink. I brace myself for the arrival of *la canicule*.

In a heatwave the white sun blinds and scorches. An oppressive mantle of polluted air smothers the city, relinquishing its stranglehold for only a few short hours before dawn. At night, my bedroom window open, motorbikes revving at the traffic lights jerk me out of my fitful slumber. At the first murmur of an approaching street-cleaning lorry, I haul myself out of bed with a groan, slamming the windows shut before the drone becomes a roar. With the windows closed the bedroom becomes a sauna, the humid silence broken only by the whine of an urban mosquito.

Tadpole was a June baby, and the first summer of her life – marred by a record-breaking *canicule* – was an ordeal. From midday until nightfall the sun struck our windows with all its force, its heat penetrating deep into the stone walls of the building. The balcony floor was hot enough to fry an egg; the curlicued railings doubled as branding irons. The geraniums in my window boxes were bleached of all colour, their scorched petals crunching underfoot.

In semi-darkness, the shutters closed, I listlessly watched one rented film after another while baby Tadpole dozed on the sofa beside me clad only in her nappy, her hands curled into fists above her head. An electric fan whirred beside us, stirring the soupy air gamely enough but providing little actual relief. When our skin touched, perspiration glued us together. We took cooling baths and I watched over Tadpole with a new mother's fearful vigilance, terrified she would overheat and dehydrate.

Thousands of elderly people perished in the heat that summer while their children and grandchildren holidayed in the south, oblivious to their plight. The morgues of Paris overflowed with unclaimed bodies: it was a national scandal.

While I had nothing so sinister on my conscience, guilt gnawed away at my insides all the same. I was horrified with myself for counting the days until the end of my maternity leave, looking forward to returning to the air-conditioned office, a haven of cool in the City of Heat. The ambient temperature wasn't the only attraction: I craved adult company. I missed meaningless banter, frivolous gossip, deconstructing soap operas over lunch. Every morning, when Mr Frog left for his office, I was nauseous with envy. He had waived his right to paternity leave, telling me it was impossible to take a holiday, he was up to his eyes in work. I felt abandoned: left to face parenthood alone, cut off from my friends and family, held hostage by the heat.

Tadpole's first summer drifted by in a hot fug of resentment. Even when it was finally over, I would never quite shake off the feeling that our home had become my prison.

My life had been irrevocably changed by Tadpole's arrival, while Mr Frog's remained the same.

Hot on the heels of Tadpole's second birthday, our unseasonably hot day out at the beach with James and his daughters heralded the return of *la canicule*. One evening after work the following week, Mr Frog, Tadpole and I waded sluggishly through the dense evening air. I felt as parched as my geraniums. A frantic day at work, the fetid stench of perspiration in the *métro* on the way home, a dash to the supermarket flanked by Tadpole to fill our empty fridge with provisions for the week ahead: all these things had sapped my energy. My batteries were almost flat.

Tadpole, who had refused categorically to be parted from her Dora the Explorer doll when we set out, infuriated me by trying to wriggle out of my iron grip at the pedestrian crossing. She'd always had a stubborn streak, and no doubt she was tired, but she had also begun exhibiting textbook 'terrible two' behaviour, challenging my authority at every opportunity. The words '*non!*' and 'no!' cropped up with alarming regularity these days, followed by an almost audible exclamation mark. I fought the temptation to snap at her, nevertheless: our expedition today was an important one, and I wanted no tears or tantrums to mar it.

'Mummy needs to hold your hand, honey,' I said, without raising my voice. 'There are cars on the road. It's very dangerous.'

'*Non! Veux pas!*' I sighed and hoisted her into my arms instead, where she bucked and squirmed, furious at being overruled.

Mr Frog strode ahead when the lights changed, a carton of assorted bric-à-brac in his arms, most of which I was secretly rather glad to see the back of. He whistled as he walked. Such cheerfulness seemed misplaced, indecent under the circumstances, and it unsettled me. Here we were, on our way to visit his future home for the very first time and, in my mind's eye, I had imagined the scene as a gloomy funeral procession. He wasn't supposed to be upbeat and happy. Surely, at the very least, the occasion called for a touch of solemnity?

'We're going to visit Daddy's new house today,' I explained to Tadpole, setting her down at the foot of the steps which led from the pavement up to the entrance hall of Mr Frog's apartment block. His *deux pièces* was perched atop one of the more modern buildings overlooking the park. '*Un immeuble de grand standing*' in estate-agent speak, which, translated into English, seemed to mean lots of marble-effect tiles and gold-coloured light fittings. Opposite the bank of intercom buttons on the first floor, a sign announced the presence of a concierge. I was impressed: so far, so *chic*.

As we filed into a mirrored lift – twice the size of its poor relation at what would soon become known as 'Mummy's house' – I glanced at Mr Frog, who was no longer whistling. His expression was impenetrable now, and I dared not ask what he was thinking. Turning my attention back to our daughter, I resumed my speech, my voice infused with a forced joviality I didn't really feel.

'Sometimes you'll be staying with Daddy at Daddy's house, and sometimes you'll be staying with Mummy at Mummy's house,' I explained as the lift drew to a halt at the eighth floor. I hoped the words were sinking in, but it was impossible to tell. 'You'll have two bedrooms, two beds, two potties . . . Aren't you a lucky girl?'

Tadpole gazed back at me gravely, but did not reply. I decided to abandon my speech for now. It was too theoretical: she needed to see Daddy's new home with her own eyes if it were to become real to her. I suspected she wasn't the only one.

Mr Frog set down his box and unlocked the door, his hands fumbling with the unfamiliar keys. The door swung open on well-oiled hinges, and we filed inside, one by one. 'This is gorgeous!' I exclaimed, amazed. The main room was spacious and bright and, as Mr Frog moved to open windows, the room was filled with a merciful cross-breeze. We were high above the surrounding buildings, and picture windows, each with its own balcony, lined three sides of the building. But the main attraction was the view from the living-room window: there, Paris was laid out at our feet.

'Wow,' I said, making straight for the largest balcony. Rooftops stretched into the distance as far as the eye could see. 'I thought the view from across the road was something special, but this tops it, for sure.'

'Yes, it's not bad, *my* view, *n'est-ce pas?*' replied Mr Frog, lighting up a cigarette and resting his arms proudly on the balustrade. Tadpole peeped through the bars between us, her eyes following a passing aeroplane which traced a hazy white trail across the early evening sky.

We spent a few moments picking out the landmarks we recognized, their spires and domes rising above the slate roofs of residential buildings: the dome of the Panthéon, the spires of Notre Dame, the primary colours of the Pompidou Centre, the faraway Tour Montparnasse. It was a bigger, better, wide-screen version of my own beloved view. Even the Eiffel Tower was visible from here. From across the road we'd only ever seen its lights reflected against the sky: Mr Frog's new building had been hiding it all along.

As Mr Frog stubbed out his cigarette, I felt the clenched muscles in my jaw relaxing. I hadn't been fully aware of how much I'd been dreading our visit until my pent-up tension began to dissipate. I'd pictured a drab apartment with peeling paint; a melancholy place where Mr Frog would eat TV dinners in front of a flickering TV screen. Imagining Mr Frog entertaining friends in his new bachelor pad, conjuring up an image of Tadpole pottering contentedly in the living room, her toys strewn across the pale parquet floor, my burden of guilt was instantly eased.

With some difficulty, we wrenched our eyes away from the view and followed Tadpole through to the bedroom, which looked out over a corner of the park. The balcony skimmed the tops of the trees on this side of the building, and when I craned my neck to the right, I could just make out the arched window of my living room.

'If I set up a tripod just here,' said Mr Frog with a sly smile, 'I'll be able to see exactly what you're up to.' He was teasing, of course, but much as I admired his ability to crack jokes at a time like this, alarm bells were also sounding in my head. I squinted down at the passers-by far below. Was it possible to recognize people from this height? Every morning I would pass by on the opposite pavement, conspicuous with my pushchair, on the way to *Tata*'s house. Would Mr Frog torture himself by watching us go by? Would I feel a prickling at the back of my neck?

It was beginning to dawn on me that his proximity, however invaluable from the point of view of sharing Tadpole's time, might also be problematic. I didn't much relish the thought of striding into the local bakery with James and finding Mr Frog there, queuing to buy a baguette. And what if I happened upon Mr Frog and a girlfriend one day as they said their goodbyes on the steps of his building? But it was too late to voice any concerns now. The benefits clearly outweighed the disadvantages and, anyhow, the lease had already been signed.

'I'm going to buy you a new bed, and we'll put it right here, in this corner,' Mr Frog explained to Tadpole, turning his back on the window. He was planning a trip to Ikea in a rented van to equip his new place, the weekend after next. Once everything was in place, he'd finally move out.

'Are you going to get curtains for this room?' I asked, regretting my question almost as soon as the words escaped my mouth. I'd have to learn to bite back the urge to give advice about feathering his new nest. It was his, not ours. The same went for everything in his life. It was time to take a step back and let him get on with the business of making this new home his own.

'I won't need curtains, no, because there are shutters outside the windows.' He grabbed a pole with a metal handle and demonstrated the mechanism. Wooden shutters descended like eyelids until we stood blinking in the darkness for a moment before Mr Frog slowly wound them back up again.

Tadpole giggled. '*Maintenant, j'ai deux* bedrooms!' she cried, clapping her hands with glee. I looked at Mr Frog in amazement: my clumsy explanation in the lift, and Mr Frog's just now, had not been a waste of breath, after all. We'd taken care to place the emphasis on everything Tadpole would gain, as opposed to what she would be losing, and our strategy seemed to have paid off: it didn't seem to occur to her that this new development could be anything but positive.

'How about we take a look at the other rooms?' I suggested. Tadpole took this as her cue to scamper off along the corridor, eager to explore. 'She seems to be taking this remarkably well,' I added in a low voice, once she was out of earshot.

Mr Frog shrugged. 'We'll see,' he said, with a clipped smile, devoid of any real warmth. 'Only time will tell.' The pride he'd taken in his new view, the joking in the bedroom had now given way to some new emotion. But whatever he was feeling, I was the last person who could offer any comfort, so

I held my tongue and followed him along the corridor after our daughter.

Back at home, Tadpole in bed, I trudged through the living room, my arms filled with damp washing. Mr Frog was slumped on the sofa, the remote control within easy reach. Half the contents of the fridge lay on a tray on the coffee table before him, his usual improvised evening picnic. On the surface little had changed. We led our separate lives under the same roof just as we always had: we fed ourselves, I wrote my blog, he watched TV or worked on his laptop. I made no protest when he left his dishes in the sink or staggered in late, his breath heavy with alcohol. There seemed little point in seeking confrontation these days, and I was cutting Mr Frog more slack than I ever had before. The wait was nearly over.

Dumping the mound of intertwined clothes on the bed, I began to assemble the white plastic drying rack by the window. 'You dropped something,' said Mr Frog. I hadn't heard the floorboards creak, and the unexpected proximity of his voice caused me to whirl round in surprise. The drying rack, not yet secured, collapsed in on itself and clattered to the floor. I held out my hand for the missing sock – or whatever it was he was holding in his fist – but he showed no sign of moving towards me, so, with a sigh, I rounded the bed. 'I've never seen these before – are they new?' said Mr Frog, his voice even and expressionless as he opened his fist to reveal my navy-blue knickers with the light-blue ribbons.

'Yes, they are quite new,' I admitted, reddening. Of all the things I could have dropped, why did I have to let go of those? It was tantamount to dangling my new sex life in his face; taunting him with the fact that I had been buying new underwear for someone else's enjoyment. It wasn't as if Mr

Frog didn't know what was going on, but spelling things out so clearly seemed unnecessarily cruel.

'You never bought stuff like that before,' said Mr Frog, his arms folded, the offending knickers still dangling from his little finger. I couldn't help wondering whether he was savouring my discomfort. His eyes were a stony shade of grey.

'Well, *you* always said you preferred cotton,' I retorted, resuming my wrestling match with the drying rack, unable to weather his accusing stare any longer.

Mr Frog left the room without another word and I hung up the washing with shaking fingers. When at last I turned, I found the blue knickers hanging from the top right-hand corner of my monitor.

'It must be excruciating, having to live together while you wait for him to move,' said James sympathetically. 'But it must be really hard for him too. I was in his shoes once, remember? When my wife ended things, I could tell she couldn't wait to move me out and her new guy in. I think I dug in my heels and stuck around for far longer than I should have done. I didn't see why I should make things easier for her.'

I wondered if Mr Frog had been dragging his feet on purpose. It was true that it had been almost six weeks since our break-up. But to be fair, given the Paris rental market, he'd done really well to find a place so quickly.

'I don't suppose you made it any easier on yourself,' I said cautiously. 'By sticking around, I mean.'

'Well, no, I don't suppose I did,' James concurred. 'But I wasn't at my most rational.'

It was Saturday evening and we were sitting in a tiny Mexican restaurant in Rennes. Sombreros hung on ochre walls; cheerful folk music played in the background – all of which seemed incongruous given the nature of our conversation. I'd noticed when we entered that the owner seemed to know him well, and I couldn't help wondering who else James had brought here over the years. His ex-wife? Eve? Suddenly I longed to go back to his apartment. We seemed to function better behind closed doors; preferably horizontal.

'Anyway, that's enough of the doom and gloom,' said James, steering the conversation purposefully away from Mr Frog. The whole point of escaping to Rennes was to leave my worries behind, not to allow them to cast a shadow over our weekend. James put his hand to his jacket pocket. 'On a happier note, I've got a little something for you.' For a split second I wondered how I would react if James withdrew a jewellery case. But there was no velvet box. Instead he handed me a jangling set of keys. 'I wanted you to have these. From now on, my place is yours. If you ever need to come here, if you ever need to get away, you'll always be welcome.'

'Thank you,' I said, closing my fist tightly around my gift. I hesitated, wondering whether to reveal what I'd been thinking when his hand went to his pocket, and decided to take the plunge. 'For a moment there, I half wondered whether you were about to pull out an engagement ring . . .'

'I hope you weren't too disappointed?' he said slowly, taking my hand in his, still clenched around the keys, and bringing it to his lips. 'As a matter of fact, I would very much like to marry you one day,' he added, his stare unflinching. 'If you'd have me, that is.'

I gasped. It couldn't be called a proposal, exactly, couched so cautiously in the conditional tense, but for the first time in my life I was with a man who could conceive of marrying me one day, and the idea thrilled me. All those arguments I'd paraded on my blog when I'd spoken of Mr Frog's reluctance to tie the knot now seemed pitiful and misguided. He'd been right all along: pragmatism was no basis for making such a decision. But I'd quietly assumed that James's divorce would have rendered wedding vows devoid of all meaning for him. Apparently I'd been wrong.

That night, as we lay spent and light-headed in crumpled sheets I finally said the words I'd held in check until now. 'I love you,' I whispered. 'And I love the way you make me feel.'

The next day, the *métro* home from Montparnasse station was packed with sticky, scantily clad bodies, the air rancid with perspiration. The connections involved what seemed like hours of trailing along corridors and moving walkways, all the temperature of a slow oven. Emerging from the exit on to avenue Simon Bolivar, I breathed hot air thick with car-exhaust fumes into my lungs. I heard the familiar growl of traffic, the wail of distant sirens: these were the sounds of my adopted city.

I'd spent most of my train journey home hovering danger-ously close to tears. Bidding James goodbye was becoming more of a wrench as every successive visit drew to a close. I felt like an amputee; as though I'd left some vital part of myself in his safe-keeping.

I pushed the heavy door open, lifting the flap of our letterbox to peer inside. As I waited for the lift to wheeze and clank its way down to the ground floor I felt for my keys in my pocket. They were heavier than usual, weighed down with the recent addition of James's set. If only the lift would obligingly deliver me to his front door, instead of my own, where an empty, eerily calm flat awaited me. Mr Frog had taken Tadpole to see his parents for a long weekend, and they wouldn't be returning until the next day.

Once inside, I let my bag fall from my shoulder, landing

with a clatter on the parquet floor, and made for the kitchen to fetch a glass of water. I was at my lowest ebb, and not even the view from my kitchen window could console me. Paris had come to symbolize everything I wanted to change about my life, everything I wanted to leave behind. The process had begun long before James and I met – work, pregnancy and motherhood had subtly altered my relationship with the city – but now it seemed irreversible.

I slid down the kitchen wall until my legs touched the cool, brick-red *tomette* tiles. Crumpled in a forlorn heap, I closed my eyes and took refuge in my memories of the weekend in Rennes, wishing myself far, far away.

18. Moving

'Catherine!' said my boss as he flung down his briefcase the following Tuesday morning. 'Why didn't you remind me that I had an early start today? I was late for my meeting.'

I sighed. Only ten o'clock and I was already off on the wrong foot with my boss. I debated whether to point out that the expensive hand-held gadget he carried at all times included a calendar, if only he would consult it, but decided it would be unwise to rile him any further.

'Sorry,' I said, my voice patently insincere, 'I'll do my best to remind you the evening before in future, if you really think that's necessary . . .'

'I just don't feel like you're looking after me as well as you used to,' he complained, his voice petulant. I rolled my eyes at his departing back. I was becoming increasingly aware of the similarity between secretarial work and caring for a demanding, often irrational toddler.

My boss had developed an antagonistic attitude towards me over the past few weeks, behaviour which I was at a loss to explain. I'd seen other colleagues suffer a similar fate, but I'd always seemed to have some sort of immunity. But now, suddenly, nothing I did could please him, criticisms rained down thick and fast and, later that day, not for the first time, Amy found me in floods of uncomprehending tears in the kitchen.

'I don't know how long I can stand this,' I wailed, taking the tissue she held out to me. 'Everything I do seems to be wrong.' I pressed my forehead against the cool windowpane and watched the tourists and shoppers milling about on avenue de l'Opéra far below, wishing I could collect my belongings and join the throng without a backward glance.

'Well, you'd find another job in a second if you did leave, wouldn't you?' Amy said reasonably. 'Although I hope it doesn't come to that. I just don't understand *what* caused the wind to change. You used to get on so well, you two.' She paused to fill the kettle and flick the switch. For all the years we'd spent in France, some instincts would never leave us. Sympathy is served with tea. No other drink will do.

'Me neither.' I shook my head sadly. 'I mean, he does know a bit about the upheaval I've been going through lately at home, but I really don't believe any of that has affected my work. And if it had, you'd expect him to make allowances, not lay into me, wouldn't you? Obviously, I've always checked in on my blog a fair bit when I'm not busy, to read new comments and even write bits and pieces, but I'm hardly even doing that right now. I'm posting about half as often as I used to, partly because I'm getting paranoid he'll find out about it and go off the deep end. The problem is, whatever caused all this weirdness, I'm so on edge now that I really am starting to make mistakes. It's becoming a self-fulfilling prophecy.' I blew my nose, hard, and turned to peer at my blotchy-skinned reflection in the door of a microwave positioned just at the right height to serve as a mirror. What a mess. I couldn't return to my desk looking like this. 'The thing is,' I continued, 'how can I change jobs now, when I only plan to stay in Paris for another year, at most, before I move in with James?' Amy knew of my plans, although no one else in the office did – and my boss certainly did not. 'I need this one thing to stay the same. So much else has changed.'

'Well, I think you need to see how things progress,' said Amy. 'But don't play the martyr and let this go on for too long. You do have other options. And if you're constantly stressed and upset, your little *Tadpole* will pick up on it.' I gave her a watery smile. Amy had become a regular follower of the blog since I'd come clean about meeting James, but it felt funny hearing the name 'Tadpole' spoken aloud.

'You're not blogging about this work stuff, I notice?' Amy raised an eyebrow.

'No!' I replied. 'Other bloggers have been fired for less, so I'm not going to tempt fate. Not that anyone from work is likely ever to find the thing, but I think it's best to play it safe all the same.' I dabbed at my eyes one last time with a piece of kitchen roll, and released my hair from its chignon, all the better to hide behind. 'I suppose I'd better get out there,' I said reluctantly, arming myself with the mug of tea Amy held in her outstretched hand.

Amy's words haunted me for the rest of the day. Was I playing the martyr? Maybe, on some level, I felt that after wrecking my family, I deserved to suffer.

'I'm not denying that you're going through a rough time right now,' said Mr Frog that evening, 'but it feels like you might be using these problems to build a case for leaving Paris sooner, rather than later.'

'No. Absolutely not,' I replied, indignantly. Mr Frog had been sympathetic, at first, when he arrived home from work to find me hunched on the sofa, my head in my hands. But the conversation had quickly veered off course, on to the thorny subject of my possible move to Brittany.

'I know there's nothing I can do to stop you going,' said Mr Frog, his voice brittle, 'but if you take my daughter away to live with *him*, I'll hardly ever see her.'

'Of course you'd see her. I'd bring her to Paris to visit and you could come to Rennes too. But there's really no point in discussing this now,' I said, feeling nauseous. Every time the subject was evoked, our fragile truce was shattered, and it took time to reassemble the pieces. 'I told you, I won't make any decisions for another year. This stuff with my boss is making life horrible right now, but my plans haven't changed. And they won't . . .'

'If you say so.' Mr Frog still looked unconvinced. 'You know, it's one thing to accept that we weren't working, but it's very different coming to terms with the idea of this other guy seeing my daughter every single day; taking my place. I hate to imagine my girl hundreds of kilometres away.'

I noted his repeated use of *my* daughter, *my* girl. We both had a tendency to say 'my' instead of 'our', subconsciously staking our separate claims to Tadpole. I could see Mr Frog's point – of course I could – but what was I supposed to say? That I would never leave the city as long as he lived in it? That I would forgo any happiness that came my way if it involved a geographical shift? All I could hope was that, over time, Mr Frog would get used to the idea; that we both would. But for now, it seemed safer to skirt around the subject, or stick our heads back in the sand to preserve our flimsy entente.

Because nothing I could say would make this bitter pill any easier to swallow.

On the day Mr Frog finally moved across the road, Tadpole and I took ourselves off to a picnic in the Buttes Chaumont, calculated to keep us conveniently out of the way for a few hours.

In a shady spot under towering sycamore trees we laid out blankets and plates of food on the parched grass. A couple of dozen bloggers had come along, in response to an invitation I'd extended on *petite anglaise*. After the first *soirée* I'd attended with Coquette, I'd plucked up the confidence to go one step further, organizing an event for bloggers who lived in Paris, like me, and who felt happy shedding their anonymity and meeting one another offline. If the truth be told, compiling the list of attendees and sending out access plans had been a welcome distraction from all the stressful things going on in my life just then, so my motives had been far from altruistic. Most of the people who had replied were fellow expats, and women far outnumbered men. For many it was the first time they had met me, let alone the infamous Tadpole, who was delighted to hog the limelight, plied with the choicest titbits from the picnic, lapping up the attention.

Despite the perfect weather – hot, but not too hot, for once – and the effort some of the picnickers had clearly gone to with the food, I was fidgety and distracted, my mind skittering inevitably back to what was going on at home. Not only was Mr Frog humping furniture and boxes across the road with a couple of friends, but I was also expecting my phone to ring at any moment to announce the imminent delivery of the mattress which would replace the one which, by now, must have taken up residence over the road. Tonight, when Mr Frog took Tadpole to spend her first night in his new home, James would be coming to stay with me. He must be getting ready to board his TGV right now, and soon he would be speeding towards Paris. My head spun and I felt detached from the conversations ebbing and flowing around me, unable to play the role of perfect hostess, let alone worry about whether I was living up to their preconceived ideas of who *petite anglaise* was and how she should behave.

One thing was certain: I felt at a distinct disadvantage. Many of the picnickers had been following recent develop-ments in my life religiously on my blog. They'd read all about the break-up, for example, about the feeling of anti-climax which followed my announcement to Mr Frog, about the limbo in which we had found ourselves over the past month or so while I waited for Mr Frog to move out, and about my first visits to Brittany, both with and without Tadpole. Fielding intimate questions from semi-strangers about my new relationship or my plans for the future was awkward in itself – although I was beginning to get used to the way people reacted and, in particular, how they often felt entitled to press me for information I neglected to reveal on the blog – but I was unable to reciprocate, and loath to demonstrate how little knowledge I possessed about what was going on in *their* lives. The polite thing would have been to have done my homework, reading up on everyone's news beforehand, but there simply weren't enough hours in every day. As it was, I'd stayed up until after midnight baking a quiche for the picnic.

When I rose to gather up my belongings – fretting about my mattress delivery, wondering where James and I would sleep if it all went wrong – I was approached by two women with children Tadpole's age in tow. I'd noticed them sitting on the periphery of the picnic, but they hadn't introduced themselves properly until now, and I'd been too distracted to wonder who they might be.

'Hi *petite*, this is Louise, and I'm Caroline.' Caroline had the remnants of a Manchester accent, and a pleasant, open face, a sprinkling of freckles dotted across her snub nose.

'Ah, yes, I remember your email now. You're both readers, rather than bloggers, is that right?'

'Yes. I comment on your blog, actually, under a couple of pseudonyms. The main one I use is Mancunian Lass.'

Caught off-guard, I let out a delighted shriek.

'Mancunian Lass? Why on earth didn't you tell me before? Oh, I wish I'd known it was you sitting over there all along!' Mancunian Lass was one of my 'regulars' – she must have left almost as many comments as James in recent months. A few days before, she'd left an essay-length comment in which she had gathered all the available evidence and concluded that 'Lover' – as I still called him on the blog – was none other than Jim in Rennes, effectively unmasking him and, although neither James nor I had confirmed or denied anything, his cover had effectively been blown. 'Your suspicions were correct, by the way, Sherlock,' I added with a conspiratorial wink.

Louise and Caroline, it transpired, were best friends who had been living in Paris for even longer than I had. Both had French partners, and two young children each. Caroline had begun following the 'adventures' of *petite anglaise* on the recommendation of a friend, although neither she nor Louise had ever read a blog before. Now they confessed to being addicted, and gossiping about my antics whenever they met up.

'When you wrote about splitting up with Mr Frog, Caro phoned me straight away,' Louise explained with a grin. 'She knew my internet connection was down. So we found ourselves discussing your personal life over the phone. It's pretty surreal, when you think about it. Your ears must have been burning.' It *was* disconcerting to imagine people talking about my dramas in just the same way my office friends picked over plotlines in their favourite soaps, and I was momentarily lost for words. People had said similar things to me by email, but never before to my face.

'Perhaps we could get together with the kids some time, and let them play together?' I suggested, once I'd recovered my composure, deliberately changing the subject. 'I actually have to leave in a minute, but I'd really love to have a proper chat some other time . . .'

We tentatively agreed to meet up again, with or without our children, and I left the picnic in high spirits. 'They talked about *petite anglaise* on the phone,' I whispered to myself as I made my way through the park, hand in hand with Tadpole. 'How bizarre is that?'

'*Bonjour Madame!*' said Mr Frog's new concierge when we stepped inside his building a couple of hours later, her greeting a thinly veiled question. I was a newcomer on her territory, and she seemed to expect me to state if not my business, then at least my identity.

A small woman with a wizened face, her coarse, dark hair pulled back severely with a tortoiseshell clip, she wore a floral-print overall over her clothes. She had waylaid us the moment I set down the Miffy bag containing Tadpole's pyjamas and clothes for the next day and hoisted her up to press the intercom button for Mr Frog's apartment. I felt sure the dustbin bag she clutched in her right hand had only been a pretext to scuttle out and get a better look at us.

'*Bonjour Madame,*' I replied. '*J'emmène ma fille chez son papa.*' I paused, unsure of how to continue, willing Mr Frog to buzz us in without delay. How should I introduce myself? How much information would constitute too much? 'I live nearby,' I added, leaving her to draw her own conclusions, no doubt staring in disapproval at our retreating backs.

Mr Frog greeted us at the front door, bending to gather Tadpole into his arms for a hug, but did not beckon me inside. His hallway was littered with empty cardboard boxes and assembly instructions for flat-packed furniture: he had obviously been busy. Shifting Tadpole on to his right hip, he dug purposefully in the pocket of his jeans and pulled out a set of keys to our apartment with his left hand. 'No, you keep those,' I said quickly, making no move to take them from him. 'I'd prefer you to have a spare set, for emergencies.' He nodded, and reached to unhook the strap of Tadpole's overnight bag from my shoulder. 'OK, well, I'm going to get going then.' I kissed Tadpole on the cheek and glanced at my watch, wondering if James was close.

'Expecting company this evening?' Mr Frog said sardonically.

'I'm just seeing a friend,' I replied evenly, determined not to rise to the bait in front of Tadpole's watchful eyes. Turning to leave, I raised my hand and gave father and daughter a feeble wave. I had planted a kiss on Tadpole's cheek, but Mr Frog I dared not touch. This was really it. Mr Frog and I no longer lived together.

Back home, I was wriggling into clean clothes, fresh from the shower, when James's text message arrived. 'Is the coast clear?' it read. 'Can I come up?'

My eye glued to the peep-hole, I flung the front door open as soon as the lift drew level with the fifth floor. James was hot and bothered from the *métro* he disliked so much, his short hair damp and dewdrop beads of perspiration outlined across his forehead. A shabby rucksack with one broken strap, chewed by Eve's dog, dangled from one shoulder. I flew into his arms, caring little that his embrace was clammy.

'So?' said James when at last I let him go, leading him by the hand along the corridor and into the living room. 'How was that picnic? And did your new mattress arrive?'

'The picnic was great, although I was pretty distracted,' I admitted. 'As for the mattress . . . Well. That's a bit of a sore point. The delivery guy called to say he had the wrong one in his truck. So, no mattress. We'll be on the sofa bed tonight, I'm afraid.'

'Hey, it's not the end of the world,' he said, smoothing my furrowed brow with his fingertips, a gesture which reminded me of Mr Frog, who used to try to erase my frowns in a similar way. 'You don't have to make that face.'

'Oh, I know it's silly,' I said ruefully, 'but I wanted so badly for our first night here to be perfect.'

'It is. It will be. You'll see. Although before we go any further, I *am* going to need a shower.'

He shrugged his rucksack to the floor and removed his T-shirt, using the balled-up fabric to mop his brow. 'All in good time,' I said, noticing the way the sweat pooled in the indentation above his top lip. 'But first you have to admire my view. The sky is a bit hazy, with all the pollution, but I think you get the general idea.'

'The picture from the blog,' he exclaimed, a smile slowly spreading across his face. 'When I think that I've been looking at this view for months, since long before we met . . . And now I'm here, with you, seeing those rooftops for real. Talk about *déjà vu* . . .'

'There's no going back now,' I warned, 'not now that you've stepped inside.' Unbuttoning his jeans, I slipped my hands inside, my palms cupping his buttocks. 'About that shower,' I whispered. 'I'm afraid it's going to have to wait . . .'

When James and I finally awoke, late the following morning, we were ravenous. The fridge was empty, so we ducked into Franprix for provisions. Despite its peeling paint and general air of shabbiness, I was rather attached to my local supermarket. Vigilance was required to avoid picking up food which was just shy of its sell-by date, and buying champagne and spirits meant finding the person who had the key to the locked cabinet near the front door, but Tadpole was always unfailingly popular with the cashiers, who slipped her free lollipops when the manager's head was turned. Today, however, Tadpole was across the road. Tantalizingly close, yet completely out of bounds.

As we moved through the aisles, picking up eggs, bread

and fresh milk, I looked over my shoulder repeatedly. I had no desire for James and Mr Frog to meet, and half wished I'd thought to make a detour to a different shop. Mr Frog had moved only a few hundred metres away, when all was said and done. This supermarket was still his local.

I began to breathe more easily when we reached the check-out without mishap. The red-overalled cashier looked puzzled to see me without Tadpole, flanked by a man who was not Mr Frog, but passed no comment. Fumbling for my purse while James packed the bags, I suddenly felt an urgent tap on my shoulder. 'Isn't that them over there?' James said in a low voice, gesturing towards the entrance, where Tadpole was silhouetted against the daylight.

'Oh God! Yes! You're right.' I ducked quickly out of Tadpole's line of vision, concealing myself as best I could behind James's stocky frame. Mr Frog had no idea what James looked like, but Tadpole did. I could think of nothing worse than her shouting his name and running over for a hug.

A few heart-stalling seconds went by before the coast was clear. Mr Frog and Tadpole passed through the turnstile a couple of metres from where James and I stood, then moved further into the shop, where they disappeared behind the shelves. I let out a long sigh. It had been an agonizingly near miss. The cashier, who had been watching the scene with unconcealed interest, ignored my outstretched hand and clattered my change down on the metal counter, stripped of her customary smile. It was as though she'd sized up our entire situation in those few panic-stricken seconds and now wished to make her disapproval abundantly clear.

'Did you see how that woman looked at me?' I groaned, as soon as we were well clear of the exit.

James shook his head. 'I was too busy packing the bags,' he replied, 'but I'm sure you're imagining things.'

'I don't think so,' I said, my shoulders drooping, as we turned the corner and passed the greengrocer's.

It seemed that both offline and online I was going to have to get used to the harsh judgements of strangers.

19. Honeymoon

The prevailing climate of tension at work, which kept me on the edge of my ergonomic chair, discouraged me from blogging at my desk. But that wasn't the only reason I updated *petite anglaise* less often that summer. Now that Mr Frog had moved out, and our separation was old news, the dust was beginning to settle, the aftershocks coming fewer and farther between.

My regular readers, on the other hand, had developed a voracious appetite for posts which shocked or thrilled; they visited *petite anglaise* for a ride on the emotional rollercoaster. My life had become entertainment to be sampled by strangers for their vicarious pleasure, safe from harm, hidden behind their monitors. When I failed to deliver, a rumble of discontent began to make itself heard in my comments box. Where was their daily fix?

'I have plotted a graph,' wrote Germain. 'On one axis the number of *petite* posts per week. On the other axis a dateline. There is a clearly visible fall in the number of posts right about the time "Lover" came along. I wish he hadn't.'

Such comments brought home to me forcefully that for some I was just a provider of entertainment, not a person in my own right who deserved a shot at happiness and tranquillity. And yet my life had taken a turn for the calmer, and for me it was a profound relief to feel able to live life more fully offline. I was posting maybe fifteen times a month – half as much as I used to – but the viewing figures showed no signs of dipping, so why not cut myself some slack?

There were however a few entries I'd been holding in reserve, out of respect for Mr Frog's feelings. Now that a couple of months had elapsed and the events were no longer so fresh, I allowed myself to describe my encounter with James in the Hôtel Saint Louis. There was no sex scene – *petite anglaise* was far too coy for that – but I did admit that we had met in a hotel when I should have been at work, and when I was still in a relationship with Tadpole's father. I wrote the post as a gift to James – just as I'd addressed my break-up post to Mr Frog – committing the powerful emotions of that day to memory so that they could never be forgotten. At the back of my mind, as I pressed 'publish', I knew my confession would shake things up, and I braced myself for the inevitable comments box fall-out.

'Do we really need to know this?' Teresa was quick to complain. 'Don't you think some things should be private . . . ? This is personal stuff you are divulging, stuff that I would cringe for anyone to know if it were me . . . Once you send something out into cyberspace, you can't reel it back in.'

Rather than letting other commenters rush to my defence, as they were wont to do, I felt it was time to address these criticisms myself. It was true that I was constantly nudging back my own boundaries, perhaps forgetting that a post written for myself, for James, might be considered too much information by a third party. 'Why do I write posts like this?' *petite anglaise* pondered in reply. 'I'm not sure I even know myself. To commit certain things to memory. To flex my tiny writing muscles. To romanticize my life. As letters to someone in particular. As therapy. To exorcise guilt. I'm not sure it matters why, as long as no damage is done.' I was reminded suddenly of the concert where James and I had first met, and how I'd felt as though I was eavesdropping on Eve's private life as John sang about their relationship. James was a source of inspiration now, and a few thousand people were listening in whenever I wrote about him.

'At the end of the day, whether or not *petite* wants to discuss her love life or the price of pears in Provence, it's entirely up to her,' said Fifi in my defence. 'Let's not forget that we are guests here, people. Take your shoes off at the door, and be polite when you leave!'

'Sometimes I wonder whether I should keep on writing *petite anglaise*,' I said to James on the phone, later that day. 'I don't seem to be able to please anyone. Either I'm not writing often enough, or it's too personal. I know I shouldn't let what people say get to me. But I can't help it.'

'I remember the days before we met, when I used to refresh your page every time I took a tea break,' said James, harking back to the days when he had been just another faceless reader, and not a character in his own right. 'But you shouldn't worry about that sort of thing. Write what you want, when you have something to say, it's your blog.'

'Did you see the comment Caroline left?'

'Caroline?'

'Mancunian Lass, sorry. The girl I told you I'd met at the picnic. She guessed that the hotel post was addressed to you, and joked that we get kicks out of being exhibitionists. Almost as though we were having sex in a public place. I suppose she does have a point . . .'

'I love what you write,' James replied, 'and I'm flattered when you write about *me*, but it's not as if you went into intimate detail . . . If some people don't want to read because they feel they are intruding on our private lives, then no one is forcing them. But just remember, you don't *owe* these people anything. I'd be sad if you stopped writing – I love reading you – but make sure you're doing it for the right reasons. Not because you feel obligated, or pressured, or because it's some sort of uncomfortable habit you can't kick . . .'

He was right, I knew he was, but I wasn't sure I was capable of kicking the habit, even if part of me thought I should. 'I can't wait for you to get here,' I said, changing the subject, bringing the focus away from *petite anglaise* and back to us. 'When you think about it, I've known you two months, but if you count the hours we've actually spent together, it adds up to so little . . .'

The summer holidays were almost upon us and, in *Tata*'s absence, Tadpole would be going to stay with Mr Frog's parents. This meant that James was free to join me in Paris for two whole weeks. Mr Frog might have moved out, but I'd been adamant that James couldn't sleep over while Tadpole was around. She needed time to adjust: she still referred to the spare pillow on my bed as 'Daddy's pillow'. It wouldn't do to rush things.

'Hold that thought,' James replied, and the longing in his voice made my spine tingle, 'while I list all the filthy things I'm going to do to you when I get there . . .'

James was wearing my least favourite pair of jeans: badly cut, with a mottled pattern that reminded me of a pair I'd owned in the eighties. I felt disloyal and shallow for entertaining such uncharitable thoughts as the *métro* pulled into Bonne Nouvelle station. It wasn't his clothes I was supposed to be in love with, and I'd be the first to clamour that beauty isn't only skin-deep, but I desperately wanted him to make a good impression. We were meeting Caroline and Louise in a bar, then planning to move on to a nearby restaurant for an Indian meal. It wouldn't be the first time I'd seen the two women since we met at the picnic; but it was the first time I'd introduced James to any of my friends. That day at work I'd received a breathless email from Louise: 'Am having a hard time dealing with the excitement of seeing Jim in Rennes!'

Caroline was already seated at a small round table in the front section of the De La Ville café, upon which a candle flickered in a red glass. Two flights of steps led up to the bar on one side, and a restaurant area on the other. On the bar side, huge mirrors reflected the gold-coloured mosaic which covered the whole ceiling. Rumour had it the building had once housed a high-class brothel, which couldn't fail to add to its cachet.

The crowd was similar to that of the Charbon: *branché*, *bobo*, exuding a very Parisian nonchalant cool. Over the road, next to the Rex cinema, were a couple of nightclubs where I'd been a regular in my pre-Tadpole days. It felt good to be out and about near my old haunts. With Tadpole away, Mummy could play.

'Caroline-Mancunian Lass meet James-Jim in Rennes,' I said, sliding into the seat next to Caroline's and catching the waiter's eye as he hurried past. 'Caroline works in translation, just like you,' I added, trying to establish a connection between the two of them which didn't rely solely on *petite anglaise*, even if it was she who had brought us together.

As James and Caroline chatted about their work, I sipped my beer and willed the butterflies in my stomach to be still. I was nervous, and it ran deeper than my usual anxiety about living up to people's expectations in the flesh, or the trepidation any girl would feel about introducing a new boyfriend. *Petite anglaise* had written James on to a pedestal. He was her commenter in shining armour, the man she'd fallen for the moment she laid eyes on him, and her words dripped with infatuation. With so much to live up to, the potential for him to disappoint was enormous.

'Sorry I'm late,' said Louise as she breezed in, looking glamorous in smart, knee-high boots and a short skirt. I was rather in awe of Louise, who managed to juggle motherhood with running a successful English-language school. 'You must be James,' she said, bending to kiss him on both cheeks. 'Gosh, this is so exciting. Like meeting someone famous.'

When James excused himself to go to the toilet, I braced myself for the verdict which must inevitably follow. 'He seems really lovely, Catherine,' said Caroline, as soon as he was out of earshot, 'and he looks younger than I expected, too.'

'I have a theory about divorced men going through a second adolescence,' I said, with a relieved smile. 'I've seen pictures of James a few years ago, and he definitely seems younger now.' I looked at Louise quizzically. Surely she must have something to add?

'Mmm. I have to say, he's not quite what I imagined,' she said thoughtfully. 'But then again, I don't know what I *did* imagine . . . Is James very different from Mr Frog? Physically, I mean?'

'They're like chalk and cheese,' I replied. 'Tall, dark and stocky versus slight, pale and fair. I ought to tell you his real name, really, we can't keep calling him Mr Frog all night . . .'

I looked up and saw James crossing the room, and for a split second I saw him as a stranger might. If I'd walked past him on the street one day, without the crescendo of emails, the electronic foreplay, would I have even given him a second glance? To what extent had I let myself get carried away by how inherently romantic it was to fall for a reader who had worshipped *petite anglaise* from afar before he'd even seen my face?

'Another drink before we make a move?' I said brightly, banishing those uncomfortable thoughts and running my hand along James's forearm as he dropped into the seat by my side. You can't divorce a person from the context in which you met, I told myself sternly. It's pointless to think that way; unhealthy to cross-examine my own motives, analyse my every impulse.

Once we'd ordered, I nudged the conversation away from *petite anglaise*. 'So, how about you two tell me all about how you came to be in Paris in the first place,' I suggested to Caroline and Louise. 'You both know so much more about me than I do about you, and it's time to even things up a bit, don't you think?'

That week, with James by my side, my feet barely touched the ground. Nothing my boss said or did could penetrate my armour. All I had to do was think of James sitting at my dining-room table, head bent over his laptop, a mug of tea steaming by his side, and I was immunized against even the most caustic remarks. James's presence took the edge off the dull ache caused by Tadpole's absence, too. But two weeks was the longest I'd ever been separated from my daughter, and as the days wore on, my longing grew more visceral.

I missed the mewls of protest she made when I woke her in the morning. I missed pulling her golden ringlets straight and watching the corkscrews reassert themselves when I let go. The memories of her tantrums receded, the good out-weighing the bad. When she was with me, bedtime often couldn't come quickly enough. But when we were apart, the sight of a fair-haired toddler in the street made my lungs constrict. There was no escaping the fact that there was a Tadpole-shaped hole in my life.

'*Allô?*' I said hesitantly.

Craving the sound of Tadpole's voice, I'd finally mustered up the courage to telephone the 'in-laws', or 'out-laws' or whatever I was supposed to call my daughter's French grand-parents.

It was my first shred of contact with the *beaux-parents* since I'd asked Mr Frog to move out, and every muscle in my body was taut. Did they hate me for wrecking their son's home? How much did they know, or suspect, of what had really happened? The news, when it came, must have been a dreadful shock. When we'd visited, Mr Frog and I had always put our quarrels on hold, papering over the cracks, presenting a united front.

Tadpole answered the phone. Or at least I supposed it was my daughter. Her voice – distorted by the telephone and unbearably distant – sounded like that of a little French stranger. '*Allô? Maman? Regarde! Un bobo!*' No doubt she was showing the offending scrape or bruise to the telephone, convinced I could see as well as hear. Muffled sounds of a scuffle ensued, and Mr Frog's mother appropriated the handset.

'It's just a scrape on her knee,' she explained hastily. 'She was running too fast and tripped on the *terrasse*. You know what she's like . . .'

'*Oui, oui, bien sûr* . . .' I replied. 'I never worry when she's with you. I know she's in good hands.'

Now that she had wrestled the phone from Tadpole's fingers, small talk would be necessary. This was the moment I had been dreading. We'd got on so well in the beginning, my *belle-mère* and I. A fizzing bundle of energy, Mr Frog's mother was perpetually in motion, congenitally unable to sit still. The kitchen was her domain and despite her own sparrow-like appetite, she'd always taken great pleasure in fattening me up. At family gatherings the womenfolk exclaimed over what a rare and wonderful thing it was to see a young woman who liked her food and rarely refused a second helping. But as my relationship with Mr Frog soured, my enthusiasm for visiting his parents also waned. On my last visit I'd feigned a migraine and taken refuge in Mr Frog's childhood bedroom with a book.

'*Vous allez bien?*' I enquired cautiously. I hadn't always been consistent about addressing Mr Frog's parents with the polite '*vous*' – after a few glasses of *Beau-père*'s best Bordeaux, a careless '*tu*' would often slip out – but I was determined to handle her with kid gloves today. Our relationship had subtly changed, and there was no sense in adding grammatical insult to injury.

'*Ravie de voir notre petite-fille,*' she replied diplomatically. '*Et vous?*'

The stock response I'd learned at school was '*très bien merci*', and the words tripped gaily off my tongue before I had time to censor myself, a reflex over which I had no control. I slapped my palm to my forehead. I had no idea whether my *belle-mère* knew of James's existence, and she almost certainly didn't know he was with me now, while her own son licked his wounds across the road. But for decency's sake, I really ought to have dampened down the happiness in my voice.

'*Bon, je vais vous repasser votre fille,*' she replied stiffly. Had I caused offence, or was she, like me, simply anxious to keep our exchange mercifully short?

'*Maman?*'

'Yes, it's Mummy. What have you been up to, darling? Are you having a nice time?' Tadpole replied in French and, although I managed to decipher the words 'swimming pool' and 'bells', the rest was incomprehensible. I decided to try a change of tack. 'Why don't you sing Mummy a song?' I suggested. 'Maybe an English one?' If there was one thing my daughter loved, it was being given an opportunity to perform. I was treated to a reasonably accurate rendition of a French nursery rhyme called '*Une Souris Verte*' in which a green mouse, caught by the tail and dipped first in oil, then water, miraculously turns into a piping hot snail. Tears welled up in my eyes at the sound of her faraway voice.

Her performance over, Tadpole soon lost interest in the telephone, leaving *Belle-mère* and me to murmur our tepid goodbyes. With a sigh, I replaced the receiver and went off in search of James. His laptop sat open on my dining table; his clothes tumbled out of his suitcase in an unruly mess on the bedroom floor; the book he was reading – one of mine – lay flat on the sofa, its spine creased down the middle.

I found James standing over the gas stove stirring bolognese. Wrapping my arms around his waist, I rested my head against his back, the top of my head barely reaching his shoulders. 'You okay? How did it go?' He had seen me pacing around the apartment earlier and it was he who had urged me to conquer my nerves and call Tadpole.

'I'm not sure speaking to her was such a good idea after all,' I said forlornly. 'I think maybe a clean break is healthier. She sounded all French. And less *mine* somehow.'

James set down his spoon and turned to face me, cupping my face in his palms. 'I know it's not easy being apart for so long, but the break will do you good. You've had an awful lot on your plate.'

'You're right. I know.' I smiled ruefully. If Tadpole hadn't been away, James wouldn't be here at all. This fortnight was the longest period of time we had spent together. We were beginning to settle into a routine of comfortable domesticity: we cooked; we watched films; we read side by side. While I soaked in the bathtub, he dimmed the lights and lit candles, then led me wordlessly through into the bedroom.

It was wonderful, but I was painfully aware of how temporary, how artificial it all was. We were living in a vacuum, but real-life obligations would soon come crowding back in. We would travel to Brittany together for a weekend to visit Eve and John, and afterwards James would remain for a fortnight in Rennes with his daughters. I would return to Paris, be reunited with Tadpole, and take a plane to England.

However much I liked to pretend that this was a foretaste of what life with James would be like, this honeymoon of ours was just another *parenthèse enchantée*.

Eve owned a *gîte* near Saint-Malo, a ramshackle farmhouse converted into apartments which she rented to holidaymakers throughout the summer months. As James brought the car to a halt on the gravel driveway, I put a restraining hand on his arm. This was the most tangible glimpse I'd had so far into the life I hankered after with James, and I wanted to sit in silence for a moment; to let myself imagine this could be our home.

'Lovely to see you,' said Eve, appearing from around the side of the house, flanked by two yapping dogs. 'I knew we'd meet again. This is so exciting!' We followed her around to the back of the cottage where John was setting up the barbecue. Watching Maisy – Eve and John's daughter – toddling around the garden on unsteady feet, sun-kissed, grimy and deliriously happy, I thought of the freedom I would be able to give Tadpole one day. Playing in the Buttes Chaumont was just not the same. I couldn't let Tadpole stray more than a few metres away: she might as well be on a leash.

As the menfolk drained small green bottles of 1664, waiting for the coals to heat up, I volunteered to help Eve prepare salads in the kitchen. Ever since our first meeting in the Charbon I'd looked forward to seeing her again, in theory. But today I couldn't help making comparisons. She was taller, slimmer and blonder than me; her full breasts strained against her tight T-shirt. I felt like half the woman Eve was. The comparison did me no favours.

'It's a shame our girls couldn't play together this time,' said Eve, over her shoulder. She stood at the wide ceramic sink next to a huge open fireplace, rinsing lettuce under the cold tap. As she bent forwards, I caught sight of a tiny G-string peeping over her worn jeans, and my mind played a cruel trick, superimposing an image of James standing behind her, slipping his hands inside the slack waistband.

'Oh, we'll be back before long,' I said confidently, wrenching my mind back to the cucumber I was supposed to be chopping. 'The summer's not over yet.' James appeared in the doorway, a sleeping Maisy limp in his arms. He climbed the stairs to her bedroom with exaggerated care and returned empty-handed, pausing to slip an arm around my waist and nuzzle my neck.

'We're ready for the meat now,' called John from outside, 'and can you bring us another beer?'

'You two don't half make us work for our dinner,' said James in mock protest, picking up the tray of sausages and steaks with one hand and two green bottles with the other. Taking a swig of my own beer, I began to attack the tomatoes. This time, I kept my eyes glued to the table.

Later that night, James and I sat in the huge whirlpool bathtub, my buttocks nestling against his inner thighs, his calves cradling mine. In the absence of paying guests, we were sleeping in the *gîte*'s master bedroom, a vast open-plan room. From our vantage point in the alcove which served as an en suite bathroom, I could see the ornately carved four-poster bed with its crisp white sheets – our next destination. The warm water was making me drowsy, and I tipped my head back, resting it on James's collarbone. His hands, cupping my breasts, slid lower, finally coming to rest on my stomach.

I was suddenly reminded of Mr Frog placing cool, tender hands on my swollen tummy to feel his daughter's first tiny movements under my skin. '*Mon écrin*,' he called me – his jewellery case. Tadpole, inside, was his pearl.

'I never thought I'd want another child,' James whispered, as though divining my thoughts, 'but I'd love to have a baby with you one day.' I placed my hands over his, my lips curving into a smile. I vaguely remembered writing a post on *petite anglaise*, long before James and I met, in which I'd spoken of my desire for a Tadpole #2. Everything that Mr Frog had hesitated over, James seemed to want.

Our weekend had been perfect, blissful. A fleeting glimpse of the future I craved, a chance to live my daydreams. And now this. This was the icing on the cake. My happiness was complete.

20. Discord

'Hello,' I said to James, brimming over with relief. 'Where have you been? I've been trying to reach you since I got home from work.' In the background, children shrieked and I could make out the distant sound of dogs barking. I'd guessed the answer to my own question before he spoke, and there was a sinking feeling in the pit of my stomach.

'I'm at Eve's,' he replied, confirming my suspicions. 'I brought Amanda and Carrie over to see her and Maisy. She gets lonely when John's away. Phone reception is always a bit of a lottery when I'm out in the sticks, sorry about that . . .'

No sooner were the words out of his mouth than I felt a tidal wave of jealousy gathering force. I bit my lip, drawing blood. It was irrational, this emotion; corrosive and harmful. But I couldn't help myself. The holidays were over and I was trapped in Paris with Tadpole once more, feeling sorry for myself. Meanwhile James and his kids were spending time cheering up another woman. And not just any other woman: James's ex-girlfriend, of all people. Even though the evening of the barbecue at Eve's place had been the high point of our relationship so far, I'd still found myself dwelling on an image of Eve bending over the sink afterwards, wondering whether James's eyes had flickered towards the space between her jeans and her T-shirt as he looked over my shoulder. I'd never met a woman so comfortable in her own skin, so effortlessly sensual.

I'd also made the mistake of looking over the early emails James had sent to *petite anglaise*, re-reading the passages which had so drawn me to him, weeks before we first met. It was into Eve's arms that James had fallen when his marriage fell apart; she who had healed his pain and made him whole again. The drama of their shared history, the intensity of emotions he'd described unsettled me now. Could our story ever rival theirs? Three whole years she'd spent with James. As I read, I hated myself for wishing I could overwrite whole sections of his past with my blog, destroying his baggage with a single controlled explosion.

'Okay, well, look, you're obviously busy, it's probably not the best time to talk,' I said, my voice tight with disappointment. I'd had another rotten day at work and all I had wanted was to hear his soothing voice in my ear. Instead, the sounds of merriment in the background taunted me cruelly. I could picture all too clearly the five of them gathered around Eve's solid kitchen table sharing a cosy meal, and it looked too much like a snapshot of the perfect family for my liking. The petulant child inside me wanted to rail against the injustice of the situation: James was with Eve instead of me; Maisy instead of Tadpole.

'You're probably right, there's actually a small person trying to climb up my leg as I speak,' James said, unaware that he was twisting the knife. He had picked up on my hostility, I was sure of that, but I was just as sure that he was refusing to acknowledge it on purpose, reluctant to be drawn into what he considered a pointless argument.

'Okay, well, maybe we can speak when you get home? I'll be up until late . . .'

'Ah, well, the thing is, we're going to stay here,' James replied apologetically. 'There's plenty of room, and the girls have a riding lesson tomorrow in this neck of the woods anyway . . .'

Something in me snapped. I couldn't *not* say anything.

How could he sleep over at his ex-girlfriend's house, while her boyfriend was away? I didn't care how convenient the arrangement might be. It wasn't that I thought anything would happen between them. But it just didn't feel right.

'Well, do enjoy your cosy evening with your ex,' I said, my voice laced with poison. 'I do hope your sleepover is worth jeopardizing our relationship for.'

I slammed down the receiver to rob him of the opportunity to have the last word, and promptly burst into tears. What had I done? If there was a relationship 'self-destruct' button, I felt sure I had just pressed it. Long-distance arguments are hell: we couldn't kiss and make up; I couldn't make him a cup of tea, or put a hand on his arm by way of silent apology. I'd just have to wait until James called back; I was too stubborn and proud to pick up the receiver myself.

A few hours later, resigned to the fact that the phone wouldn't ring, I tried to exorcise my jealousy the only way I knew how: by writing about it. I wanted *petite anglaise* to make my apology: she had a knack of expressing complex feelings so much more vividly than I ever could on the phone. James could reassure me until he was blue in the face, but irrational jealousy wouldn't bow to reason or logic. I wanted him to know that I was painfully aware of the danger it could represent if left to fester. Together, *petite anglaise* and I would confront my feelings head on. If there was one thing James professed to love about my alter ego and me, it was our disarming honesty.

I bared my soul, up to a point, but my ugliest, darkest thoughts I kept off the page. Writing brought the usual clarity, and I came to understand as I typed that it wasn't James's close friendship with Eve that pained me, it was the affection he lavished on Eve and John's daughter, whom he'd known from birth. James got along with Tadpole just fine, but anyone could see that he loved Maisy deeply. I knew it was early days, that love for a child – even your own – doesn't develop overnight, but I couldn't help wondering whether he would ever feel as close to my daughter as he did to Eve's. The thought was a malignant tumour eating away at my insides.

So the truth *petite anglaise* told, in this instance, was not the whole truth. 'I'm not jealous of anyone in his present,' I wrote on my blog. 'It's his past I have a problem with.' Not only did I fail to admit that Eve still posed me a problem in the here and now, but I edited all mention of Maisy out of the final draft. It was then that I realized the rules of engagement had been subtly altered now that my lover was hanging on my every word. Writing honestly, using the blog as therapy, needed to be weighed against the damage I could wreak if I revealed too much. *Petite anglaise* might have brought us together, but she could just as easily be our undoing.

Once I'd finished, I decided to give Amy a call. It was past eleven, so if she didn't pick up the phone straight away I resolved to hang up. But my luck was in: she picked up on the first ring.

'Hi, what's up?' She sounded dejected, or weary, or both.

'I just had a horrible fight with James,' I replied. 'I didn't wake you, did I? Is it a bad time?'

'You know what, I was about to go to bed, so if you don't mind, you can tell me about it tomorrow,' said Amy. 'Unless I end up reading about it first.' I was momentarily stunned by her words. They seemed so unnecessarily harsh. What was going on?

'Er, okay. I . . . I guess we'll speak tomorrow then,' I stuttered. 'Sorry if I caught you at a bad time . . .'

I hung up and stared at the phone accusingly, wishing

I hadn't taken it into my head to call anyone. This evening, it seemed, I was hell-bent on destroying everything I touched.

The office was quiet the next morning, my boss away on a business trip. Amy had called in sick, which made me feel even worse about our exchange the previous evening, and my 'get well soon' text message elicited no reply. And although supportive comments were pouring on to the blog thick and fast, commending the honesty with which I'd tackled the thorny subject of jealousy, there was still no word from James. Unable to endure his silence any longer, I shut myself in the ladies' and called his mobile. He picked up at once, and I was profoundly relieved to hear that his voice bore no trace of the previous night's impatience. 'Hey, special girl. Feeling better today?'

'A little,' I conceded. 'I wrote some stuff, and that helped.'

'I thought you might,' he replied. 'I haven't had a chance to read it yet, mind. I'm at the stables. But I think I can imagine the gist of it.'

'And you're not cross with me?'

'No. I'm really not. But you do know you have nothing to worry about, don't you? I just hope you're not planning to ask me to stop seeing Eve. She may be my ex-girlfriend, but she's also my best friend, and it's an unusual situation, I'll admit, but it's just the way it is.'

'I'm not that much of a fool. I'd never ask you to do that,' I said indignantly, although the thought had briefly crossed my mind.

'Anyway, we can talk about this face to face next time I see you, on your birthday,' James said, putting an end to the discussion. 'Concentrate on looking forward to that, please, instead of creating problems where there are none.'

Mr Frog was due to collect Tadpole that evening and I had

no plans of my own, so I decided to drop in to see Amy on my way home. As she lived all the way out in Vincennes, at the end of the number one *métro* line, it wasn't so much dropping in as making a huge detour. Amy raved about how wonderful Vincennes was, but it had always reminded me of a rather bourgeois retirement village. She'd better be in, I thought to myself grimly as I buzzed the intercom on the gate. I've come an awfully long way just to find out the meaning of one throwaway remark.

When Amy opened her front door in her dressing-gown she looked astonished to see me. Her skin was pale and the smudges under her eyes had made a comeback. 'Hope you don't mind me popping by,' I said hesitantly. 'But I was at a loose end and I wanted to see how you were. When you didn't reply to my text, I started to worry . . .'

'Oh, that's very sweet of you,' she said with a wan smile, 'I probably forgot to charge my phone, nothing more dramatic than that. But come on in. I'll stick the kettle on.'

Before the kettle had even boiled I'd learned that aside from a rotten cold, the real culprit was Amy's boyfriend. She saw Tom about as often as I saw James, but he was blowing hot and cold, driving her mad with his ambiguity. I sipped my tea and interrupted little, letting her get everything out of her system. After I'd risen to make a second cup I decided the time was ripe to broach the subject of last night's call.

'On the phone last night, you sounded a bit annoyed with me . . .' I began tentatively.

'I may have been a bit sharp,' conceded Amy, looking down at her tea for a moment. I set down my own drink, sensing that she was about to say something important. 'I suppose,' she continued, 'I've been feeling like things have got a bit one-sided lately. I don't know if it's this blog of yours. You get very wrapped up in your own dramas. You're really good at unburdening yourself, but I'm not sure you pay enough attention to the people who are right in front of your nose, and their problems . . . Last night I just wasn't in the mood to listen. I had problems of my own.' I remained silent for a moment, digesting what she'd said, colour rising to my cheeks. Her words stung, but I knew they weren't unjustified. I was guilty as charged.

'I'm sorry if I've been a terrible friend,' I said, blinking back tears which had sprung from nowhere. 'You're right, I know. I have been far too self-absorbed lately. It's always me, me, me. I should probably think about laying off the blogging for a while . . .'

'There were a couple of times when you wrote about something and I kind of wished I'd been invited too,' added Amy. 'Like that picnic, for example. I felt a bit left out. I would have liked to come along.'

'I wish you'd said something earlier,' I said, shaking my head. 'It never even occurred to me that you'd want to come. Come to think of it, I have been keeping my *petite anglaise* social life separate, but I'm not even sure I understand why. But I promise, next time I organize something you'll be the first to know.' I was being a little disingenuous, because I did have some inkling as to why I tended to keep people like Amy – who had known me long before *petite anglaise* – out of the equation. Supposing I did act differently with my blogging friends – more confident, more self-assured – she would notice this and comment on it immediately. I wasn't sure I'd be entirely comfortable with my two worlds colliding.

'I'd like that,' said Amy, apparently mollified. 'Just so long as I don't actually have to start a blog of my own, mind. This blogging lark is most definitely *not* for me . . .'

21. Birthdays

Anyone would have thought that my birthday weekend had been cursed.

First, my boss refused to sign off on my holiday request for Friday, the day of my actual birthday, meaning that Tadpole and I had to take an impossibly late train to Rennes after work, arriving long after her bedtime. Wilting visibly by the second, but hell bent on fighting the urge to sleep, Tadpole did not endear herself to our fellow passengers.

Once she was finally tucked up in the travel cot in the tiny utility room James had converted into a bedroom for her, he poured me a large, celebratory glass of wine and I snuggled into his side on the sofa, my legs tucked under my bottom. 'Happy birthday, beautiful,' he said, clinking his glass against mine. 'It was brave of you to travel so late. I know it's not easy.'

I took a sip of wine and set my glass on the floor. Putting a hand on his thigh, I caressed it through the threadbare fabric of his jeans. 'Now, I may be exhausted, but I wonder if there's some way we could salvage this birthday of mine . . .' Just then, a choking sound emanated from Tadpole's bedroom. I cried out in alarm, swinging my feet to the floor and toppling my wine glass. James was already halfway across the room, and he flung open the door, fished Tadpole out of the cot and deposited her in my arms. She coughed again, disorientated, blinking in the bright lights. I patted her back ineffectually, and looked questioningly at James. He'd been a parent for far longer than I had: I tended to defer to his greater experience.

But James barely had time to open his mouth to reply before Tadpole emptied the contents of her stomach all over the sofa. The cause of her discomfort was suddenly copiously clear. She'd eaten cherry tomatoes on the train; tomatoes which she had evidently neglected to chew. Tiny tomatoes which now decorated the sofa, many completely intact, their skins unbroken. Tadpole, who had scared herself witless with her own performance, began to howl. I looked down at my dress and my hair, which were splattered with flecks of cherry-red.

Birthday sex, I suspected, might no longer be on the menu.

'This place is lovely!' I exclaimed as the waiter led us into a whitewashed room with a stone floor and ancient exposed beams in the ceiling overhead. It was Saturday night. Tadpole had made a speedy recovery – the same, sadly, could not be said for James's sofa – and a friend of his had offered to babysit. James had made a reservation at a French restaurant nearby for a belated birthday meal. The room was softly lit, and a candle flickered on every table. Delicious gamey smells wafted out of the kitchen, making my tummy rumble. A glance at the menu chalked up on an old-fashioned *ardoise* confirmed that it was also rather expensive. James was really pulling out all the stops tonight, and I hoped he could afford it.

'Choose whatever you want,' he said, seeing me hesitate. 'It's a special occasion.'

'That's very sweet of you,' I replied, 'but only if you let *me* pay the babysitter.' James looked as though he was about to protest but I cut him short. 'Birthday girl's prerogative,' I added, my tone making it clear that I would not take no for an answer. I chose seared *foie gras* and a venison stew, while James plumped for a rather less adventurous steak with pepper sauce.

'It's been a long time since I ate anywhere so French,' I remarked, between mouthfuls of velvety *foie gras* which melted on my tongue. 'I didn't realize how much I've been missing French food, until now.' James and I had been living inside a cocoon these past few months. He'd brought out my British side. Instead of croissants, I now ate granary toast and marmalade for breakfast, washed down with a bottomless cup of tea, in place of my bowl of *café au lait*.

'Well, I did wonder whether you might.' James set down his knife and fork and looked at me intently.

'It's not that I don't appreciate your cooking,' I added hastily. 'I love it when you cook for me, but it's true that we tend to eat as if we were back in England. Shepherd's pie, sausages and mash. It's lovely, but I do miss French dishes sometimes.'

'I suppose that's what I've always eaten,' said James, a hint of defensiveness in his voice. 'I *was* married to an English-woman all those years. Whereas you were living with a French guy . . .'

The waiter appeared to clear away our empty plates in readiness for the main course and set down fresh cutlery on the starched tablecloth. I was silent for a moment. James looked very handsome in the candlelight. He'd worn my favourite shirt with his smartest jeans, and was unshaven, with just the right amount of stubble. After all the trouble he was going to, I sincerely hoped I hadn't hurt his feelings. But, unwittingly, by bringing me here, he had managed to put his finger on something my new life with him sorely lacked: the 'Frenchness' I'd been so drawn to when I first met Mr Frog.

It wasn't just about what James and I ate, of course; it ran much deeper than that. We spoke only English when we were together, whereas with Mr Frog at least half our conversations had always been in French. At James's place we watched

British TV, or leafed through British magazines, we drank at an Irish bar on the Place du Parlement de Bretagne in the evenings. At weekends James even played the occasional game of cricket with a local expat team. When we'd first met, I'd found this 'Britishness' appealing. The shared cultural references, the books and TV shows we had in common, all these things were shortcuts, allowing us to get to know each other more quickly, giving us an easy familiarity from the outset, over and above the head start which *petite anglaise* had given us. But now, a few months down the line, the novelty was beginning to wear off. I'd caught myself cringing a couple of times when I overheard James speaking his rather stilted French in shops, or on the phone. In the long term, did I really want to live a British life in France?

Our meal over, we strolled hand in hand through the quiet, pedestrianized streets, my body tingling in anticipation of what would follow once the babysitter had been paid and we were finally alone. But all the same, I couldn't quite shake off the feeling of unease which had overtaken me in the restaurant. By throwing in my lot with James, my inner voice whispered, wouldn't I be turning my back on the very reason I'd come to France in the first place?

'*Va voir* James?' enquired Tadpole, turning in her pushchair to look at me as we sped through the park.

'No, honey,' I replied. 'James has gone back home now.'

Tadpole's face fell. Over the past week she'd grown used to a new presence in the mornings and evenings. Arriving home from *Tata*'s, she tapped insistently at the door, chanting James's name over and over until he opened it, just a chink, and peeped at her through the gap. Every day the same routine; every day the same delighted giggle from Tadpole. He was entitled to a kiss and a hug after her bedtime story;

in the mornings she hopped into my bed and snuggled up between us.

When Mr Frog had first moved out, at the beginning of July, I'd only allowed James to stay with me in Paris when Tadpole was away. But it was September now, and four months had flown by since we first met. I simply couldn't bear to keep the man I loved at arm's length any longer. The beauty of James's translating job was that he worked from home – my home or his – and needed to return to Rennes only when it was his turn to spend the weekend with his daughters. I could no longer see any earthly reason why we should deprive ourselves of precious time together. We couldn't survive on telephone calls alone.

I'd broken the news of James's impending visit to Mr Frog as gently as I could when I delivered Tadpole to his apartment one night, soon after my birthday.

'He's coming to stay next week?' said Mr Frog, his voice choked with anger and disbelief.

'Yes, he'll stay for a few days,' I said quietly. 'Look, I don't expect you to be happy about this, but if I'm ever to work out whether our relationship is built to last, I need to spend time with him. It's easier for him to come here than for me to go there.' I lowered my eyes to the floor, noticing the fuzzy clumps of dust which lined the skirting boards. Mr Frog had never been fond of housework. But now was definitely not the time to draw attention to his shortcomings.

'So, my daughter will wake up in the morning and find a stranger's head on my pillow,' he said flatly. It was a figure of speech: I'd bought new bedding when Mr Frog left, to symbolize my fresh start.

'He's not a stranger,' I countered. 'She's seen James plenty of times in Rennes. And there's no question of him taking your place. Don't forget that he's had to deal with another man living with his own kids, he's really sensitive to the whole situation . . . He's not there to replace her daddy, he's just Mummy's friend who comes to stay.'

Mr Frog nodded, his expression sullen, but resigned. 'So what you're trying to say is that you both have my best interests at heart,' he said bitterly. 'That's awfully big of you.'

'Don't be like this,' I begged, my eyes mutely imploring him not to let things get ugly. Tadpole had raced into the bedroom when she arrived, but I knew neither of us wanted her to overhear any harsh words. 'I know it's not easy, any of this, but let's not make it any harder than it has to be.'

Now the week was up, James had taken himself back to Rennes while I was at work, and I was feeling desperate. Not because he'd gone, but because I'd promised Tadpole we would ambush Daddy with a birthday cake and candles. Less than a fortnight after my own birthday, it was now Mr Frog's turn and, in less than half an hour, he would materialize to whisk Tadpole off for the weekend. Whether out of a sense of guilt, or just for her sake, I wanted to do something to make Mr Frog's birthday special. What I'd failed to remember was that our local bakery was closed for refurbishment. It was almost seven o'clock, and our options were severely limited.

I peered half-heartedly through the window of the Chinese *traiteur* next door to the hairdresser's. *Perles de coco* and almond tarts stared blandly back at me – nothing that would look appropriate with birthday candles. I squinted across the road at the kosher sushi shop. Maybe they sold brownies? But no, the metal shutters were pulled obstinately closed. I would have to think again.

With a sigh, I dragged Tadpole back to the petrol station we had passed five minutes earlier, with its 8 à Huit mini-market. Cake out of a packet would just have to do. It seemed nothing short of sacrilegious in a country where *pâtisseries* are so outstanding, but there was no alternative. Hopefully Mr Frog would be so bowled over by the thoughtfulness of our gesture that he would overlook the poor planning and execution.

I dithered in front of the tired-looking *madeleines*, *cake anglais* – a pale fruit cake containing glacé cherries which resembled nothing I'd ever eaten in England – and bags of individually wrapped *fondants au chocolat*. Settling for the soft-centred chocolate cakes, we dashed home with only minutes to spare.

When Mr Frog arrived, Tadpole took his hand and led him into the living room to show him the jigsaw she'd just finished, while I slipped into the kitchen to fetch a tray. I had arranged three cakes on a plate, a blue and white striped candle lolling at a drunken angle in the centre of each. As I paused in the doorway, I saw Mr Frog, his back to the door, busy shrugging off his overcoat. He didn't hear his daughter – the soul of indiscretion – saying, 'Happy birthday cake, Mummy!' in a stage whisper as I approached.

'Time to sing,' I whispered back, and Tadpole began to sing, in English, just as we'd rehearsed on the way home. Mr Frog wheeled around, clearly startled, his lips forming the most genuine smile I'd seen on his face in a long time, his grey-blue eyes shining in a way which made me wonder if he wasn't fighting back tears.

'I help you blow, Daddy?' offered Tadpole generously once I'd set down my tray on the coffee table, bending her head rather too close to the dancing flames for my liking.

'*Mais bien sûr, ma puce,*' he said, kneeling by her side at cake-level. 'But first we have to count: *un, deux, trois . . . souffle!*'

Once the cakes had been reduced to a small pile of crumbs, I dabbed at the corners of Tadpole's mouth with a tissue, then ducked into her bedroom to fetch her overnight bag. Leaning against the doorframe while the lift clanked and groaned its way up to the fifth floor, I inhaled the dinner smells escaping from the neighbouring apartments and filling the stairwell. The smell of united families, I thought to myself. Families who sit down and eat square meals together.

'Thank you, Cath,' Mr Frog said as he pulled the lift door open and Tadpole stepped inside. '*Ça m'a beaucoup touché . . .*'

As the doors slid closed behind father and daughter, for a second or two my faith in the rightness of my actions wavered. I caught myself wishing that we could share moments like this more often; moments which would never have quite the same resonance with James. Because, however much I loved him, Tadpole was not, and never would be his.

22. Jinxed

The towering sycamores which lined the avenues along the route to *Tata*'s house had begun to shed their leaves, carpeting the pavements with a rustling layer of red, gold and brown which dissolved into a soggy mulch when the weather turned wet. The summer, with its dramas, its stresses and its idyllic moments, was well and truly behind me now; the *métro–boulot–dodo* routine had reasserted itself with a vengeance.

Hot on autumn's heels came an army of green-overalled street-cleaners. Working around the clock, their mission impossible was to combat the leaves, keeping the pathways in and around the park unencumbered. Approaches differed: old-school sweepers were armed with brooms and clear green plastic bags, while others used leaf-blowers, whirring engines strapped to their backs, and blasted the debris forcefully in the direction of the gutters. Road-cleaning lorries trundled lethargically along the roadside while a lone figure walked behind, hoovering up piles of rotting leaves from the kerbside, his task hindered by the cars parked bonnet to bumper along his route.

'Look, Mummy! They all crispy, just like cornflakes,' Tadpole cried as golden-brown leaves crunched under her shoes, and I made a mental note to make use of her observation in a blog post someday soon. She had insisted on getting out of the pushchair halfway to *Tata*'s and, as a result, we were making excruciatingly slow progress. Glancing at my watch, I winced. But faced with a choice between a barbed comment from my boss and wrestling a screeching Tadpole back into the pushchair against her will, the former won hands down.

'Please be careful where you put your feet,' I begged. Just because you couldn't see the pavement didn't mean that there was nothing to fear. The dogs and pigeons hadn't gone on holiday; the evidence of their presence was simply better concealed. Just then, Tadpole noticed a leaf-blower up ahead moving purposefully towards us. She grasped my hand tightly in hers, almost crushing my fingers, and cowered against my thigh.

'*Regarde*, Mummy! A hairdryer!'

'Don't worry, sweetie. He's a street-cleaner. He's just tidying up the leaves. There's no need to be scared.' I adjusted my trajectory all the same to give the green man the widest possible berth. Tadpole had an irrational fear of hairdryers.

The man's face was pitted, the skin above his bushy eyebrows deeply lined. The engine on his back smelled strongly of petrol, and he wore protective headphones to drown out its deafening roar. Courteously, he switched it off for a few moments while Tadpole and I sidled anxiously past. I rewarded his thoughtful gesture with a warm smile of gratitude.

My smile soon vanished, however, when I cottoned on to the fact that the old man was slowly, deliberately, looking me up and down. '*Ça va, ma biche?*' he said, his face contorted by a decidedly lewd grin.

Good grief! Surely he didn't think that I'd been flirting with him? I made no reply and, my cheeks reddening, quickened my step, forcing Tadpole to break into a canter to keep pace with me. A few steps further, however, I stopped dead. Something had just dealt a glancing blow to the back of my head.

'Owww!' I yelled, letting go of Tadpole's hand and wheeling round to confront the culprit. Surely it wasn't possible the man had thrown something at me? But the leaf-blower had his back to us now, his motor turning at full throttle, and I doubt he'd even heard my cry. Aside from a clutch of firemen in navy-blue sweatshirts jogging parallel to us in the park, there was no one else in sight. I put my hand up to rub the top of my head and my fingertips came away spotted with tiny flecks of blood.

'What's matter, Mummy?' asked Tadpole, her brow furrowed with concern. My eyes fell on a spiky horse-chestnut casing which lay shattered in two on the pavement behind me, a gleaming conker by its side. I had found the culprit.

'A conker fell out of a tree and hit Mummy on the head,' I said slowly. I supposed I should be thankful that it hadn't been a pigeon dropping, although the French do say, for some reason, that a direct hit brings good luck. Conkers, however, bring only pain, and for the most part lie unwanted on the pavement once they fall, as there are no French playground games which call for *marrons* to be strung up and used in duels until their hard shells shatter.

'I kiss your *bobo* better,' said Tadpole maternally, delighted to have an opportunity to look after Mummy for a change. Squatting low on the pavement for a moment, steadying myself against the pushchair, I bobbed my head so she could touch her lips to my hair.

The day had not got off to a particularly auspicious start, but Tadpole's presence had a way of righting every wrong. 'Come along then, sweetie,' I said, hauling myself to my feet. 'Mummy's all better now.'

However, things did not improve once I made it, late and flustered, to the office. My boss was dictating at full tilt that day, striding over to my desk at regular intervals to place yet another tape on top of the towering pile of typing the juniors had already generated. Every time I heard the unmistakable rattle of a cassette being prised from a Dictaphone, it set my teeth on edge. The other secretary on my floor – a French girl with a perpetual pout who rarely deigned to give me the time of day – had called in sick and, to my dismay, I'd been left to pick up the slack single-handedly. It had been truly frantic. I'd scarcely glanced at my blog – infuriating, as I was itching to post about my eventful journey to work that morning – and lunch had been a five-minute break, barely long enough to wolf down a sandwich.

Wilting fast, I glanced at the clock, willing the hands to speed up. Thank God it was Friday, and six would mark the beginning of the weekend. I was planning to go out for a few drinks with Amy, making a conscious effort to be a better friend to her on this rare weekend when I wouldn't be travelling to Rennes. I might even pop into a few clothes shops first, I thought to myself, while she was finishing up in the office. Mr Frog was on duty tonight, but I had no intention of staying late, no matter how much unfinished work I'd have to leave in my in-tray.

'Have you printed out the attachment to the email I've just received?' my boss called from his office, without looking up from his paperwork.

'No, I was finishing your letters to catch the post,' I shot back, my eyes still riveted to the screen, 'but I'll do it now.' A cursory glance at Outlook revealed a message from Mr Frog, sent an hour ago. I opened it quickly while the printer spooled loudly into action by my side.

'Are you around this weekend?' his message read. I fired off a rapid response in the affirmative: 'I'm here, yes. James is in Rennes.' At a guess, Mr Frog was trying to establish whether he'd risk running into his nemesis over the weekend. When I'd finally come clean about our near miss in Franprix, months later, he had blanched noticeably. He still had no desire whatsoever to be introduced to James.

But the real reason for his enquiry became clear half an hour later, when a second email popped into my inbox: 'I'm sorry to do this, Cath, but I have a meeting which has been rescheduled at the last minute, and I won't be able to get to *Tata*'s for six thirty. Can you please go? I'll try to come by before bedtime or, if it goes on really late, tomorrow morning.'

I groaned out loud, then glanced furtively around the office to see if anyone had heard me. I could kiss my relaxing, childless evening goodbye. Likewise tomorrow morning's *grasse matinée*, as the French so distastefully call a lie-in. Instead I would have to race to *Tata*'s, and field Tadpole's disappointed questions about why Daddy wouldn't be coming to collect her, as planned. Let Amy down, on the one Friday I was actually in town and free for a girls' night out, and spend the evening home alone instead, all the while cursing Mr Frog under my breath. We might not be together any more, but he still had the unique ability to back me into a corner and make me burn with an all too familiar mixture of anger and resentment. I was at the mercy of his job, even now; the precious little free time I had would never be sacrosanct.

'This is not on!' I retorted, my fingers stabbing the keyboard angrily. 'Tonight is *your* responsibility! I have plans of my own.' Two minutes later, impatient at having received no reply, I seized the telephone and called Mr Frog's office. My blood was at boiling point; I was too furious to work.

Mr Frog barely had the chance to say '*Allô?*' before I launched my offensive. 'I can't believe you're doing this!' I raged in an angry whisper, mindful of my boss, who was working with the door to his office ajar. 'What exactly would you have done if I *had* been away for the weekend? Left her with *Tata* overnight? Tonight is *your* responsibility! I'm not some sort of glorified babysitter who can pick up the slack at a moment's notice . . .'

Mr Frog was unmoved by my arguments. He knew that all he needed to do was stand firm and there was nothing I could do but capitulate. *Tata* didn't do overtime, and I wasn't about to trample all over our good relationship with her, or turn my back on Tadpole, no matter what I might say to the contrary. I'd cave in, all the while raging at my own impotence. What else could I do?

'The fact is that you *are* here and I can't pick her up,' he said flatly. 'I need you to do this for me. Now, we'll have to talk about it later, because I'm leaving for my meeting in a minute.'

'Well,' I said, forgetting to whisper as my hackles rose, 'next time, the answer will be no. Whatever the question is.' I slammed down the receiver, causing the junior nearest to me to jump half out of his skin.

It was then that I noticed, for the first time, the rain falling in determined sheets outside my window. I pictured my waterproof poncho, the only protective clothing worth its salt in a rainstorm when both hands are occupied pushing a buggy. This morning I had taken the poncho out of my bag, of course, thinking I wouldn't need it. I may, or may not, have packed an umbrella in its place, for all the good it would do me. I groaned again. And this time, I didn't care who heard me.

When I rang *Tata*'s doorbell, an hour later, I was conscious of my coat dripping on to her doormat. On the short walk from *métro* Laumière I'd already received a thorough soaking. '*Ah, c'est vous ce soir?*' she said as she opened the door and stepped aside to let me pass. Even *Tata*, I noted wryly, seemed disappointed to see me.

'Yes, there's been a change of plan,' I replied, making no

232

effort to conceal my irritation. 'A meeting rescheduled. I didn't really have much choice. Thank goodness I wasn't away for the weekend.'

'Ah, well, we would have worked something out, I'm sure,' replied *Tata*, wisely refraining from getting drawn into the crossfire. She had a soft spot for Mr Frog, and had blinked back tears the day I broke the news to her that we were no longer living together.

Tadpole was sitting with her playmates at a small table, a paintbrush in her hand. Her eyebrows were matted with green poster paint, and there was a splodge of blue on the tip of her button nose. French nursery rhymes were playing on the stereo, and she hadn't yet heard me come in. At the sight of her, the stress of the office and my anger with Mr Frog began to evaporate, and I smiled, waiting for her to notice my presence.

When she did, her face showed surprise and the briefest flicker of pleasure. But as soon as she remembered she'd been expecting Daddy, the corners of her mouth began to droop. Sometimes, watching her face, I felt as though I could read her every thought. She hadn't learned how to conceal her emotions yet; every nuance was transparent to me.

'*Non! Je veux Papa!*' she cried, turning away, throwing down her paintbrush in a fit of pique. However determined I was not to take her reaction to heart, there was no denying that it smarted like an open-handed slap in the face.

We trudged home, Tadpole safe and dry under the protective sheath of her pushchair cover but still wailing for her daddy, while I bent my head low and skated forwards across the slippery leaves, blinded by the droplets on my glasses. My hair was plastered to my head and rivulets of chill water ran down the back of my neck, soaking the clothes under my wool coat, which had doubled in weight. I was beyond miserable. Was it possible for this cursed day to get any worse?

An hour later, wearing dry clothes, a towelling turban wound around my wet hair, I pottered in the kitchen, a cup of tea steaming by my side. I was grilling fish fingers for Tadpole's dinner, and planned to console myself with a fish finger and ketchup sandwich.

Out of the corner of my eye I registered Tadpole's approach. Her shoes were back on, albeit unbuckled and on the wrong feet, and she wore the Miffy bag – which we now referred to as her weekend bag – slung across one shoulder. It was open: inside I spied a book or two, her sippy cup, a car and a plastic harmonica.

'*Maman*, I ready to go to Daddy's house now,' she announced. I stood, speechless, a wooden spatula dangling limply from my right hand. Turning as if to leave, Tadpole strode towards the front door. I followed, still clutching my spatula, wondering how best to deal with the situation.

'*Ouvre la porte*, Mummy. I going now,' she cried. I sighed, and shook my head, but this only made Tadpole more determined. She began to hammer with her fists against the front door.

'Honey, Daddy's coming later. And if he can't come later, he'll see you tomorrow. I'm sorry, but you'll have to stay with me for a while.' Is it so terrible to be sentenced to an evening with me, I wanted to add? What on earth does Daddy have that I don't?

The corners of Tadpole's mouth drooped once more, a sure sign that she was about to cry, and I crouched low and pulled her to me. She resisted, at first, but a few moments later she hugged me back, allowing me to console her. I held the spatula carefully away from her clothes and savoured the feeling of her warm cheek against mine. 'Mummy,' she said suddenly, pulling back and wrinkling her nose. 'What's that stinky smell?'

'Oh shit!' I yelled, just as the smoke alarm began to peal. In the process of placating my daughter, I had managed to burn our dinner. There are some days, I said to myself as I reached into the freezer and grabbed the last of the fish fingers – enough for Tadpole, but not for me – when you are jinxed; when nothing will go right. A French saying has it that if you put your left foot down first when you get out of bed, the day gets off to a bad start. Perhaps it was best, I thought to myself superstitiously, to consider today a total write-off, and pay special attention to my footwork the following morning.

James's tone was sympathetic, and he was saying all the right things, as usual. But for some reason hearing his voice that evening on the phone made everything worse, not better.

'I hate feeling so powerless,' I railed. Even as I spoke, I realized that Mr Frog must have felt this way when I told him I wanted us to live apart. Maybe this was his way of punishing me?

'He was wrong to back you into a corner like that, of course,' James said reasonably, 'and I can see how frustrating it must have been for you not to be able to stand your ground. If I've learned anything from my divorce, it's that you have to build up a lot of goodwill before you start asking for favours. And even then, you ask, you don't impose . . .' Tadpole was sleeping; my hair was almost dry. I had retreated under my duvet with the phone pressed to my ear to recount the events of my day of misery.

'I just wish you were here,' I said in a small, desolate voice. 'It's good to talk, but what I really need is a hug. If you'd been waiting here when I got home dripping wet, you'd have laughed, and I'd have seen the funny side . . . Being here alone, it's just too hard.'

'I'll visit as soon as I can, babe,' he said gently. 'You know I'd be there if I could.'

The word 'babe' made me bristle. I'd told James it reminded me of the cartoon pig of the same name. But the real reason I hated it – the reason I hadn't told James – was that a nickname like 'babe' was too impersonal, too transferable. Had he called his wife 'babe', or Eve?

'I think I'm going to try and sleep now,' I mumbled. 'All I want is to put an end to this truly horrible day.'

Sleep proved elusive, however. I was still too furious with Mr Frog, too bitter about my cancelled plans. My brain was stuck in a loop, endlessly rehearsing the angry speech I would make when he showed his guilty face the next morning, and the venomous blog post I was sure I'd write afterwards. So when I did fall asleep, it was Mr Frog – not James – who inhabited my dreams.

23. Keys

'Ooh, arrabiata sauce, my favourite,' said Amy as I ladled a generous serving of steaming pasta on to her waiting plate. To make amends for our aborted evening out, I'd invited her over for dinner. A bottle of Chianti stood half-empty on the coffee table and we ate on the sofas, our dinner plates balanced on our knees. It had been a while since our last girls' night in, but as the wine began working its magic, fuzzy warmth spreading through my body, I made a mental note to myself to invite people over more often.

Before long the conversation inevitably turned to the men in our lives, and the frustrations caused by our long-distance relationships. 'I'm just getting fed up with spending all my evenings on the phone when he's not here,' I confided. 'I mean, I want to talk to James – I'd be upset if he didn't call – but by the time I've got *mademoiselle* into bed, and James and I have made small talk for an hour, the evening has disappeared.'

'At least your situation is only temporary,' said Amy ruefully. 'I have no idea if Tom and I will ever end up living in the same city. I think he actually likes it this way. If I announced I was upping sticks and moving to London, I wouldn't see him for dust.'

'You don't know that for certain,' I said, making a sympathetic face as I refilled our glasses. 'But as for my situation being temporary, I suppose it is, but moving in with James seems an awfully long way off right now. And, in the meantime, I feel as trapped as I did before, in some ways. I've traded one absent guy for another . . . I don't know how I'm going to cope with eight more months of this waiting and wondering . . .'

'Wondering?' said Amy warily. 'Don't tell me you're having doubts?'

'Oh. I don't know, maybe sometimes.' It was the first time I'd actually given voice to such feelings, and it was as though they had crept up on me so stealthily that even I hadn't noticed, at first. 'I was looking at a few job ads today online, for example, and it got me worrying about what kind of job I'll be able to find in Rennes, and whether we'll be okay for money. I really love James – I've never felt so strongly about anyone before – but I have to be practical too. At the end of the day, it's not just *me* moving, I'll be uprooting my daughter's life as well.'

'And remind me again why *he* can't move to Paris?'

'Lots of reasons. His girls are in Brittany. He could never afford to live here. Most of what he earns goes into various taxes, and he has child support to pay to his ex-wife too. And, anyway, he hates Paris – he only puts up with staying here so often because he wants to see me. And the fact is, I do want to leave. I've been hankering after a house and a garden ever since I got pregnant.'

'Fair enough,' said Amy, picking up the bottle, realizing it was empty, and putting it down again. 'But have you told James about any of your doubts? You've certainly kept quiet about them on the blog . . .' Amy had a point. Sometimes it felt like the blog had morphed into one of those mirrors you get in fairgrounds, a looking glass which distorted my reflection. The girl in the mirror – *petite anglaise* – frequently smiled when I did not.

'Well, that's the thing,' I said slowly. 'I don't think he ever has doubts, and that makes me feel guilty for having negative thoughts myself . . . And of course there are some subjects which are tricky, like money. Guaranteed to get him on the defensive. Too dangerous to broach on the blog.'

'Ah yes, that old chestnut,' said Amy. 'Modern men: they say they don't mind when the woman is the main bread-winner, but when it comes down to it, they usually hate it.'

'You're right though,' I added. 'I have kept very quiet about it all on the blog. And because of that, I'm short of things to say. I can't have written more than ten posts in October. That's about half as many as I was writing in the same month a year ago . . .'

I collected our empty plates and took them into the kitchen, returning with a second bottle of wine and a cork-screw. Amy was standing by the window, her arms folded, looking out across the city.

'Won't you miss all this?' she said, gesturing at the skyline. Despite the late hour, a random pattern of yellow-orange squares across the face of the Tour Montparnasse betrayed the presence of office workers clocking up overtime. I could no longer look at it these days without thinking of the station it towered over: my gateway to Brittany.

'I'll miss this view,' I said, fiddling with the cork, which seemed intent on splintering into tiny shards. 'But I'm so used to it that I mostly take it for granted anyway. I probably stare at it on my blog more often than through this window . . .'

It was well past midnight when Amy left. As I rinsed the wine glasses under the kitchen tap, humming to myself, it occurred to me that I hadn't felt the need to speak to James all evening.

'Bla bla black sheep, have you any wool?'

Tadpole sang at full volume, prompting passers-by to stare at her with undisguised interest. A child who loves to sing in public is one thing; a child who sings in English, switches seamlessly into French to ask for a biscuit, then resumes her English song, draws looks of awe and admiration. I envied Tadpole sometimes: to her, speaking two languages was as natural as drawing breath.

I walked home in a daze that evening, my eyes barely registering the pavement ahead, let alone the stares my daughter was drawing. The previous night's wine with Amy had taken its toll. I'd woken feeling sluggish and heavy-limbed and, although the fog in my brain had finally begun to recede, I felt sure I'd be in bed not long after Tadpole.

The trees were now stripped bare of leaves, and the winter sun had dipped blindingly low, making my eyes water behind my glasses. For the time of year, the weather was mild and, although I was wearing only a long-sleeved top under my unbuttoned coat, I was clammy from the exertion of pushing Tadpole uphill. Suddenly I brought the pushchair to an abrupt halt, cutting Tadpole off at the third bag of wool. My red jacket! I'd been wearing it under my coat when I set out that morning, but in my haste to leave the office on time I'd left it dangling over the back of my chair. I knew without even putting my hands to my coat pocket that it was empty. I'd left my keys behind.

'*Merde!*' I muttered under my breath, glancing at my watch and considering my options. Either I could return to the office with Tadpole by *métro*, keeping my fingers crossed that someone was working late, as I had no office key. Or I could call a taxi, although the round trip would take just as long in the gnarly rush-hour traffic, and would cost me a fortune. There was one other option: call Mr Frog, who had a spare set of keys, and see whether he could be prevailed upon to leave work early and ride valiantly to our rescue on his gleaming white Vespa.

'*J'ai fait une énorme connerie!*' I wailed when Mr Frog answered. 'I've gone and left my keys at the office! We're halfway home from *Tata*'s and it will be an absolute nightmare going back for them. Is there any way at all you could come and let us in?'

For a few tense moments I heard only silence, and I began to think my phone had dropped the call. 'You're in luck, you caught me on a good day,' Mr Frog said, finally. 'I suppose I could leave in twenty minutes or so and work from home afterwards.'

'Oh, thank you! I owe you!' I was giddy with relief. 'Give me a call when you arrive. We'll be somewhere nearby.'

Mr Frog arrived half an hour later, and neither of us saw him approach at first. Sitting at a red Formica window table in the Café des Buttes Chaumont, Tadpole pored over a Dora magazine I'd bought in the newsagent's next door, while I gazed blankly out over square Bolivar, my brain stuck in first gear, my fingers closed around an empty espresso cup.

Hearing her name, Tadpole looked up, overjoyed, her magazine sliding to the floor, forgotten. I flashed Mr Frog a grateful smile as he bent to retrieve it. I'd texted to tell him where we were, but hadn't expected him so soon.

'Daddy, DA-ddy, DADDY!' Tadpole chanted, clapping her hands in delight. '*Viens t'asseoir avec nous!*' Mr Frog took a seat beside Tadpole, who leaped on to his knee and threw her arms around his neck.

'Can I buy you a drink?' I offered. 'To thank you for coming all this way at such short notice?'

'Okay, why not? I'll have a *pression*,' he replied. 'It's not often I get out of work in time for an *apéro*.'

When the waiter appeared at Mr Frog's elbow Tadpole turned to him and introduced herself, holding up two fingers to illustrate her age. '*Aujourd'hui, je suis avec ma maman ET mon papa!*' she added with a wide smile. The waiter raised an eyebrow. As far as he was concerned she was only stating the obvious. He couldn't be expected to understand what a rare occurrence this was.

Looking from my daughter, to her father, and back again, I felt a lump in my throat. I was adept at justifying everything I'd done – to my readers, to my friends, even to myself – reasoning that because Mr Frog now spent far more one-to-one time with his daughter, and they were closer than ever before, everyone was better off. But that meant glossing over the fact that I'd robbed Tadpole of the chance to be with us both at the same time. Seeing how ecstatic she looked now made my heart heavy.

Mr Frog appeared to be wearing a new suit. It was well cut, a change from the jeans and T-shirts James worked in from home, and I had to admit he looked quite handsome. I wondered if he was seeing anyone. He never talked about his personal life to me, and no doubt I'd be the last to know if there was someone special. 'Yes, it *is* new,' he said, seeing my appraising stare and anticipating my question. 'Do you like it?'

'I do,' I replied simply. 'It suits you.' Not so long ago I would have tutted over how much it must have cost, and made a barbed comment about how Mr Frog spent all his money on himself, and never saved for the future. Now, as long as he paid Tadpole's maintenance on time, it was no longer any of my concern: there were far fewer subjects for us to do battle over these days. 'Thanks again for getting away so quickly,' I added. 'We'd probably only have been halfway to my office by now.'

'Yes, well, perhaps by way of thanks you could write a post about it,' Mr Frog joked, taking a long sip of his beer. 'After what you wrote about me shirking my responsibilities when

I called you at work, that time, it would be nice to show those readers of yours that I'm not entirely evil. Give me an image makeover.' I blushed. I had no idea Mr Frog was following *petite anglaise* so closely. How ironic that he should be taking more interest in the blog now.

'I'll see what I can do,' I replied grudgingly. 'No more Mr Frog the bad guy. As long as you behave, of course . . .'

As I counted out the correct change and we rose to leave, my thoughts already turning to what on earth I could make for Tadpole's dinner, I hung back with the pushchair, watching Tadpole walk hand in hand with Mr Frog to the front door of my building. I feared there might be tears when we parted. It must be confusing for her to see Daddy unexpectedly like this, and it would be cruel to wrench her away from him so soon after he'd arrived.

'*On se voit jeudi, ma puce*,' Mr Frog explained gently when we reached our destination. 'We're going to visit your school together on Thursday.' Tadpole nodded, apparently satisfied with this arrangement, and Mr Frog and I exchanged relieved smiles over her head. Handing me the keys, he bent to kiss Tadpole lightly on the cheek.

As I watched him walk away, his Vespa helmet swinging from his right hand, I couldn't help thinking that, in spite of everything we'd been through, our family was in remarkably good shape.

On the phone with James later that evening, I played down the impending school visit as much as I could.

'I'm doing it for her dad really,' I explained. 'So he feels involved. And so that when I tell him about visiting the school in Rennes, in a few months' time, he'll have a point of comparison. But in many ways it feels like a pointless exercise, wooing the headmistress under false pretences when we all know I have no intention of staying in Paris . . .'

'Hey, you're doing the right thing,' said James. '*Maternelle* is a whole ten months away. A lot can happen in ten months.'

'I suppose so,' I replied, disappointed with his response. I'd rather hoped James would react by telling me the visit was a waste of time; that I was being over-cautious. I craved reassurance. His unwavering certitude was the best antidote to the doubts which had begun to surface in my mind since I'd first given voice to them, in conversation with Amy. 'I wish I didn't have to do all this lying,' I added. 'Well, not *lying* exactly, but holding back information. At first it was just keeping the blog secret from my colleagues. Now I'm keeping quiet about leaving Paris so my boss doesn't find out, lying to the school admissions people . . .'

'You're doing the right thing,' said James firmly. 'You'll tell them the truth if and when they need to know.'

'*If* and when?' I was suddenly fearful. 'Are you giving yourself a get-out clause?'

'Of course not,' he said sharply. 'You know what your problem is? You read far too much into every little word. You over-analyse.' His remark stung and for a moment I was too taken aback to respond.

'An occupational hazard,' I replied defensively, once I'd gathered my wits. 'Don't pretend you didn't know that about me long before we met . . .'

'I did,' James said, interrupting me before I could finish, 'but I'd like to think that together we should be able to conquer some of these insecurities of yours.'

'And we will,' I said decisively. 'When we really are together, instead of hundreds of kilometres apart. You'll see.'

When I saw Mr Frog striding towards Tadpole and me on the day of the infamous school visit, I was struck once more by how handsome he looked in his new suit. I'd made an extra-special effort that morning too, both with my clothes and Tadpole's and, outwardly, at least, we looked the part: a well-turned-out family.

'We'd best get a move on,' I said, looking pointedly at my watch. 'Our appointment's in five minutes, and we don't want to make a bad first impression, or make ourselves late for work.'

The school was a typical sandstone municipal building dating from the turn of the century, and I noticed as we drew closer that the ground-floor windows were all barred, which gave it the air of a prison rather than a place of learning. It wasn't a patch on the pre-school I had my eye on near James's place, nestled between the Thabor park and a seventeenth-century Benedictine abbey. The headmistress, to whom I'd spoken on the phone a few days earlier, had a rasping voice suggestive of a forty-a-day Gauloise habit. I sincerely hoped she'd forgotten I'd initially mistaken her for a man when she answered the phone, addressing her as '*Monsieur*'.

'*Nous avons rendez-vous avec la directrice,*' I said to the elderly African lady who'd answered the front door when we rang the buzzer and now stood, arms folded across her batik-print tunic, guarding the door. I supposed I should find it reassuring that not just anyone could waltz into a French school, but was it too much to ask for a welcoming smile?

'*C'est par ici,*' said the woman with a curt nod. Leading us through a hall where children clattered around on makeshift stilts made from upturned buckets on strings, she abandoned us at the foot of a flight of stairs, gesturing for us to turn left at the top. As we made our slow ascent, Tadpole clutching both our hands and gazing spellbound at the gaudy artwork which filled every spare centimetre of the walls, I spoke to Mr Frog in a low voice.

'Now, no mention that we're separated, or living apart,

and nothing about moving to Rennes in the summer,' I said in a tense whisper, not quite able to meet his eyes. 'There's no need to complicate matters at this stage, it's none of their business.' We were getting our stories straight; lying by omission. It would be a relief when I could bring my life out into the open, dispensing with the web of half-truths.

Mr Frog, his face impassive, did not reply. The word 'Rennes' always produced that effect, and I couldn't blame him for reacting that way. It tore me to pieces too, imagining how hard the transition would be; how excluded Mr Frog would feel when we moved away. I could insist until I was blue in the face that my plans weren't all about putting my happiness first and giving myself to James, that I wanted to give Tadpole the picture-postcard school, the cottage I dreamed of with a rambling garden. But poor Mr Frog would only ever see the future in terms of what he stood to lose.

'*Les poux sont de retour!*' warned a poster taped to the door which I supposed must lead to the *directrice*'s office. Seeing the picture of a head-louse tap-dancing across a child's head, I put a hand to my hair instinctively and scratched a phantom itch.

'*Entrez!*' said a gruff voice, in response to my hesitant knock.

'I thought you said it was a *directrice*,' whispered Mr Frog, 'not a *directeur*.'

'I did. And it is,' I said, stifling a giggle. 'Although let's just say you're not the first one to make *that* mistake . . .' Mr Frog smirked, raising his eyebrows, and I smiled widely. Without any need for further explanation he had understood my gaffe. It was a rare moment of complicity, and I savoured it. All tension between us had dissipated and, for once, Mr Frog smiled with both his mouth and his eyes.

Composing a blog entry about the school visit later that

day, I dwelled on the awkward exchange in the stairwell, failing even to evoke the moment of complicity between Mr Frog and me outside the headmistress's door. Homing in on one and not the other, I wasn't being dishonest, exactly, because it would be impossible to document every waking second of my life. But why leave it out? Maybe I wasn't ready to confess – to James, or to myself – that over the past week or so, between the café and the school, my happiest moments had been spent with Mr Frog.

24. Lemsip

'I don't want my life to be perpetually mapped out like some sort of military campaign,' objected James, an uncharacteristic hint of irritation creeping into his voice when I prodded him, for the sixth time, about his daughters' Christmas whereabouts.

'I'm sorry. I know I keep hassling you,' I said, squeezing my teabag with the back of a teaspoon, cradling the phone awkwardly between my ear and my shoulder. 'But playing at happy families isn't easy. We have to take so many different people into account: your ex, my ex, all our children's grandparents . . . So we can't just play everything by ear. I'm only wondering whether to post the girls' presents in advance, or to bring them with me, that's all.'

That wasn't all, of course. I was wondering whether Christmas would be an adult celebration or a cosy, family affair. Secretly I craved the former, although I wasn't about to admit to that and risk being accused of plotting to sideline James's children.

The festive season had been carved up so that everyone in Tadpole's life got their timeshare slot. First Mr Frog would take her to stay with *Mamie* and *Papy* while I spent the holiday weekend in Brittany with James, with or without Carrie and Amanda. On Boxing Day evening I would leave James with his leftovers, TGVing reluctantly back to Paris for a few morbidly quiet days in the office. When Tadpole returned, she and I would fly to Yorkshire together to spend New Year with my family.

Plotting Tadpole's movements, ensuring that no one felt left out, slighted or short-changed was challenging, to say the least, and my plans had been laid months in advance, a fact which was clearly not to everyone's liking.

'Okay, well, look, I'll speak to the girls' mum and see if I can pin down exactly what's going on at our end,' said James grudgingly. 'If they are going to be spending Christmas with us, I'll have to work out where on earth I've hidden the decorations.'

'Good luck with that!' I said sarcastically, immediately wishing I'd held my tongue. The first time I'd visited James, his apartment had been spotless; on subsequent visits, less so. It wasn't dirty – just cluttered and riotously untidy – but if Tadpole and I were to move in, I was adamant that James would have to change his ways, if only to make space for us. Whenever I visited I had to hold myself in check, even though I was itching to sort the paperwork fanned across the floor around James's desk, or to gather up the clothes strewn across every surface of his bedroom. That was how he liked things, James insisted and, until I moved in for good, that was how things would stay.

'You getting a tree?' asked James, wisely preferring a change of subject to a petty argument.

'I haven't decided yet,' I confessed. 'With all the to-ing and fro-ing, I'm wondering whether to bother . . .'

If I did succumb to temptation and buy one of the over-priced trees huddled on the pavement outside the local florist's, the poor *sapin* would spend much of the Christmas period home alone, shedding needles which would embed themselves between the floorboards, only to reappear months later, as if by magic, whenever someone ventured barefoot across the living room.

It wasn't as though there weren't plenty of other thrills on offer to get Tadpole in the Christmas mood. The *mairie* was frosted with tasteful white lights, outlining every window and hanging like stalactites from the roof. On the cobbled square in front of the town hall a Christmas market had taken up residence, a multitude of tiny stalls selling chocolate Yule logs, gingerbread Santas and plastic cups of *vin chaud* which spiced the crisp winter air with the lingering scent of cloves and cinnamon. Nearby, a free merry-go-round span in giddy circles, the yelps of children competing with the tuneless Euro-disco blaring from the sound system.

Our route home from *Tata*'s made this monstrosity impossible to avoid, much to Tadpole's delight. Every evening I shivered stoically on the sidelines, my breath conjuring white clouds from the icy air, while Tadpole careered past in a shiny blue car, one mitten-clad hand on the steering wheel, the other vigorously waving.

Tadpole had even learned 'Away in a Manger' off by heart and I'd managed to record her rendition of it in readiness for a Christmas posting on my blog, to be accompanied by a photograph of her wearing reindeer antlers, voluntarily blurred in the interests of preserving her anonymity.

But there was still a vital something, or someone, missing from our Christmas, and I finally caved in and wheeled a tree home in Tadpole's pushchair a week before the holiday season got underway. Anything that might make my first Christmas as a single parent feel more festive had to be worth a try, even if it was futile to try to deflect attention away from the conspicuous absence of the two men in my life by using shiny baubles and a few balding strands of tinsel.

'Which *sapin* do you like best?' I said to Tadpole, bringing her pushchair to a halt outside the florist's on avenue Laumière. 'How about this one?' I fingered a small but perfect specimen with branches like bottle brushes, the needles an attractive blue-green. Soft-focus images swam around my head: Tadpole passing me decorations one by one, carol singers warbling on the stereo in the background. This might be the first Christmas Tadpole remembered in years to come. I owed it to her to make it special.

'I like *that* one better!' Tadpole cried, pointing at a scrawny, parched-looking apology for a tree which towered high above my head. It looked as though the lightest of touches would dislodge any remaining needles, leaving it prematurely bald. This was definitely not what I'd had in mind.

'Well,' I said diplomatically, 'that one is very pretty, yes, but Mummy hasn't got quite enough money to buy it, and it would be very difficult to carry home . . .' The journey through the park awaited us still and, as it was, Tadpole would have to walk alongside her pushchair while the *sapin* rode home in comfort.

Plumping for a middle-sized tree, I winced at the price and we set off for home, eager to begin decorating. Only then did the limitations of my fantasy become fully apparent. I'd forgotten just how fragile the eggshell-thin baubles were. I'd overlooked the fact that the assorted bent paperclips and safety pins I always used to hang the decorations were treacherously sharp. As for the carol CD which had featured in my daydream, it was nowhere to be found, and after the third 'No, not like that! Careful, it's going to break!' Tadpole lost interest in the proceedings altogether, stomping off to her room in disgust. If she couldn't juggle with the shiny balls or pop sharp objects into her mouth, where was the fun?

My daydream in tatters, I finished hanging the baubles alone. Standing back to admire my handiwork, I had to admit our tree looked the part, even if I'd done a rotten job of making us feel festive.

'Sweetie, can you come back into the lounge? Mummy's

going to switch on the pretty lights now,' I hollered, hand poised ready to plug the flex into one of the wooden two-pin sockets I suspected our landlord ought to have replaced years ago. Tadpole dawdled slowly back along the corridor, excited in spite of herself, but unwilling to give me the satisfaction of seeing her hurry. She hovered in the doorway, a felt-tip pen clutched tightly in one hand.

Although only half the fairy lights twinkled into life, the overall effect was still impressive enough to warrant a burst of applause from Tadpole, her pen rolling across the floorboards forgotten, destined to be found lurking under the sofa months later, its tip completely dry.

'Father Christmas is going to leave presents for you under this *sapin*,' I whispered, hoisting her up so that she could admire the decorations at close range, a constellation of fairy lights reflected in her eyes, 'and under *Mamie* and *Papy*'s tree too, and even in England, at Grandma and Grandad's house.' In Tadpole's eyes Christmas hadn't been carved up, it had simply been multiplied.

'But of course,' I couldn't resist adding, 'only if you're a *very* good girl . . .'

Amy and I climbed the flight of steps which led from *métro* Pont Marie to the Quai des Celestins. Buffeted by the icy cross-winds, we were relieved to dive into a narrow, sheltered side street leading us into the southernmost tip of the Marais.

In milder weather the Marais was one of my favourite places. When I first arrived in Paris, I'd spent long hours padding up and down every single street north and south of the rue Saint Antoine, gazing through ornate wrought-iron railings across formal gardens to the *hôtels particuliers* beyond. I was reading *Dangerous Liaisons* at the time, and it was all too easy to imagine the Vicomte de Valmont seated at an *écritoire*, writing to the Comtesse de Merteuil, or a group of aristocrats in powdered wigs taking a turn around the garden while they waited for horses to be saddled to their carriages. Private residences had given way to museums and offices, or been carved up into smaller apartments, but I never could shake off the feeling that I was stepping back in time when I walked through those narrow streets.

'So, what's this year's restaurant like?' said Amy. We were on our way to the office Christmas meal, a rather tame affair, on account of the fact that it was always held at lunch-time, and you were never entirely sure whether you'd be required to return to the office once the festivities were over.

'I haven't the faintest idea,' I replied with a frown. 'Nobody's really told me anything.' In previous years I'd been in charge of organizing the outing myself but, back in October, when the plans were laid, I was still out of favour with my boss so the task had been given to someone else.

'Things are getting better between you two now though, aren't they?' Amy said, gesturing ahead to where my boss's receding back could be seen amidst a clutch of colleagues. The whole office was on the move; Amy and I were bringing up the rear.

'Yes, slowly improving,' I said, nodding. 'Although I still can't say I really understand what went wrong in the first place, or what has changed for the better now. I'm just going to keep my head down and enjoy it while I can. If things could stay like this until I leave next summer, that would be ideal . . .'

It was the first time I'd had a chance to catch up with Amy since the party she'd thrown a couple of weeks earlier, as work was getting frantic with the year end approaching. I'd brought James along – as he'd been staying with me at the time – and Amy had liked him, or at least she'd said she did.

I'd been plagued all evening by the nagging feeling that James didn't quite fit in, but that was hardly surprising. He was forty, whereas most of Amy's guests were only in their mid-twenties. And at the end of the day, he didn't have to fit in with my Paris life. I was the one who would be moving, not him.

'Only another six or seven months to go!' said Amy, lowering her voice just in case anyone might be listening in. 'It's going to fly by.'

'I hope so,' I replied. 'I want to have a real relationship; I'm tired of waiting.'

'Well, at least James has the freedom to come and stay for weeks at a time,' Amy said wistfully. 'I wish Tom could do that.' Tom hadn't even made it to her party, and I knew she had felt his absence keenly.

'I am lucky in that respect,' I said. 'Although, having said that, he's not planning to come back until the New Year. I get the feeling he's starting to get a bit sick of living out of a suitcase.'

'I'll miss having you around, when you go,' Amy said, suddenly serious. 'You're one of the few people I can really talk to. I know I'll be able to read about what you're up to on the blog, but it's not the same . . .'

'I'll visit,' I said, touched by her admission. It was confirmation, if confirmation were needed, that since we'd cleared the air that day when she was off work ill, our friendship had deepened. 'And I'll only be a phone call or an email away. You must come and stay with us too, as soon as we've got space. But it's quite a way off yet.'

I boarded my train on Friday evening after work, two days before Christmas, trembling with anticipation. Amanda and Carrie were away with their mother and her new partner skiing in the mountains, so James and I would spend Christmas alone, exactly as I'd hoped. I pictured us eating a candlelit meal for two, retiring early with a bottle of champagne. I'd been looking forward to this trip for three long weeks and now there were only three hours separating me from James's waiting arms. As the train eased itself out of Montparnasse station, I fizzed with pent-up excitement.

At first, as the TGV hurtled in the direction of Rennes, I put the tightness in my throat down to the air conditioning. But when my nose started to drip like a leaking tap and my sinuses began to ache, I knew I was in trouble. By the time the train pulled into Rennes station, I was feverish and dizzy and laying my throbbing head on a cool pillow was the foremost thing on my mind.

'I can't believe this,' I croaked, two days later. 'I so looked forward to seeing you, and I've been too ill the whole time to do anything. It's so unfair. The only festive thing about me is my red nose.'

'Hey, it's a pity, I know, but there's no point getting all worked up about it, love,' James said reasonably, putting his palm to my clammy forehead. I resisted the urge to swat his hand away. I didn't want reasonable. I wanted romance and passion; our old intensity. I wanted, at the very least, to see some evidence that my bitter disappointment was matched by his. Where had he gone, the James who sent me all those knee-weakening, eloquent emails back in April? The man who once confessed he was so captivated by the movement of my hips every time I walked across the room that he constantly had to suppress the urge to pick me up and carry me to the nearest bed?

I collapsed back on to the pillows, clutching a handful of tissues, feeling cheated, robbed. James had broken the news to me that he would be away for much of January, staying with his parents in England and, as I kept repeating, we'd barely seen each other in December. I'd desperately wanted our first Christmas together to be magical, to mean something. It could and should have been perfect. Instead, the weekend had passed by in a feverish blur, and now our time had almost run out.

'Just think, next Christmas you'll be living here with me, and we'll laugh about this,' said James, smoothing back my hair with a paternal gesture which I'd seen him use before, with Amanda and Carrie. 'Now, you stay there, and I'll go and make you some more hot lemon.'

'Thanks,' I said weakly, curling into a tight ball of disappointment under the bedclothes when he left the room. I'd asked for passion, and Father Christmas had brought me Lemsip. Try as I might, I couldn't shake off the uneasy feeling – yet another emotion that I wouldn't be in a hurry to document on my blog – that for James and I, the honeymoon period had come to an end, just as Mr Frog had predicted.

25. Relief

'You look really tired,' said Amy as I leaned back in my chair, letting my body sag against the kitchen wall and closing my eyes. I'd listlessly picked over my salad, then pushed it to one side, unable to muster any further enthusiasm. The lettuce was like rice paper in my dry mouth.

'I'm feeling low at the moment,' I replied, with a sigh. 'Fed up with being on my own. Just plain depressed. I don't seem to be able to snap out of it. There's nothing I can do but ride it out.'

In the fortnight since Christmas, I'd felt as though I were slowly sinking in quicksand. The world around me seemed different: monochrome, tasteless and bland. Getting up in the mornings, readying Tadpole for her day and dragging my sorry carcass to the office required a supreme effort of will. It was as though a black cloud were following me around, casting a melancholy shadow.

I'd begun a blog post about my feelings, hoping to chase away the gloom by facing it head on. It had worked, to some extent, when I'd been plagued by jealousy, but this time it didn't seem to be the answer. I could describe *how* I felt, but not *why*. Unpacking my doubts, examining them on the blog in full view of James, would wreak untold damage. Besieged by pessimism, I was too afraid that if I took hold of a single thread and tugged, hard, our whole relationship might unravel.

James detested his powerlessness in the face of my bleak moods, but there were no words he could say which would magically bring me to my senses. The clouds would lift, or disperse, eventually, of their own volition. Sobbing into the telephone, I craved physical contact, the reassuring warmth of skin. I wanted to rest my head against his chest and hear the steady, regular beating of his heart.

Amy pushed back her chair and moved purposefully towards the kitchen cupboard. After rummaging around behind the packets of tea favoured by our French co-workers – herbal infusions claiming to possess all manner of miraculous slimming and 'draining' properties – she produced a large bar of dark chocolate which had been concealed at the back of the shelf. 'Here, have a piece of emergency chocolate,' she said, setting it in front of me. 'Sometimes it really is the only cure.'

'You know what the worst thing is?' I continued, peeling back the copper-coloured foil and breaking off a single square. 'I've been awful to James. I twist his words, push him away, hold petty things against him . . . It's really nice of him to spend a fortnight with his parents in England while his dad is convalescing. But I'm making him feel guilty for doing it . . .'

'The recommended dosage is two squares,' said Amy sternly. She sounded more like a school nurse administering vile-tasting medicine than a friend offering chocolate and, in spite of myself, I let slip a smile, albeit a feeble one. 'I'm sure he knows it's only depression talking,' she added, taking a couple of squares of chocolate herself, then sliding the packet back across the table towards me. 'So he can hardly hold that against you. But isn't there some way you can get yourself over there? Visit him while he's in England?'

'I don't think his parents need a toddler around right now,' I said doubtfully. Mr Frog was going to be away for two consecutive weekends. His timing couldn't have been worse. 'But having said that, his parents do live quite close to mine . . .' The germ of an idea had been planted, and as soon as my boss went into his afternoon meeting I started making enquiries.

'I've got great news!' I announced as soon as James picked up the phone that evening. 'I spoke to Mum earlier and she offered to babysit the weekend after next! I could fly over on Friday, meet my parents at the airport, then come to stay with you, and meet your parents. If you think that would be okay of course . . .' I faltered. What had started out as a triumphant, gleeful announcement had fizzled out into a cautious question, my confidence faltering at the halfway mark. Supposing he said no? What then? His father *was* ill, and James was ostensibly there to help. His parents might not appreciate a social call. There was an excruciating pause, and I held my breath anxiously.

'Okay? Of course it's okay, silly girl. That's fantastic news! Mum and Dad would love to meet you, and there are so many people from home I want you to meet!'

'Oh, thank God! For a moment there . . .' I was so relieved I laughed out loud. Tadpole, who was splashing in the bathwater by my side, looked at me with interest. As much as I'd struggled to hide my gloom from my daughter, she was as attuned to my moods as ever. Instinctively, she seemed to know that all those other smiles I'd forced hadn't been the real thing, whereas the one I wore now was unmistakably genuine, and her grin now mirrored my own. 'The logistics will take a bit of working out, of course,' I added, my happiness clearly audible, 'but I'll phone Mum and Dad back now, we just need to iron out the details.'

'Fantastic. Well, get your flights booked straight away in that case. Listen, I have to go now, my mother's putting dinner on the table, but that's great news. I'll phone a few friends later and see what I can organize.'

'Will do!' I promised. 'Thank goodness it all worked out. The idea of not seeing you all month was horrible.'

As I lifted Tadpole out of the bath, I caught myself humming a favourite song. The stormclouds were scattering. I would see James in just over a week's time. Not a moment too soon.

Grabbing Mr Frog's keys the day before I was due to travel to England, I bundled a protesting Tadpole out of the front door, praying that she wouldn't pull the previous day's stunt, which had consisted of rolling around on the carpeted floor and screaming at a pitch calculated to set my teeth on edge. Full-scale tantrums had become a familiar part of our daily routine, and I pitied our neighbours.

'I want to finish my jigsaw, Mummy!' Tadpole shouted indignantly, ignoring the finger I had pressed to my lips.

'Later, darling,' I muttered, secure in the knowledge that by the time 'later' came, she would have forgotten our exchange. The lift rattled its way down to the ground floor – the noises were getting worse, surely it must be ready for a service? – and after strapping Tadpole into the pushchair, I set our course for 'Daddy's house'. Mr Frog was away on a business trip, but he'd forgotten to attach the rain cover to Tadpole's buggy when he dropped her off at *Tata*'s the previous morning. The skies were looking particularly ominous, and no doubt the forecast for Tadpole's weekend in Yorkshire with her grandparents wouldn't be much better, so I'd hastily phoned his mobile earlier that morning to ask permission to drop by and collect the cover in his absence.

The door swung open and Tadpole darted inside, immediately at ease in her home from home. I paused on the threshold. It felt wrong to be there without Mr Frog, as though I were an intruder prowling around a stranger's home.

My own apartment had changed little since Mr Frog's departure, but his was the embodiment of his fresh start, filled with furniture he'd bought without me. Stepping inside was akin to trespassing on his new life.

I spied the pushchair cover immediately, but didn't bend to pick it up just yet. Instead I drifted into the bedroom, following Tadpole's lead. The room was sombre, the shutters at half-mast. The rumpled covers on Mr Frog's futon bed I recognized; the Dora the Explorer pyjamas laid out neatly on Tadpole's pillow were new. There had been talk of buying her a proper bed, but for now she was still using her travel cot, with the addition of a thicker mattress. It made the arrangement seem temporary, even though six months had elapsed since Mr Frog moved out.

So engrossed was Tadpole in the book she had picked up as soon as she entered the room that she didn't notice when I slipped away, this time with no valid pretext. Curiosity had gained the upper hand: I was snooping now.

I stole into the kitchen, the least 'lived-in' room, the surface of the gas hobs so spotless that I suspected they'd never been used. Packets of chocolate biscuits and sweets littered the work surfaces – precisely the sort of junk which Mr Frog used to sneak into the shopping trolley at Franprix when he thought I wasn't looking – and I was willing to bet that if I opened a cupboard I would find some of the dried noodles he'd lived on when we first met.

I drew the line at peering inside his cupboards, but paused, remembering the tiny room we shared on rue de Vaugirard with its sloping floor. We'd travelled a long road since then, but from what I could see today, Mr Frog had reverted to his bachelor ways as though the clock had been wound back eight years and we had never happened. Hearing Tadpole's footfalls approaching I suddenly felt uncomfortable, as though

I were about to be caught doing something I shouldn't. 'Sweetie? Time to go now!' I called. Retracing my steps I scooped up the rain cover, grabbed Tadpole's hand and stepped back out into the stairwell.

But the glimpse I'd been given into the world Mr Frog had rebuilt from the ashes of our relationship haunted me for the rest of the day. I was reminded of just how much I'd put him through, saddened by the loneliness I'd sensed as I stood in his kitchen. Compared to what Mr Frog had endured, my post-Christmas gloom suddenly began to look trivial. I might be lonely now, but in six months' time I'd have everything I'd been dreaming of since I first met James last May. What on earth did Mr Frog have to look forward to?

'Friday is gin and tonic night in this household,' said Jane the following evening, busily slicing lemons while her husband, Nick, poured a generous helping of gin into glasses, the waiting ice cubes crackling enthusiastically. 'You'll join us, won't you, Catherine?'

'It would be rude not to,' I replied gamely, looking around their kitchen, trying to pinpoint what it was that made it so quintessentially English, despite the fact that most people in both France and England shop at Ikea these days.

A curvy brunette a few years older than me, with a dry sense of humour and attractive laughter lines around her eyes, Jane seemed happy with the cards life had dealt her, and rightly so. She'd met Nick, a dashing entrepreneur, in her mid-thirties, and they were now married, with two young children, who'd just been put to bed. The fleeting twinge of envy I'd experienced when James and I walked into their tastefully decorated townhouse was quickly neutralized by how down to earth the couple seemed. They'd done their best to put me at ease the moment I crossed the threshold; it was impossible not to warm to them.

Nick was one of James's oldest friends. They'd attended school together as teenage boys, not far from where Nick and Jane now lived, and had remained close throughout James's exile abroad. It was fascinating to watch James unwind in their presence; to witness the years falling away. I've always thought that, in the company of their oldest friends, people get back to the basics of who they really are, so I'd been eagerly looking forward to the insights this trip to James's home town would bring.

'You're thinking of moving to Rennes in the summer, I hear,' said Nick, handing me a glass. 'That'll be a change from the big city.'

'It will.' I gave James a sidelong glance. 'But Rennes does have a few things going for it . . .' James slipped an arm around my shoulders. I sensed that he was proud to show me off: no doubt the fact that I was a good few years younger than most of his friends' wives or girlfriends didn't hurt. All the same, I couldn't help wondering how I compared, in their eyes, to Eve, or James's ex-wife. I'd never quite managed to shake off the ghosts of girlfriends past.

'Now,' said Jane, taking a seat opposite me in the conservatory they'd tacked on to the back of their kitchen and sweeping aside a pile of toys to put her pedicured bare feet up on a footstool. 'You must tell me about how you two met. Is it true that you fell for each other on the *internet*?'

I blushed, and the hand holding my glass, which I'd been about to bring to my lips, stalled in mid-air. Where on earth should I start? How much did they know already? Did she even know what a blog was? Thankfully, taking his cue from my hesitation, James launched into a detailed explanation while I slowly sipped my drink, watching Jane furtively to gauge her reaction.

The reason for my discomfort was simple. Our story – however romantic I could make it sound in my own head or on my blog – sometimes sounded a little tawdry in the re-telling. There was no escaping the fact that I'd been living with the father of my child when we met; that I'd cheated on him, then left; that what James and I now shared was born out of the ruins of another relationship. Jane was a mother too. What on earth must she think of me? What sort of selfish, impulsive fool leaves her partner for someone she has met only twice?

But if Jane was surprised, or shocked, she hid it well, and the conversation soon drifted back to the blog itself. Nick began quizzing me about my visitor statistics, exclaiming that my readership figures put most of the corporate sites he worked on to shame. I gave examples of the sorts of subjects I posted about – toddler tantrum problems, adjusting to the separation from my daughter's father, day-to-day trivia – conscious that I'd only written half a dozen posts in January and was actually finding myself rather short of material these days. Later, when Jane and I moved back through into the kitchen to mix a second drink, she returned to the subject of James and me, but still I detected no hint of disapproval or reprimand in her voice.

'It can't have been easy. Dealing with the fall-out from your break-up and coping with a little one alone,' she said, pouring me a refill, while James and Nick studied a takeaway menu from a nearby curry house. 'I'm just really glad to see James with someone nice. You both look so happy. I bet you can't wait to move to Brittany . . .'

'You're right. I can't wait,' I said emphatically. I really meant it. From the moment I'd met James at the airport, my faith in us had been renewed. My parents drove away, Tadpole waving gaily at me through the back window, and he pulled me close, kissing me with an intensity that told me everything I needed to know.

'Well, do make sure we get an invitation to the wedding,' said Jane as she dropped an ice cube into my glass and handed it back to me. I took it, my head spinning. Had James mentioned marriage, or was this just Jane's way of fishing for information? Probably the latter, I surmised, although I might never know for sure.

'You'll be among the first to know, when the time comes,' I replied with a knowing smile.

Jane raised her glass in a silent toast. As we clinked our tumblers together, James and Nick glanced up as one, no doubt pleased to see that Jane and I had hit it off so well. James hadn't the faintest idea what we'd been discussing, and I had no intention of enlightening him. Instead, I drained my glass, set it down on the sideboard and enquired about what we were ordering for dinner.

26. Adrift

Back in Paris, two weeks later, I dashed home from work, anxious to snatch some precious time alone with James before Amy was due to arrive. She and I – along with half my office – had been invited to a colleague's hen night. Tadpole was with her daddy, and James would be staying home alone. He didn't mind me abandoning him in the slightest – or so he'd said – insisting he had plenty of work to be getting on with, even though it was a Friday night. I still felt guilty, nonetheless. I'd agreed to this girls' night out ages ago, never suspecting that it would fall within James's first visit to Paris since Christmas. I'd been tempted to bail out, but neither Amy nor James would hear of it.

As the *métro* screeched into Buttes Chaumont station and the doors parted with their familiar spring-loaded sound, I plotted. I'll jump into the shower, I thought to myself, then drag him to bed for a while, until it's time to get my glad rags on. Before I go, I'll order him a pizza. Yes, that would be a nice gesture. Save him cooking for one.

'Hi, honey, I'm home,' I called as I stepped inside, aiming for some approximation of an American accent but failing miserably. There was no reply, which was puzzling. Usually, at the merest hint of the lift door opening, or of my footfalls on the landing, James would rush to the door before I'd even had a chance to touch my key to the lock. I glanced along the corridor. The slice of living room I could see from the hallway revealed only an empty seat before the dining-room table; a lifeless laptop with a blank screen.

I found James sitting motionless on the sofa, a crime novel hanging limply from his hand. He was chalky pale. Either he'd had some bad news – his father perhaps? – or he was coming down with something nasty. So much for diving between the sheets for a while, I thought, crestfallen, conscious of how selfish my inner voice sounded.

'You okay? You look pretty rough . . .' I made no move to join him on the sofa: there was something about his posture that didn't invite contact. Instead I hovered uncertainly in the middle of the room.

'Something I ate, I think.' He put a hand to his stomach. 'I'm not feeling too good.' Now I came to think of it, James had complained of the very same thing last time he visited, almost three months ago, in early December. Something about Paris didn't seem to agree with him.

'That's odd,' I replied, frowning, 'because I'm fine, and we both ate the same meal last night. Maybe you picked up a bug on the train the other day . . .'

James was cleanshaven, and wore a biscuit-coloured jumper, both of which exaggerated his pallor. I definitely preferred him with a five o'clock shadow, and was prepared to weather any amount of stubble rash, if necessary. He'd put on weight since we first met, we both had: contentment was taking its toll. My trousers fit more snugly around my hips than before, but in James the gain was most visible in his face: no longer taut and angular, the skin around his jaw line was slackening.

'Are you going to be okay on your own?' I said doubtfully. 'Because I can cancel my plans, if you . . .'

'No! Don't do that,' said James quickly, not letting me finish. 'I'll just get an early night and sleep it off. Don't worry about me.'

'Well, okay, if you're sure,' I said with an inward sigh of

relief. An early night with James might have been what I was craving earlier, but tending to an invalid on his sick bed wasn't quite what I'd had in mind. 'In that case, I'm going to have a quick shower and start getting ready to go out. Unless you want a cup of tea, or something, first?' James shook his head. I moved into the bedroom, still wearing my coat, and sat on the edge of the bed, bending to unzip my boots and free my calves from their prison. Oh yes, I'd definitely put on weight: my boots didn't use to pinch.

I was rubbing the angry red imprint below my knees when James appeared in the doorway. Out of the corner of my eye, I saw him lower himself on to the stool in front of my computer. It looked comically small all of a sudden, dwarfed by his size.

'Catherine?'

Something I detected in his voice, in the way he said my name, derailed me, and I straightened up with a sharp intake of breath, waiting mutely for what in a blinding flash of sixth sense, I suddenly knew must follow. He closed his eyes for a second and swallowed with a grimace, as though clearing his throat of bile. 'I'm sorry,' he said finally, 'but I just can't do this any more.'

There was a ringing in my ears and for a few seconds I thought I would faint, side-stepping my body to avoid hearing whatever he was about to add. But my vision clouded then cleared: there was to be no escape. 'I wish I didn't feel this way,' he continued in a pained voice, 'I wanted so much to make this work.'

'I don't believe I'm hearing this, after everything we . . . after everything I . . .' But there seemed no earthly point in finishing my stunned protest. I pressed my fingertips to my temples and bowed my head forwards until my elbows touched my knees, curling into a tight, defensive ball. The brace position, as it is referred to on those laminated cards tucked into the seat pocket of aeroplanes, an instinctive, futile pose offering no real protection from the cruel, lancing words which kept on coming.

'I can't let things go any further. I can't let you uproot everything and come to live in Rennes. Because I don't think I want to spend the rest of my life with you. Not any more.' I could not raise my head. I had no desire to see the face that went with that voice.

'You don't love me any more,' I said flatly. Silent tears finally began to drip on to the inside of my glasses, down the sleeves of my coat, dampening my forearms.

'I did. I still do. But not enough. I'm so sorry.' I couldn't be sure, but I thought he might be crying, too.

It was over. A handful of innocuous-sounding, everyday words had demolished every hope, every dream, every promise I'd clung to since the day we'd met. I saw us standing on the street corner welded together that first night, before I tore myself away and leaped into a taxi. I saw us entangled in the hotel, my toes curling with pleasure. I saw his hands cupped around my belly in the bathwater. A house of cards, destroyed by one cruel gust of wind. My world was imploding before my horrified eyes.

When I left Mr Frog I'd foolishly, recklessly pinned everything on James, projecting every second of my future on to him. I was aware of the risks, I knew love came with no guarantees, but I'd hurled myself headlong into this new adventure all the same. I'd wanted so desperately to feel things intensely, and my wish had been granted, at a terrible price.

'I want you to leave,' I said suddenly, my words clipped and precise. I would not debase myself by begging him to stay. Let the incision be clean; let the scalpel be sharp and sure. I listened as he gathered his belongings with merciful speed, his suitcase already packed, the manoeuvre anticipated. I heard him zip his computer pouch closed, ease his arms into the sleeves of his jacket, tie his shoelaces.

'I'm sorry,' he said again, from the doorway. Tears dripped from my chin, mingled with my hair; my mouth filled with brine. Still I would not look.

When the front door closed behind him with a dull thud, I finally raised my head. My gaze was drawn to something glinting by the computer, which had not been there when I entered the room: his copy of my keys.

Crumpling on the bed, still wearing my coat, I sobbed noisily, messily, into my pillow until my head throbbed, howling until my throat grew hoarse. Less than a year ago, Mr Frog had sat on this very same spot while I delivered my speech. Now my turn had come. Two relationships had begun in the Café Charbon and ended here, in this very room, mocking me with their perfect symmetry.

'Can't make it tonight, sorry,' I told Amy by text message when the first round of sobbing finally subsided.

'Why ever not?' she shot back immediately. I could sense that she was angry, probably assuming I'd fallen victim to nothing more than post-coital torpor, but I couldn't bring myself to explain what had happened, not yet, so I made no reply. If I called her, my voice would fail me. She would come here, witness this sorry spectacle, try to persuade me to go out, anything to stop me from marinating in my own tears, home alone. But a hen night was the last place on earth I needed to be right now. And maybe, just maybe, there would be a knock at the door. James would crawl back, begging my forgiveness. He knew now he had made a dreadful mistake. He'd tried to leave, but found he simply couldn't.

By midnight, however, I was resigned. James wasn't

coming back; in fact, he was probably in Rennes by now. Dry-eyed, terrifyingly calm, I knew what I had to do. Let *petite anglaise* be the bearer of my bad news. Let her distil my pain, my shock, my disbelief, into a series of neat sentences; let her pin the confused tangle of emotions to the page with words. Our relationship had been born out of the blog, so wasn't it fitting to announce the ending there, for the whole world to see?

Once I hit the 'publish' key, there would be nowhere left for me to hide. I'd have no choice but to face up to the grim finality of what had happened, to nip any futile hope of reconciliation in the bud. This is what I wrote:

> I am a rudderless boat turning in dizzy, uncomprehending circles on a sea of noisy tears. He doesn't want me any more.

I disabled comments for the second time in the blog's history, sending my howl of anguish across cyberspace then beating a hasty retreat. I had no desire to hear a chorus of 'I told you so's and 'poor you's echoing back at me, and I also knew instinctively that my readers would be quick to condemn James, on the basis of the scant information at their disposal.

Once it was done, I crawled into bed: spent, exhausted and fully clothed.

It was the familiar sound of his breathing, deep and regular, which alerted me to his presence a few hours later. I stretched out a sleepy arm, resting it on the smooth, hairless warmth of his chest, feeling its rise and fall. I raised my head so that I could study the shadowy contours of his sleeping face. He was here, with me; all was right in my world.

Until in one nauseating instant the memory of his words slammed into me with all their force, shattering the cruel illusion. 'None of this is real,' screamed a voice inside my head. 'He can't be here!' I struggled to swim up through the velvety layers of sleep, willing myself to wake. My dream was about to morph into a nightmare, I felt sure of it, and I wanted out. With sickly dread I watched as James's eyes flicked open. I tried to withdraw my arm, but he clutched at it, restraining fingers gripping tightly on to my wrist. 'Let go of me!' My scream was strangled in my throat, the sound which emerged only a risible croak.

Suddenly James's body was wracked with hacking coughs, increasing in violence until the force of them made him retch. Recoiling in horror, I watched as he vomited something black and viscous on to the bedclothes, his eyes as appalled as my own. I clawed at my face with my free hand, biting my own fingers, desperate to jar myself awake.

But there was nothing I could do. James began to decompose before my eyes, moaning as if in excruciating pain. Soon, all that remained in the bed beside me was a pool of something foul-smelling and brackish where his body had been.

Drenched with perspiration, heart thudding, I opened my eyes to find the bed empty. The nightmare was over, but when I held my right arm up to the red light cast by the digits on my alarm clock, a part of me still half expected to find livid fingerprints encircling my wrist.

27. *Mouchoir*

The next morning I sifted through every single thing James had said, every look he had given me over the past few months, searching for clues, signs, hints. Holding every tense moment, every harsh word up to the light I examined each one closely. Just when did he stop mentioning marriage, or a baby? When did the brochures of barns and cottages in the countryside stop appearing in his apartment? How different, how altered everything looked, knowing what I now knew, eyes narrowed to squint through the prism of hindsight.

'I can't do this any more,' he'd said, as though being with me made him physically ill. I'd been so preoccupied with battling my own anxieties, I never suspected that James was having silent doubts of his own, quietly wrestling with his demons. Probing, measuring the depth of his feelings. Finding them wanting.

Long periods of time staring vacantly into the middle distance gave way to occasional bursts of frenetic activity. Gathering up every possession of his I could find in an act of ritual cleansing, I stuffed them into a large envelope: my keys to his apartment, a borrowed DVD, a stray T-shirt from my laundry basket, a razor left on the side of the bathtub. There wasn't a great deal: he'd been a perpetual visitor, living out of an overflowing suitcase, never hanging his shirts in my wardrobe, or buying a spare set of toiletries to leave in my bathroom.

On my computer's hard drive I found only a handful of photos. A self-portrait James had sent to my phone, a week or so after we first met. A picture, taken by me, of Tadpole dressed as a fairy, with James a shadowy figure on the sofa in the background, an unwilling subject. Not a single image of us together. As an entity, a couple, it suddenly seemed as though we had only ever truly existed on the page. Because there was no shortage of words to prove what we had once been: text messages stored in my mobile phone, hundreds of archived emails, scores of comments on *petite anglaise*, both before and after we met. In a drawer by my bedside I found a handful of Post-it notes he'd left for me to find in happier times. An 'I love you' on my pillow, an 'I'll miss you' on my computer screen. Our relationship had begun with words, and now words were all that remained.

I ran a bath and retreated under water, where some sounds were muffled, others oddly amplified: footfalls in the apartment above, the distant sound of a television, the frantic rocking of a washing machine as it reached the climax of its spin cycle. A memory surfaced, of days spent off school with ear infections as a child. Inside a cocoon of pain, I'd listened to the faraway, otherworldly sounds of my mother washing up, hoovering or talking on the phone while I lay upstairs in bed. I felt the same detachment now I'd felt then, listening to life continuing elsewhere, as normal, while mine stood stock-still. I was wispy, insubstantial; a ghostly shadow of my normal self, unable to connect with the world around me.

When the water grew cold, I hauled myself out, shivering. Finally, swaddled in a white towelling bathrobe, I picked up the phone and, hesitating for only an instant, instinctively dialled a number, one of the few I knew off by heart.

'*Oui?*'

'It's me.' My voice sounded hollow. Last time I'd used it, it had been to ask James to leave.

'*Quelque chose ne va pas?*'

'James left me. Last night.' Silent tears welled up, and my nose began to run. 'I'm a mess. I'm sorry, but I didn't know who else to call . . .'

There was an incredulous silence. No doubt Mr Frog had prayed for this outcome – anything which would prevent me leaving with his daughter – and I was probably the bearer of the best news he'd heard all year. I pictured him smiling, or punching the air jubilantly. But when at last he found his tongue, his voice betrayed nothing but concern.

'Come over, if you want,' he suggested. 'She's having her nap. It's probably better if she doesn't see you like this.' At first I was taken aback by his suggestion. Surely Mr Frog was the last person who should be comforting me right now? But the idea of company – any company – was so appealing that I cast my reservations aside.

'I . . . Okay, yes, I'll just pull on some clothes. I'll be there in five minutes.' I caught sight of myself in the hallway mirror as I unlocked the front door. I cut a sorry figure: puffy eyes, a corned-beef complexion, damp hair matted. He was right – it wouldn't do for Tadpole to see me in this state.

Sitting cross-legged on the warm tiles of Mr Frog's living-room balcony, I rested my back against the sliding glass door. The weather was mild for early March; the skies pale and cloudless. I closed my eyes and tried to concentrate only on the feeling of the cool breeze caressing my face, erasing the track marks left by my tears.

'Here you go,' said Mr Frog, handing me a cup of mint tea, which I cradled in my hands, waiting for it to cool. Lowering himself to the floor beside me, he lit a cigarette. We sat in silence for a few minutes, looking out across the rooftops. Paris, the city I'd been about to turn my back on, stretched as far as I could see in every direction, and sunlight glinted off a hundred metal chimney stacks.

'You know what's weird?' he said finally. 'I think I feel angrier with him now than I did when he stole you away from me.'

'I suppose you're relieved,' I replied, trying to keep bitterness from tainting my voice. 'That I won't be leaving Paris any more, I mean.'

'Well, yes, of course I am,' he admitted. 'I'd be lying if I said I wasn't. Just imagine if you *had* left, and it had gone wrong a few months later. Think how much worse that would have been . . .'

'I know,' I sighed. 'But I just can't quite believe it's really happened, yet. That I got everything so wrong. Or how much it hurts.'

I was bracing myself for an 'I told you so' which, oddly, never came. Instead Mr Frog listened quietly while words spilled out of my mouth, silently taking my cup and refilling it with tea when he noticed it was empty. He'd always been a good listener, I thought to myself, but I'd been so intent on seeing my glass as half empty that I'd spent most of my time criticizing him for not talking enough. The only thing he didn't do was touch me. I had forfeited the right to any physical expression of sympathy: he couldn't even seem to bring himself to put a comforting hand on my arm.

When the time came for Mr Frog to rouse Tadpole, I slipped away and pulled the front door quietly closed behind me. In an hour or so, Mr Frog had promised he would bring her over to spend the rest of the weekend with me, so that I needn't be alone. I straightened up my flat, picking up the damp tissues scattered around my bed and replacing the mascara-smudged pillowcase. Once all the evidence had been concealed, I picked up the telephone again, this time to break the news to my mother. I knew she hadn't read *petite anglaise* yet. If she had, I would have heard from her by now.

'I did worry sometimes, about how the two of you would cope in Brittany,' she admitted, once she'd got over her initial shock. 'Financially, I mean. And all that travelling back and forth to share custody at weekends, I was afraid it would really wear you down.'

'I worried about those things too,' I confessed. 'I never imagined it was going to be a walk in the park. But James seemed so sure. He brushed away my concerns. I can't believe I let him make me feel guilty for having doubts . . .'

'He's let you down, love, whether he meant to or not. He wasn't as strong as you thought he was. He made a lot of promises he simply couldn't keep.'

I bit my lip. My instinct, even now, was to rush to James's defence. I loved him, and although a day would surely come when hearing him criticized and diminished was of some comfort, that day had not yet come. A tapping at the front door provided me with the excuse to cut short our conversation. 'I'll call you back later, Mum,' I said, silently thanking Mr Frog for his perfect timing. 'I think they're here now.'

'Well, you take care of yourself, and give my granddaughter a big cuddle from me,' she said with a sigh. It must be unbearably difficult, I thought suddenly, being a long-distance mother. Maybe one day I would experience this first-hand, trying to console a heartbroken Tadpole over the phone, cursing the hundreds of kilometres of land and sea between us.

The very first thing I saw when the door swung open was a bouquet of pale-pink tulips wrapped in cellophane, which Tadpole brandished triumphantly, the blooms obscuring her face. Mr Frog hung back, letting Tadpole hog the limelight, but I sensed he was feeling extremely pleased with himself. He'd never once surprised me with flowers in all the eight years we'd spent together – an irony not lost on me – but this gesture meant more than any birthday or Valentine.

Words were the weakest currency at a time like this, as well he knew.

'How lovely of you! My favourite flowers! What a surprise!' I cried, dropping to Tadpole-level, laying the flowers gently on the floor and pulling my daughter into a needy embrace, ravenous for physical contact.

'What's matter, Mummy?' Tadpole raised an inquisitive finger to touch my damp cheeks.

'Mummy's crying because she's very, very happy to see you.' I caught Mr Frog's eye over her shoulder and gave him a wobbly smile.

'I get a *mouchoir*.' Tadpole tugged herself free and scampered into the bedroom, returning with the box of tissues. 'Look! I make it better!' Grabbing a liberal handful, she dabbed clumsily at my cheeks, knocking my glasses askew.

'*Je vous laisse*. If you think you'll be okay?' said Mr Frog, still hovering in the hallway, as though he were reluctant to cross the threshold.

'Thank you . . . for everything,' I said. My voice sounded small and thin, but did not break. 'She really is the best medicine.'

'I know, remember?' he said with a nod. His half-smile removed the sting from his words, but I winced all the same.

It wasn't exactly clear to me *who* was looking after *whom* that day, but maybe it didn't really matter. For the rest of the afternoon I snuggled up on the sofa with my daughter while she watched cartoons, savouring the warmth of her body as she nestled in the crook of my arm, matching the rhythm of her breathing with my own.

Shortly before Tadpole's bedtime tears threatened to well up again and I decided some sort of explanation was probably necessary. I was bound to have unsteady moments over the next few days, and the last thing I wanted was for Tadpole to think she might be in some way responsible for my sadness. Setting down *The Very Hungry Caterpillar*, which I'd just recited tonelessly from memory, I hoisted Tadpole on to my knee, her eyes level with mine, and groped for the simplest words I could find.

'Mummy is feeling sad today. Because Mummy's friend James has gone home, and he isn't going to come back and see us any more. We won't be going to visit him on the train either, and we won't see Amanda and Carrie. Mummy didn't want James to go, so she's feeling very sad. And sometimes it makes her cry.'

Tadpole listened solemnly but said nothing. I doubted she had any grasp of the gravity of the situation. To her, James had been a friend, an occasional visitor. She had no inkling – as far as I knew – of our plans. No idea that James's home should soon have become ours, that we would have seen him every day. I'd refrained from kissing or hugging James much in her presence, and more often than not he had waited patiently in the background until Tadpole was safely tucked up in bed. I thought once again of the photo I'd found: James a benign presence on the sofa, hovering on the periphery of Tadpole's vision.

Switching off the fairy lights above her bed, I pulled the covers up to her chin, and said goodnight, first to the collection of soft toys with which she shared her bed, and then to Tadpole, planting a kiss on her forehead. The ritual complete, I turned to leave with a heavy heart, reluctant to begin the long evening alone.

I was about to step into the hallway and pull the door closed behind me when Tadpole finally spoke. '*D*ever mind, Mummy,' she said brightly. I smiled. She always said '*d*ever mind.' I could protest until I was blue in the face and it wouldn't alter her conviction that '*d*ever' was a word.

'Never mind,' I repeated quietly. 'Mummy will be better soon.'

The next day I was pathetically grateful for the opportunity to lose myself in routine activity with my daughter.

In the morning we walked briskly to the Grange aux Belles teaching pool near the Canal Saint Martin. I wrestled Tadpole into her swimming gear, then shyly changed into my swimsuit, self-conscious in the unisex open-plan changing rooms. The indoor pool, filled with lukewarm water which barely grazed my nipples at its deepest point, was filled with an assortment of polystyrene shapes, yellow plastic ducks, balls of every colour, floating platforms and slides. *Bébés dans l'eau* was more of an aquatic playground than a swimming class. But seeing Tadpole's delight as she seized a floating plastic turtle, watching her overcome her reticence and hurtle down the slide into my arms, these small things made our expedition worth the effort. I followed her as she bobbed around the pool in an inflatable ring, not so much swimming as walking upright through the water.

Mr Frog had been bringing Tadpole here on weekends when she was in his care, but on my weekends we'd been away in Rennes, more often than not, so I'd seldom visited the pool. Daunted at first, I began to relax once I'd established that most of the toddlers were accompanied by a lone parent, no doubt while the other savoured a skilfully negotiated lie-in or looked after a second child. Whatever the reason, it was a relief to blend in. When I was with James – even when he was hundreds of miles away – I'd rarely given my status as a single parent a second thought. But now that he was out of the picture, I suddenly felt more vulnerable than I ever had before. I was a *single* single parent now. An anomaly in a world of couples.

Later that afternoon, enticed outdoors by the gentle promise of March sunshine, we braved the weekend crowds in the Buttes Chaumont. Taking the main avenue leading across the top of the park, Tadpole teetered along the kerb, her arms outstretched like an aeroplane, while I pushed her empty buggy listlessly, a few paces behind. Exposed to the sun, my skin felt like a stiff parchment stretched over my cheeks. Crying had wrung every drop of moisture from me and my body felt brittle, insubstantial. I was a dry autumn leaf – which had no business being there in springtime – and the slightest gust of wind might blow me away.

The park was filled with painful, jarring reminders of what I'd lost: an elderly couple sitting on a bench, gnarly, arthritic fingers interlaced; a handsome young man in a baseball cap whispering something in his pregnant wife's ear, his arm draped protectively around her shoulders.

Taking a shortcut along a narrow path at Tadpole's insistence, we almost blundered into a couple of dark-haired teenagers kissing under cover of a weeping willow. At the sight of them, my lungs constricted. I remembered writing about the young couple kissing in the *métro* all those months ago. Then I'd only felt wistful: pining for something I thought I would never taste again. Now I was an open wound: I'd felt like they did, for a while at least, but it had slipped through my fingers.

'Mummy,' begged Tadpole, 'can I go on the *manège*?' We had emerged from under a low bridge into the area of the park she knew best, where *Tata* and the other childminders converged with their charges on weekday afternoons. People milled about everywhere, children clamoured for ice cream and helium balloons, pony rides or candyfloss. Usually I was reluctant to bow to pressure, but I didn't have the strength to refuse anything today. Fumbling in my pocket for loose change, I bought a plastic *jeton* from the kiosk. Tadpole clambered inside a fire engine, delighted, and I flopped on to a bench as the roundabout began to turn slowly. I waved every time my daughter whizzed past, forcing a smile. But when the carousel carried her out of my line of sight, I abandoned my charade, the smile curdling on my lips.

'James, where *war* you?' Tadpole called expectantly when we returned home, reaching the front door before me and knocking insistently on the bottom panel. I gripped the door handle with bloodless knuckles, steadying myself for a moment before I put the key to the lock.

'James isn't here,' I said quietly. 'Remember what I told you at bedtime, yesterday?' The concept of 'never' – or '*d*ever' – was too abstract for Tadpole, who lived mostly in the present tense. I half wished I could do the same, no longer regretting the past, or fearing for the future.

Once we were inside, James's imprint was everywhere; he was superimposed across every room like a watermark. His ghost was seated at the dining table, head bent over his laptop, brow furrowed in concentration. In the kitchen there was an echo of him towering over the hobs, making dinner. Drawing the bedroom curtains at nightfall, I skirted around an imaginary suitcase.

With Tadpole in bed, the evening yawned ahead, mocking me with its emptiness. I took a seat at my computer and stared at my inbox, which brimmed over with messages of concern, virtual bouquets, kisses and hugs. Scrolling through them one by one, I began to compose short replies of thanks, signing '*petite*', as always, my hands shaky at first. I didn't copy or paste. That would be cheating, and the task would be over too quickly. As time wore on, my hands shook less.

'I read your post late last night and my stomach just flipped over,' an anonymous stranger wrote. 'I don't even know you, but I lay awake in my bed worrying about you.' There were scores of messages like this one: readers who reached out to put a virtual hand on my arm, who passed me a box of cyber-tissues, who shared their own break-up stories in the hope that, after reading them, I would feel less alone.

'I just wanted to say I'm really, really sorry,' wrote Anna Red Boat. 'I've been thinking about you all weekend and didn't know whether emailing was the right thing to do or not, supposing that all your readers were doing the same thing.' I smiled, touched to see that Anna saw herself as a virtual friend and set herself apart from my other readers. After all the emails we'd exchanged over the past year or so, that was definitely the way I saw her too.

When I'd cleared my inbox, I glanced at the clock and shook my head incredulously. It was midnight already. Four hours had slipped by since I'd opened up the first email. I wasn't sure if I felt better, exactly, but I was certainly grateful for the distraction. Anything had to be better than staring unseeing at the white walls of my apartment, or sobbing silently into my pillow.

The new-message icon appeared just as I was about to shut down the computer and make myself a cup of hot milk. Seeing the name of the sender, my heart stuttered. James. His message was untitled. Opening the body of the email, I scrolled down to see two pages of dense, meticulously crafted prose. I could sense that he had weighed every word carefully, typing and re-typing, re-reading and editing.

I haven't written until now because I wanted to try to make sure I said something worthwhile. I don't know if I will, but I'll do my best. If what I say makes no sense to you or seems stupid, cruel or just contemptible then I'm offering no defence. How can I?

There were sentences which made me groan out loud; paragraphs which confirmed all my worst suspicions. He confessed to feeling defensive about his ability to provide for Tadpole and me, and to doubting his strength to become a father again. He lamented the fact that his emotional baggage had turned out to be weightier than he had ever imagined. But there it was again, the razor-sharp phrase which had cut me to the quick. 'I *do* still love you, but – and this is the bit that hurts to say and to hear – I don't love you *enough* to be able to give you the things we dreamed about and planned.'

I could argue with everything else, try to convince him that together we could vanquish his demons, we could make things work, but against the finality of that statement I was powerless. You can't *make* someone love you enough. His intensity had not survived the months of waiting intact. Instead there had been a slow, silent unravelling.

A chill, accepting calm descended upon me. This ending, however wretched, was necessary. Neither of us deserved to settle for less than what we had shared in the beginning, before it waned.

28. Shredded

'You seem distracted today,' remarked my boss, looking up from the work he was reviewing to where I dithered in the doorway. It was Monday morning, my first day back in the office since James had left. I was dry-eyed but still felt strangely detached from my surroundings, my brain out of gear. I'd got up to fetch something from the filing cabinet in my boss's office, but in the space of five or six steps my mind had gone as blank as a computer screen in sleep mode.

My boss and I had been getting on far better since Christmas. He'd even resumed his old habit of taking me out to a local wine bar for lunch from time to time, refilling my glass until I wondered how on earth I'd function back at the office, swimming through the afternoon in a red-wine haze. So whereas a few months earlier his question would have dripped with reproach, today his tone implied curiosity, and even some genuine concern for my well-being.

'Oh, yes, sorry, it's just personal stuff,' I replied, my eyes drifting evasively to the view through his office window. Across the rooftops, I could see the Sacré Cœur, its milky-white dome contrasting with the powder-blue of the sky. It was safer to admire the view than to meet my boss's enquiring gaze. The last thing I wanted to do right now was lose my composure. 'Had a bit of a rough weekend,' I added, keeping things deliberately vague.

I was wary of sharing my personal life with my boss, even if we had mended our fences. And supposing I did tell him everything, he still wouldn't understand the full ramifications of the break-up. I'd never let slip that I was planning to leave for Brittany in a few months' time, afraid of shattering our new-found harmony.

'Okay, well, I'm here if you need a chat,' he said, sounding disappointed that I wasn't prepared to elaborate further. A female colleague appeared at my elbow, coat slung over her arm, to take him out for lunch. I stepped aside to let her pass, grateful for an excuse to withdraw.

Amy took their departure as her cue to pounce. She'd been shooting me quizzical looks across the top of the cubicles all morning, but so far I'd taken great pains to dodge a *tête-à-tête*, avoiding the kitchen and dashing to the ladies only when I could see she was tied up on the phone. Baring all on the internet, where no one could see my face crumple as I wrote, was one thing; saying the words aloud, in public, without breaking down was another. I'd sobbed down the phone to my mother, shed silent tears in front of Mr Frog, but today in the office I wanted desperately to hold it together. The last thing I needed was colleagues pausing as they passed by my desk, enquiring as to whether I was okay: their words of concern and sympathetic glances would be my undoing.

'I just read your blog,' Amy said breathlessly as she drew to a halt by my side. 'Why on earth didn't you call me? I could have cancelled my plans and come over. There I was, cursing you for pulling out of the hen night, thinking you'd blown us all off just so you could have another early night with James . . .' In her eyes I read sympathy, but also chagrin. I'd obviously hurt her feelings by keeping her at arm's length, letting her find out from *petite anglaise* when she deserved to find out from me.

'I'm really sorry,' I replied, my bottom lip wobbling dangerously. 'Please don't take it the wrong way, but I needed to be on my own for a while.'

'You could have told me that, I'd have understood and given you some space. But it would have been nice to hear the news from you directly,' she said, still not placated. 'I'm sure all your internet friends have flocked to the rescue as usual, but they're no substitute for real people who know you and care about you. Don't shut me out, that's all I'm saying. How can I be a proper friend to you if I have to read your blog three days later to find out what's going on?' I nodded, unable to meet her eyes. 'And as for James, I can't believe he's done this to you!' she said incredulously. 'I mean, when I saw him on Pancake Day everything seemed fine. And yet he must have known what he was going to do, even then . . .'

I'd invited Amy over for *crêpes* on Mardi Gras, along with a few other friends from the office, just three days before James left. We'd taken turns flipping pancakes in the kitchen, fielded questions about our plans for July, and the subject of marriage had even come up amidst chatter about preparations for the looming hen night. Were there signs I'd missed that night? Had James been unusually quiet? Was he wrestling with the grim knowledge that none of the things we were discussing were ever likely to come to pass?

'From what he said when he emailed last night, he was still trying to convince himself he could make things work,' I said, finding myself in the uncomfortable position of defending James once again. I remembered his sickly pallor on Friday. Biding his time until he simply could not keep a lid on his feelings of doubt any longer had made him physically ill.

'It must have been an awful shock for you, Cath, I'm so sorry.' Amy put a hand on my arm. 'But, wait,' she said, her eyes widening, 'didn't you say on Tuesday that you'd already given notice on your apartment?'

'I'm sure that was what prompted James to act when he

did,' I said dryly. I pulled open the top drawer of my desk to reveal the letter I'd composed to my landlord a few days earlier. It was ready to post, lacking only a stamp. Amy let out a long, low whistle. It had been a close call.

'Listen, I have to dash,' she said, glancing at her watch. 'I've got a client lunch. But if you do want to talk about things – or if you just don't feel like being on your own – I could come round one evening, if you like. I know it's easier for me to come to you, so you don't have to get a babysitter . . .'

As she turned to leave, I took out the letter to my landlord and tore it into tiny pieces, scattering them into the waste-paper basket like ragged confetti. A few feet away stood a mechanical shredder with gleaming metal teeth which would have devoured the envelope with a growl and turned it into thin paper streamers. But there would have been no satisfaction in that. I needed to feel the paper tear, see the fragments fluttering slowly downwards, carrying my shredded dreams with them.

I spent my lunch hour working on a new blog post. A phrase from a reader's email had lodged inside my head. 'The first forty-eight hours are always the hardest.' My forty-eight hours were up, and the desire to sob out loud and stare blankly at walls seemed to have left me, so maybe there was some truth in that statement. I began to write and, letting my fingers drift across the keyboard, I composed a post about how I *wanted* to feel.

I will never regret our paths crossing back in May. Wouldn't trade the panic-inducing intensity of that first evening for all the stability in the world. I felt reborn. Indescribably happy. The future was suddenly filled with unexpected promise.

The more I wrote, the more the words breathed life into the feelings they described.

> We shared some perfect moments, he and I. Moments which marked my life indelibly; moments which my present anguish cannot erase.

How could I ever forget? After all, the highs and lows of our relationship were documented on my blog, preserved for posterity. All I had to do if I wanted to relive our first night in the hotel, my first trip to Brittany or our day at the beach was rummage through the archives of *petite anglaise* and re-read what I had written. Those memories would never leave me.

As I wrote, I became conscious of a weight lifting: it was a relief no longer having to deal with doubt, no longer repressing the nauseous guilt I'd felt at the prospect of separating Tadpole and Mr Frog. Examining my feelings in public, prodding my bruises to see how much they really hurt, despite everything I'd been through, blogging still felt natural, necessary and cathartic. I could write myself back to health, I realized, finding solace in *petite anglaise* as I always had.

When I'd finished, I enabled comments once more. Something told me that, in the absence of James, *petite anglaise* would step into the breach and do her best to fill the empty space he had left in my life.

'You should leave this place,' said Mr Frog, gesturing from the fireplace to the arched window with a sweeping motion of his chopsticks. We sat on separate sofas. A wide expanse of coffee table stood between us, littered with aluminium takeaway containers, their contents covered with a thin film of grease. I'd bought Chinese food from the *traiteur* downstairs after work, partly to stall Mr Frog into hanging around for longer, but also as a gesture of gratitude for his unexpected support over the weekend.

I brought a forkful of rice to my mouth. I'd barely touched my food, but I knew I needed to make a show of keeping my strength up. I didn't want him worrying about whether or not I was in a fit state to look after Tadpole. The daily routines I'd built around her were the scaffolding holding me upright.

'I know I can't afford to stay here in the long term,' I sighed. 'I could justify it when I thought I was leaving Paris in July. But now I'll definitely need to think again.' I leaned over to my bag and pulled out a classified-ad magazine. 'I had a quick look at what's on offer on the way home. Cheaper means smaller, probably a one-bedroom flat, which is a depressing prospect. The only way to make it palatable might be to buy a place, instead of renting.'

I pictured myself ditching my bed and mattress in favour of a sofa bed which I would pull out every night, transforming our living room into a bedroom. Or the alternative: sleeping above Tadpole on a mezzanine bed. I'd always been impatient to clamber on to the first rung of the property ladder, as Mr Frog knew only too well, but it had never occurred to me that I'd have to do it in quite such a literal sense, by sleeping in a glorified bunk bed. It was a sobering thought, after daydreaming about a cottage with a garden for the best part of a year.

'Wow. That's a big step,' said Mr Frog. 'And not something you should rush into, either. But it does make sense . . . I could help you move, when you do find something. Get some of the guys from work to help with the heavy lifting.' I smiled. It was true that my friends, people like Amy, Caroline and Elisabeth-Coquette would be no match for five flights of stairs and all my furniture.

'I never imagined you'd have it in you to be so *nice* to me.' The words tripped out of my mouth as though I were thinking aloud. It was all I could do to stop myself from finishing the sentence with '. . . after everything I put you through.' I'd never dared such directness before. What I'd done to him and how he felt about our break-up were taboo subjects we still tiptoed around. And his feelings for me now – whatever they might be – were a no-go zone.

'Well,' said Mr Frog cautiously, 'I'll always care about how you are doing. If you're okay, our daughter's okay.'

'Thank you,' I said awkwardly. 'I will need help. I need to make a lot of changes in my life. A new home. A new job, eventually. I'm starting to think the hardest thing wasn't losing James, it was losing all the plans we'd made, everything we'd mapped out. Now I have to face up to whatever I don't like about my life, on my own, without running away to Brittany.' I'm right back to where I was before I met James, really, I thought to myself. I've spent the best part of a year describing a complete circle.

'Well, you won't be completely alone. I'll be here,' said Mr Frog. 'And what about all those friends you've made through your blog?'

'I neglected them from the moment I met James,' I admitted. 'I had so little free time, and I didn't see the point in investing too much of myself in Paris people when I was so sure I'd be leaving. So I've got my work cut out now. Some of them probably won't want to know. I can't exactly blame them.'

'Oh, don't be so hard on yourself. They'll rally round. And you're stronger than you think. *Ça va aller, j'en suis sûr.*' Mr Frog reached for the last dumpling.

Gathering up the remains of our meal after he'd left, his words echoed in my head. 'I'll always care about how you are doing.' Was I reading far too much into his caring behaviour over the last two days? Or could it be that he still had feelings for me?

Later that evening I stared at the computer screen, my mind in turmoil, my forefinger hovering uncertainly above the mouse button. Would it be healthier to delete James's emails with one merciless click? If they were no longer there, I wouldn't be tempted to read and re-read them, playing back my favourite memories time and time again, unable, or unwilling to lay them to rest. Was it safer to forget how ravenous I'd been in the beginning; how I'd yearned to crawl inside his skin?

In my mind's eye, I pictured James delivering the news to his parents, his daughters, Eve, his friends from home. A part of me hoped, cruelly, selfishly, that they had told him he had behaved like a fool – that he was unlikely to get another chance like that in this lifetime. The James I saw in my head was gripped with remorse.

But I could never take him back, never erase those caustic, wounding words which I summoned to the forefront of my mind whenever I was tempted to pick up the phone and beg him to reconsider. 'I don't love you enough,' I heard him say. 'I just can't do this any more.'

And so, for now, I left his emails intact, undeleted. Replaying those memories made me wince, but I knew it was a necessary form of self-torture.

29. Opaque

Tadpole trotted ahead of me down the aisle of the plane as I scanned the seat numbers for row twenty. We passed an assortment of pensioners, children in full Disney regalia, couples cuddling up in warm anticipation of a romantic weekend in Paris, businessmen armed with laptops. We were on our way back home to Paris after spending a weekend in Yorkshire with my parents. Long talks with my mother – I talked, she listened – and a change of scenery had done me the world of good. As for Tadpole, their first and only granddaughter, she'd been spoiled rotten as always, lapping up all the attention lavished upon her as if it were her birthright.

After much stopping and starting while fellow passengers grappled in slow motion with hand luggage and coats, we eventually reached our seats. Tadpole clambered across to the window and began fiddling with her seatbelt, a look of fierce concentration etched on her face. 'Mummy, help me put on my strap-*on*!' she cried, after a couple of unsuccessful attempts at fastening the metal clasp. I put a hand to my mouth to stifle a giggle, wondering if anyone had overheard.

'Wait a minute, honey, we need to take your coat off first,' I replied, shoving my bag under the seat in front with my foot and removing first my jacket, then Tadpole's. When I turned, I saw an attractive man stowing a bag in the overhead locker. 'Can I help you with those?' he enquired, gesturing at our coats. He was in his late thirties, at a guess, and wore smart jeans and a patterned shirt, his dark hair gelled rather too liberally for my taste. His voice was pleasant, educated, his accent difficult to place.

'Thank you, that's very kind of you,' I mumbled, flashing him a shy smile as I handed over my mac and Tadpole's lightweight jacket. The man sat down in the aisle seat to my left and I contemplated him surreptitiously through my eyelashes. He was balancing a laptop on his knee, but made no move to open it.

As I unpacked my Tadpole entertainment kit – crayons, a drawing book, a Mr Men sticker book – I became aware of a certain restlessness in my travelling companion. Was it my imagination, or was he casting around while the last few passengers filed in, trying to gauge whether there were likely to be any free seats left elsewhere? Sure enough, no sooner had the hostess heaved the main door shut and pulled the red tape diagonally across it than my handsome neighbour sprang to his feet.

'I'm just going to move and give you two some space,' he apologized, looking from me to Tadpole. 'No offence intended.'

'None taken,' I muttered, hoping I'd managed to sound nonchalant; the opposite of how I actually felt.

How I felt was afraid: afraid that in this inconsequential little exchange I'd just seen the shape of things to come. For the first time in years I was single. And this time I was not just a single woman, but also a mother; part of a package. The little person occupying the window seat by my side – her rag doll wedged between her seatbelt and her tummy – was the sum total of what was most precious, most valuable in my life. But she could also be grounds for rejection. Seeing Tadpole by my side, some men would assume I had a partner; others simply wouldn't want to know.

I was in no hurry to find someone new, I just wanted to

be able to tell myself that an attractive man might be pleased to be allocated the seat next to mine. By changing places, he had unwittingly dealt my self-esteem a glancing blow, forcefully bringing home to me what an uphill struggle might lie ahead.

'What are you still doing here?' said Amy, looking pointedly at her watch. It was five past six. Usually by that time I'd have been long gone. 'Don't you have to dash off to the nanny's?'

'It's my night off,' I explained, shaking my head. 'It's silly, I'm not even working, I'm just faffing around really, putting off going home.' Home wouldn't be much different, mind. I'd shut down my office computer, then power up the one in my bedroom instead. Writing, commenting, chatting, surfing, these were the only activities I could manage right now. If I tried to read a book, my mind constantly wandered off the page, and no matter how many times I jerked it back again, it wouldn't hold still. Television was worse: I found myself staring at it blankly, without the faintest idea of what I was watching.

'Well, listen, if you've got no plans tonight, I'm joining a friend for a birthday drink, although I have to shop for a present for her first. Why don't you come? She won't mind if I bring someone along, and I could do with some help choosing the pressie . . .'

I wasn't dressed for going out – in fact I'd go so far as to say it looked like I'd put my outfit together in the dark that morning – and I didn't even have a powder compact in my bag, but anything had to be better than pining at home, alone. I still hadn't had the willpower to delete James's messages and, as if that wasn't masochistic enough, I'd started scanning the visitor statistics to see whether he was still reading *petite anglaise*, looking for a single footprint on a road trodden by thousands.

'Okay, you're on,' I said. 'For the present-shopping, at least. I'll play the rest by ear. I suppose I should be making more of my nights off; although I don't want to be out too late, what with work tomorrow . . .' It was tempting, while I still felt so fragile, to stay at home and hide behind my computer monitor, burrowing deep into my blog. *Petite anglaise* had become my refuge, and the frequency of my posts had doubled since James had left. But I couldn't hide there for ever.

As we walked along the avenue de l'Opéra towards Havre Caumartin and our final destination – the Printemps and Galeries Lafayette department stores – Amy talked at length about Tom, who still didn't seem to know his mind as far as Amy was concerned, oscillating wildly between infatuation and indifference. It was soothing to listen to someone else's problems for a while, instead of thinking or writing about my own. A couple of times I bit my tongue, suspecting that I was feeling too negative – both about men, and about long-distance relationships – to be able to offer Amy any advice of real value. Rejection left a tart aftertaste: whatever I had to say would be tainted by my own disappointment.

As we drew close to the Opéra Garnier and came to a halt at the first of several pedestrian crossings, Amy turned to me suddenly and changed the subject. 'So how are *you* doing? I mean, really? Because brave words on your blog are all very well, but no one gets over heartbreak that quickly.'

'I miss him,' I said sadly, my voice almost drowned out by the roar of the rush-hour traffic. 'I miss the silliest things, like the sound of him snoring in the night. It woke me up sometimes, and this probably sounds stupid, but I was just happy to be reminded that he was there.' Amy didn't laugh;

if anything, her eyes encouraged me to go on. 'I miss the physical stuff too, of course,' I said with a coy sideways glance. Since James had left, I'd felt my body reverting slowly back to how it was before, as though the nerve endings had shrunk far beneath the surface. 'But I don't want him back. There's no future for us now.' I twisted the ring I wore on my middle finger as I spoke, a gift from Mr Frog many years ago.

The green man had just lit up, and we crossed the road in silence. 'I have to ask this,' said Amy when we reached the opposite kerb, our trajectory taking us past the *terrasse* of the Café de la Paix, 'even if it sounds cruel. Do you ever find yourself wishing you could wind back the clock to that lunch we had the day before you came clean about James, so that you could do things differently?'

'No,' I said, without hesitation. 'I don't regret what I did. I think it had to happen. If James was never meant to be more than just a catalyst, then so be it. I was unhappy, and I needed a push to do something about it.' My eyes alighted on a well-dressed couple who were drinking champagne at an outdoor table, their hands interlaced, not two metres away from us, and I almost flinched. When I was pregnant, I remember seeing pregnant women everywhere I turned. Right now Paris was being cruel: surrounding me with happy couples, rubbing salt into my wounds.

'Well, at least now you're not dashing off to Rennes at every opportunity, you'll have some weekends in Paris to yourself. That'll be good for you,' said Amy. 'It took me a while to get back on my feet after my break-up – and I certainly wasn't ready to meet anyone new for a while – but I did force myself to go out, see my girlfriends. It did me a lot of good, although my liver might not agree . . .'

'You're right,' I said with a sigh. 'I need to get out and see more people. Force myself to switch off the computer and live more in the real world. How about I start by coming along with you to the birthday drinks? If you're sure no one will mind?'

'Brilliant,' said Amy, visibly pleased with herself. 'I *knew* you'd come round. But first things first. We need to choose a gift.'

Crossing the boulevard Haussmann, we pushed open the revolving door and stepped inside the brightly lit foyer of Printemps.

'I saw a billboard in the *métro* today that made me think of you,' wrote one of my commenters the next day in a private email to my *petite anglaise* address. 'I'll leave you to work out which one I'm talking about . . .' I was intrigued, but too snowed under with work to investigate and, as I scampered around the office binding documents for a meeting, the cryptic message flew clean out of my head.

That evening I happened to glance up from my book as the train screeched into Gare de l'Est and there it was, displayed alongside one of those Galeries Lafayette posters showing a Laetitia Casta lookalike wearing little more than a liberal coating of baby oil. A poster twice my height depicted a huge pink heart inscribed with the words '*petite anglaise raffinée cherche compagnon de route pour chanter sous la pluie.*' My book fell into my lap and I brought a hand to my mouth. So that's what he was referring to!

I posted a picture of the advert on my blog the next day, describing the jolt I'd experienced at seeing my name writ large across a billboard, even if the advert was *really* part of a campaign for a loan finance company and referred to a small English car seeking an owner and not an English girl looking for a love match. It soon became apparent from the comments left, however, that many of my Parisian readers had been doing double takes – just as I had – when first they saw the poster.

'Funny, I don't live in Paris,' said Aude, 'but I was there today and I saw this advert twice. The first time, I didn't have time to read it from start to finish, and I really thought it was an advert for YOUR blog.'

Aude could have been sitting right beside me in the *métro* on my way home and neither of us would have been any the wiser. I was anonymous, I went about my business incognito, and yet there I lingered in the minds of complete strangers. Strangers who knew me only as *petite anglaise*; strangers who had never seen my face.

Combing through the visitors' logs that night, I wondered whether I lingered in James's mind too. He left no comments, and he wasn't my only reader in Rennes, so the search was worse than futile. However much I liked to imagine him hunched in front of his computer, reading my posts with a haunted expression, in truth, his thoughts and feelings had become opaque to me now.

I decided to come clean about these feelings, partly in a bid to smoke James out if he really was silently following the blog, but mostly because I wanted to admit that behind the brave face *petite anglaise* had been presenting to the world, I was still in pain.

'If you are out there, ex-Lover,' I wrote, moments before I disabled the visitor log, determined to go cold turkey, 'then you have the advantage. Because here I am, an open book, with a broken spine. While you, you remain unfathomable.'

30. Stirring

The signs were unmistakable: a buoyancy, a lightness, a renewed bounce in my step. The familiar sensation of seeing the world through a feel-good movie filter. I hummed as I walked and, when I caught sight of myself reflected in a shop window, the girl who looked back at me was pale, but smiling.

It was foolish to let myself feel this way, so soon, but I was vulnerable, receptive; as soft and malleable as putty between warm fingers. I didn't stand a chance. Paris opened her arms to me, and I fell into them, gratefully.

It all began on my first Friday evening without Tadpole since James had left, two weeks earlier. Nestling among the latest batch of sympathetic emails from readers I'd spotted a message from Elisabeth-Coquette and we'd made arrangements to see a film near Odéon. Shivering in the cold, my breath fogging before my face, I wished I'd had the foresight to dress more warmly.

March is a fickle month in Paris. A mild spell lures the trees into a false sense of security, tricking them into yielding their blossoms prematurely. But a cold snap inevitably follows, bringing them brutally back to their senses, arresting their development. I'd been caught out too, and now regretted checking my heavy winter coat into the dry cleaner's. Digging my hands deep into the pockets of my thin mac, I weighed up whether or not I had time to slip over to the *crêpe* stand across the road before Elisabeth arrived. I probably didn't, but the persistent aroma of vanilla sugar and warm chocolate sauce was steadily weakening my resolve.

I stood waiting for Elisabeth at the base of the statue of Danton, a popular Left Bank meeting point. I couldn't remember who Danton was, but I noted with a smile that his pedestal had been tagged with space-invader graffiti, the pixels picked out in contrasting mosaic tiles. I was surrounded by young people; their chatter drawing frosty speech bubbles in the air. Lone girls waited breathlessly for friends to arrive. Nervous faces and tentative, shy smiles of greeting were reserved for first dates; pouts and reproaches of '*t'es encore en retard*' for long-term boyfriends. Groups of students, their faces illuminated by the neon signs which blazed above the cinemas and cafés lining both sides of the boulevard Saint Germain, argued earnestly over which film to see, and disjointed fragments of conversation littered the air. '*Il va être nul, ce film là . . .*' '*Tu l'as déjà vu?*' '*Je déteste Tom Onks . . .*' '*Mais si, ça va être bien . . .*' '*Oh là là, non, hors de question . . .*' Mobile phones were pressed to ears tinged red with cold, numb fingers fired off text messages over the airwaves. Strangers asked each other for a light, or even for a cigarette. The air buzzed with excitement. Standing there, alone, I felt something stirring.

A younger me had often stood guard by the *métro* exit here, a *Pariscope* magazine in her hand, flashing anxious looks at her watch and scouring the crowds for a glimpse of Mr Frog's blue duffle coat. His *chambre de bonne* was just a short walk away, at the Sorbonne end of the rue de Vaugirard. Things were so much simpler then: we were both in stop-gap jobs, as opposed to careers, and all we had to argue about was which film we'd rather see, or whether to buy our popcorn *salé* or *sucré*.

My vision clouded by ghosts, I didn't see Elisabeth approach until she drew to a breathless halt in front of me. Copper curls escaped from a knitted hat and her cheeks were flushed scarlet from the cold.

'So sorry I'm late,' she said, out of breath, as though she'd run all the way. 'I got a phone call from the States just as I was about to head out . . .'

'Oh, don't worry about that,' I replied, brushing aside her apology. 'It feels *so* good to be out. I can't remember the last time I saw a film in this part of town. I'm much more of a *rive droite* girl, at heart, but I do have a soft spot for this neighbourhood.'

'You certainly seem to be holding up okay,' she said cautiously, surprised to see me so upbeat. She'd probably thought she was on some sort of mercy mission tonight, playing chaperone to the walking wounded. 'I'm so sorry about what happened . . . But it's great finally to catch up with you. We don't do this nearly often enough.'

We watched a film – *Capote* – giggling like schoolgirls when the Frenchman in the queue in front of us pronounced it the French way, as though the writer's name had been Truman *Condom* – then drifted along the boulevard Saint Germain to a no-frills Tex-Mex on a side street which Elisabeth knew well. We talked until the second-hand cigarette smoke made us hoarse, and I lost all sense of time, almost missing the last *métro* home. Was it the wine, I wondered, as I leaned my head against the windowpane and watched the stations file past, that had filled me with this feeling of tired elation? Or was there something in the air?

The next morning, on my way to an apartment-viewing, I paused halfway along rue Piat to lean over the parapet and look down on the Parc de Belleville. Landscaped on a steep slope, where centuries ago vineyards and orchards once grew, staircases plunged, pathways spiralled and, beyond it, the rooftops of Paris stretched as far as the eye could see in every direction. I should come here more often, I thought to myself. I haven't even been making the most of my own neighbourhood, let alone the rest of Paris.

I'd begun actively searching for a new place to live, close to Tadpole's school and 'Daddy's house'. The *deux pièces* I visited that morning wasn't quite right, but I was filled with cautious hope nonetheless. The idea of moving, a reluctant, pragmatic decision, initially, was growing more appealing with every passing day. The quest had given me a new sense of purpose. A place of my own in Paris – hadn't I dreamed of that for years? Instead of running away, I owed my adopted city a second chance.

Although the air was still crisp and cold, the sky was a cheerful periwinkle blue, and birds chirruped in the branches above. After my appointment, I decided on a whim to take a stroll. Narrowing my eyes, blocking out the cars parked bumper to bumper along the kerbside and substituting the tarmac for cobbles, it was easy to imagine I was walking through a village, far from the capital. Belleville was full of surprises: culs-de-sac of terraced houses with walled gardens hidden in the shadow of high-rise blocks, private courtyards filled with greenery concealed behind heavy double doors, one- or two-storey buildings that had once been farmhouses or workshops in the days when Belleville lay outside the city limits. I wandered without purpose, revelling in my new-found freedom to improvise. The exhilaration I'd felt the night before hadn't faded. If anything, it was intensifying.

After lunch, I decided to take a *métro* over to the Left Bank, to browse in the boutiques around Saint Germain, just because I could. Feeling a bit like a tourist, I ordered hot chocolate in Café Flore, sitting in the panelled room upstairs, where the pace was slower and there were more free tables. It was served in two jugs, one containing chocolate the consistency of molasses, the other filled with frothy warm milk, and I stirred the mixture vigorously, pausing to suck the remaining chocolate from where it lingered on the spoon.

Shrugging off a vague, half-formed plan to buy books at W H Smith, near Concorde, I drifted along the rue de Seine, passing deserted art galleries and sleepy restaurants. Dawdling in front of the wooden kiosks which lined the riverbanks, I stopped to finger antique postcards and advertising posters, yellowing pre-war magazines and classic comic books, all wrapped in protective cellophane. The elderly stallholders sat on deckchairs, drinking coffee from Thermoses and watching the tourists stroll by, seemingly unconcerned that most people had no intention of actually buying anything.

When I reached the Pont Neuf, I remembered the last time I'd seen it, from the taxi taking me to the bloggers' *soirée*, before James and I had even met. I smiled at the sight of couples pressed together in its curved alcoves. Such a stereotype, this obligatory parade ground for lovers, but I was bemused to note that such public displays of affection no longer seemed to cause me pain. It was mid-afternoon now, and the temperature was rising. I unbuttoned my jacket and breathed deeply. The air smelled strongly of spring.

I walked for hours that weekend, content with my own company, self-sufficient, drinking everything in, my senses overwhelmed. There was such pleasure to be found in the little things: breaking the end off a warm baguette, savouring the contrast between the crisp shell and the warm, yielding dough; brushing half-heartedly at the dusting of flour on my coat; smiling sweetly at a passer-by who mockingly wished me '*bon appétit*'.

Losing James had left me vulnerable, but in a good way. I

was as porous and permeable as the sugar cube I held to the surface of my espresso, watching the coffee rise towards my fingertips. Sipping the bittersweet liquid, feeling its warmth permeate my body, I couldn't imagine anywhere else on earth I'd rather be. I'd forgotten how much it was possible to love this city.

'You ready for me to take over?' I enquired as I neared the top of the steps outside Buttes Chaumont station, my phone pressed to my ear.

'We're still in the park,' Mr Frog explained, unnecessarily. I could have deduced as much from the shrieks of children at play in the background. 'We're about to leave the play area with the slide near Botzaris. *Et toi?*'

'Just out of the *métro*, five minutes away,' I replied. 'Why don't you stay on the main path and I'll meet you halfway?'

It felt curious, walking through the park without Tadpole, especially at the weekend. The benches which lined the main avenues were the preserve of gossiping pensioners, as always, but the wide avenues favoured by joggers during the week were now overrun with couples and families. I weaved self-consciously around the pushchairs and tricycles, my excitement mounting at the prospect of seeing Tadpole. I'd barely spared her a thought all weekend – growing more and more able to enjoy these short periods of separation as time wore on – but now I couldn't wait to see her face light up with pleasure at the sight of me approaching.

I spotted Mr Frog in the distance, walking alongside an empty pushchair which was being propelled forwards as though by an invisible force. Tadpole had taken to insisting on pushing the buggy herself lately. A frustrating habit, as she often advanced at a snail's pace or was liable to run other people inadvertently off the pavement, unable to see where she was going. I altered my course now so as to meet the pushchair head on. I could see determined fists gripping the handles, but Tadpole's head was bowed, her face hidden from view.

'Good weekend?' enquired Mr Frog with a tired smile.

'Lovely,' I replied. 'It was a real novelty to have some time to myself in Paris. And this weather, this light . . . It makes you glad to be alive, doesn't it?'

At the sound of my voice, Tadpole's eager face emerged from behind the pushchair. 'I *goed* on the slide with Daddy!' she cried, as I swooped down and hugged her tightly for a moment. Then, falling into step with Mr Frog, and with Tadpole between us – still pushing the buggy – we slowly made our way to the park gates, in the shape of a family.

31. Charmed

Mr Frog took Tadpole to a family gathering at his parents' house the following weekend. I panicked as the weekend loomed closer: my renewed enthusiasm for Paris was undiluted, but there was a fine line between enjoying my time alone and feeling apprehensive about how I would keep loneliness at bay. Swallowing my pride, I sent an SOS email to a few of the people I'd met through *petite anglaise*.

'I'm home alone this weekend – half my office is going to a wedding, and I'm not invited – so, um, I'd love to catch up with anyone who might be free,' I wrote bashfully. I didn't enjoy having to beg, but I knew it was up to me to make the first move. I'd been too wrapped up in James to devote enough time to my budding friendships before. But if people were willing to give me a second chance, I was keen to start over.

Caroline Mancunian Lass replied almost immediately. Her mother was staying, so she had a ready-made babysitter on-hand. She suggested we head to rue Montorgueil, the neighbourhood she'd lived in before she had children, to have a drink and a bite to eat. I received other invitations too: on Sunday I would have lunch with Joanne, the reader who had found James's dating profile all those months before. Begging had paid dividends.

Rue Montorgueil had become rather chic in recent years, trading on its proximity to the fashion boutiques of nearby Etienne Marcel. The pedestrianized street was still lined with speciality food shops selling ripe cheeses, aesthetically pleasing stacks of fresh fruit and vegetables or fragrant mounds of coffee beans, their display tables spilling out on to the cobbles and helping to preserve some of the former market atmosphere. But the street had also been infiltrated by a handful of trendy restaurants and, on the way from the *métro*, I was disconcerted to see a shiny new Starbucks on the corner of rue Réaumur.

We met in a bar I'd never been in before, a former haunt of Caroline's called La Grappe d'Orgueil, which owed its charm to still having one foot firmly in the last century. Everything was curved, in art nouveau style, from the edges of the mirrors, to the zinc bar and even the doors leading through to the toilets. Couples and small groups of friends sipped aperitifs in wooden booths upholstered with dark-green leather, while the older generation propped up the bar. The air was heavy with cigarette smoke. Caroline was already sipping a kir when I arrived. She'd managed to snag a tiny booth below a glass display case full of antique crystal glasses.

We lingered far longer than we'd intended over our drinks and peanuts, then wandered up the street to Il Tre, one of the more modern places I'd passed, with walls painted black and red and sleek tubular spotlights hanging from the ceiling. 'There's nothing like an over-attentive Italian waiter when you're in need of a pick-me-up,' Caroline said with a smile as we waited by the bar to be seated. 'That's why I chose this place. These guys can do wonders for your self-esteem, single or not . . .'

'You know that time we went out for dinner with Louise to the Indian place?' I asked Caroline once we were seated, hastily moving my napkin off the table as the waiter, a rather handsome Italian, appeared with two steaming platefuls of spaghetti with clams. 'Well, I've often wondered what you two really thought of James, that night . . .'

'I thought he was really nice,' said Caroline slowly. 'Very down to earth, very besotted with you. Young-looking. Louise was less convinced though . . . Partly because I think she'd imagined him differently – you know, devilishly handsome and athletic, whereas he was nice-looking, but nothing out of the ordinary – but more because she didn't think that you'd be happy burying yourself in a provincial town like Rennes.' I pondered this for a moment.

'I must say, I am finding it harder to picture myself in Rennes now that it's all over,' I admitted. 'Paris has charmed me all over again. It's such a cliché, but there's something irresistible about springtime in Paris, isn't there? And I know I shouldn't really think this, let alone say it out loud, but I'm enjoying being a part-time mum more, now that I'm single. Having whole weekends to myself so I can recharge my batteries, indulge myself with a lie-in or two. It's such a luxury . . .'

'Stop, you're making me jealous!' Caroline protested, picking up the wine and, if I wasn't very much mistaken, pouring twice as much into my glass as she did into her own. 'I'll be getting up to two toddlers in the morning, and they'll show no mercy, hangover or no hangover. I don't even remember when I last had a lie-in.' We touched our glasses together in a silent toast, although to what, I wasn't sure. 'I've never been separated from my girls,' she confided, 'not even for a weekend. I don't know if I can imagine what it would be like.'

I picked up my cutlery and made an attempt to swirl the slippery spaghetti around my fork. I'd chosen the dish out of nostalgia; it had been Mr Frog's favourite when we visited Sicily, years ago, for our first ever holiday. What I'd since forgotten was how difficult it was to eat gracefully.

'Spending time apart wasn't something I thought I'd be comfortable with in the beginning,' I said thoughtfully. 'The first time she went to stay with her grandparents she was only one, and we had no choice really. *Tata* was away, and I had no holiday allowance left. I was apprehensive beforehand, and I think there were tears, but as the days went by I enjoyed the break, almost in spite of myself. We went out for dinner, to the cinema . . . It was almost as though we'd rewound to a time before we were parents.' I paused for a moment, frowning. 'Do I sound horribly selfish?'

'No, not at all,' said Caroline emphatically. 'I think it's important to claim some of yourself back once you've got used to being a mum. It sounds healthy to me, you shouldn't feel guilty. Don't you go paying too much attention to the negative comments some people write on the blog. I reckon any mother who claims she wouldn't jump at the chance of some time off is lying to herself.'

As we sipped our coffee, our meal over, my phone vibrated energetically in the pocket of my coat, which hung over the back of my chair. It was a text message from Elisabeth-Coquette. She was at a housewarming party – did I fancy joining her? I leafed through the miniature *Plan de Paris* I carried in my handbag at all times. 'It's only a ten-minute walk away,' I said to Caroline, a smile slowly spreading across my face. 'How about it? Shall we go?'

We made it to the party just before midnight, tipsy and rather sheepish at arriving empty-handed. We'd banked – rather foolishly – on finding a corner shop selling wine en route, but once we'd left the bustle of Montorgueil behind and headed north towards the party we found ourselves in a wasteland of apartment buildings and garment workshops and had to concede that our plan had been fatally flawed. If the hostess – a friend of Elisabeth's and fellow blogger whom I knew only as *Maîtresse* – thought us rude, she certainly hid it well. A slender blonde with an endearing air of vulnerability, Lauren welcomed us warmly and immediately put us at our ease.

'Come on in,' she said cheerily, swaying in her little black dress and knee-high boots. 'It's really exciting to meet you, *petite*, let me get you a drink and introduce you to everyone . . .'

'Oh, call me Catherine,' I said hurriedly. Between bloggers I didn't mind so much if the name *petite* stuck but, in mixed company, meeting new people, I had definite misgivings about being introduced as *petite anglaise* first and Catherine second.

I gazed around Lauren's apartment with the shrewd eyes of an apartment hunter, noting the marble fireplaces in every room, the intricate mouldings on the ceilings and the varnished oak floor. The twenty or so guests were mostly sitting or standing in sedate clusters in the living room, but I felt more comfortable chatting to my host and her French boyfriend in the narrow corridor leading to the kitchen. After a tumbler of vinegary wine – the sort of vintage people always seem to bring to parties but never actually drink themselves – caused the room to spin, I quietly switched to mineral water, leaning my back against the wall for support. Standing a few metres away, Caroline was deep in conversation with Elisabeth, whose blog she'd been following for as long as mine.

I didn't see the stranger approach until he was at my elbow. Wearing my long hair loose had its pros and cons: it provided a perfect veil behind which to hide, but it also reduced my peripheral vision to a disconcerting minimum.

'Hi, I don't think we've been introduced? I'm Toby.' To my surprise, the voice belonged to an attractive guy I hadn't noticed when I'd arrived, about my age at a guess, with ink-black hair and dark eyes to match. His features were boyishly handsome, his clothes casual, but I sensed they had been chosen with care.

'I'm Catherine,' I said cautiously. 'Pleased to meet you.'

'And how do you know Lauren, Catherine?' I tried to place his accent. Life abroad or education had smoothed the rough edges, but I thought I detected a flattening of the vowels I recognized; a hint of Yorkshire underneath.

'Oh, I'm friends with Elisabeth, the redhead over there.' I gestured in her direction. 'This is the first time I've met *Maîtresse* actually. I mean Lauren.' I flushed at the unintentional slip.

Lauren had evidently been listening in. 'Catherine happens to be the most famous blogger I've ever met,' she chimed in. 'She has, like, thousands of readers.' I was blushing deeply now, simultaneously flattered and embarrassed. What if Toby thought my pastime was odd? What if he thought I was some sort of exhibitionist?

'Fame on the internet is a very relative thing,' I mumbled, wishing now that I did have wine in my tumbler instead of water, anxious to change the subject. 'So, what brings you to Paris, Toby? And how did you meet Lauren?'

Toby, it transpired, was an actor turned academic, which explained a lot about his bearing, a certain theatrical resonance to his voice and his ability to slip effortlessly into character when he launched into an anecdote. There was a touch of camp in some of his gestures, and it did briefly cross my mind that he might be gay but, if I wasn't misreading the signals, Toby seemed to be interested in me, and this even after I'd managed to ease the fact that I was a single mother into the conversation.

As the night wore on and the guests thinned, we ended up sitting side by side on the sofa in the next room, reminiscing about our schooldays. I had been right about the Yorkshire connection. Somehow we ended up discussing a field trip to Whitby, a coastal town an hour's drive from where my parents lived which our junior schools, his in Leeds, mine in York, had visited when we were nine years old.

'We had these wire coat-hangers, bent into squares, and at regular intervals along the beach we had to put them on the ground and write down everything we found inside them, for our seashore project,' I said, the memories flowing freely, surprising me with their detail.

Toby laughed a short, barking laugh. 'Yes, we had those too. And inside every one the answer was seaweed, more seaweed, and – if you were really lucky – a coke can or a used condom.' I wasn't sure that my nine-year-old self would have been able to identify a condom, but I grinned all the same.

When Caroline materialized by my side and tapped me on the shoulder, I turned to face her, feeling suddenly guilty that I'd allowed Toby to monopolize my attention. 'I'm going to head home now,' she said apologetically. 'Got to get up early with my girls in the morning. No weekend off for me . . .' I rose and followed her through to where our coats were stacked on Lauren's bed, wondering what to do. I knew I should offer to leave with her, so that we could share a taxi. But sensing my indecision, Caroline was quick to reassure me there was no need. 'Don't worry about me,' she said with a wink. 'You look like you're enjoying yourself. You can't leave now . . .'

'Toby does seem nice,' I said hesitantly, fishing for some sort of blessing.

'Yes. He does. And very interested.' She turned to go. 'Now you have fun, and don't forget to get in touch tomorrow and tell me all about it.'

Not long afterwards the party fizzled out completely and Elisabeth, Toby and I made our way to Place de Clichy in search of taxis. Elisabeth was headed south of the river, back to the Left Bank, but Toby was going east, as was I. 'Might as well share a cab then?' he said as a taxi pulled up alongside us, its sign illuminated.

'I suppose that would make sense,' I replied, as casually as I could manage. We bundled Elisabeth into the first taxi so that she wouldn't have to wait alone and, as it pulled away, she waved at me through the window with a knowing smile.

'*Où allons nous?*' growled the driver of the second taxi as we slid into the back seat, barely audible over the sound of his radio, which was tuned into a radio station playing North African music.

'Place Sainte Marthe,' Toby replied. His accent, in French, was as convincing as my own. Much better than James's, I thought to myself, uncharitably.

'*Et ensuite, à l'avenue Simon Bolivar,*' I added pointedly. I didn't want it to look as though I presumed anything about how this night would end.

As we turned off the boulevard de la Villette in the direction of Place Sainte Marthe, Toby fumbled in his coat pocket for his wallet. 'This is me . . .' he said, leaning across to give more precise instructions to the taxi driver. I wondered what would come next. A kiss on the cheek? An exchange of phone numbers? Or just a 'Well, I had a good time, see you around sometime . . .' I was woefully out of practice at this sort of thing. James and I hadn't met in a particularly conventional way, so a whole decade had passed since the last time I'd had to play all the games single people play.

'Do you fancy getting one last drink somewhere?' he said, suddenly, as the taxi drew to a standstill. I was flattered, gleeful on the inside, but knew at once that I wouldn't accept his invitation. It was 4 a.m. The bars which usually spewed tables across the square had retreated behind wooden shutters, their lights extinguished. I was wobbly on my feet, I'd drunk too much already but, above all, it was too soon.

'I think I'm going to call it a night,' I replied. 'But we could meet up some other time, when you're back in Paris.' From what I'd been able to piece together, Toby led a nomadic life, involving lots of Eurostar journeys, with one foot in London, the other in Paris.

'Okay, well, let me give you my card . . .' He dug once more in his wallet. My hand closed around the white rectangle as he leaned in and planted an awkward kiss on my cheek, then jumped out of the car and disappeared into a nearby building. I gave the driver my address and let myself fall back on the fake-leather upholstery, drowsy but rather pleased with myself.

That might be the last I ever see of Toby, I thought to myself as the taxi began to climb the rue de Belleville and the language of the signs above the shops changed from Mandarin back into French. I was prepared to take the risk. A one-night stand – which was surely where 'one last drink' would have led us – was the last thing I needed right now.

But meeting Toby – and having the opportunity to turn him down – had given me a welcome dose of confidence. An attractive man had flirted with me. And when I'd told him I was a mother, he hadn't so much as flinched.

32. Chéri(e)

'It's kind of small, but perfectly formed,' I explained to Mr Frog as we made our way briskly to my early morning rendez-vous, Tadpole skipping along between us. 'I'm thinking of putting in an offer, but I'd really like to see what you think of it first.'

The search for a new place to live was starting to bear fruit. Was it a case of 'extreme retail therapy', as one of my commenters had suggested? It was only just over a month since James had left. But however reckless or impulsive my apartment-hunting spree might look to other people, I didn't feel like I was rushing into anything. Hadn't I been visiting flats in Paris for years, dreaming about owning property with Mr Frog long before James came on the scene? If anything, I was simply picking up where I'd left off, a year earlier. The only difference was that Mr Frog was no longer part of the equation.

Going it alone made matters almost frighteningly simple. There was no need for compromise, or protracted arguments about whether the apartment was right for our family. No agonizing over whether now was the right time to take out a loan. With hindsight, I knew those discussions had been nothing but wispy smokescreens. Bickering about price, lay-out or location had been safer than focusing on the thorny issue of why Mr Frog and I found ourselves increasingly reluctant to take the plunge hand in hand. Now the decision was mine, and mine alone. I was seeking Mr Frog's opinion, as a friend, but I didn't need his blessing.

'How many places did you say you'd visited?' enquired Mr Frog. Nearing the pedestrian crossing, we grabbed Tadpole's hands in unison.

'Five, including this one. On top of the dozens we visited before . . .' I could feel myself bristling, sensitive to the implied criticism that I was being over-hasty. 'But this one really does stand out. I don't see any point in dithering. I'll only end up regretting it if someone else snatches it from under my nose . . .' I glanced at the traffic lights – stubbornly lodged on green – then down at Tadpole, who was frowning up at my nostrils, baffled by my figure of speech.

'Oh, by the way,' added Mr Frog, lowering his voice so that Tadpole wouldn't hear him above the roar of passing traffic. 'She told me at the weekend you'd been crying. Said you were feeling sad because James doesn't visit any more.'

'Oh gosh, did she really?' We'd had that talk weeks ago. Did she really remember it as clearly as if it had happened only yesterday? I was dismayed at the idea that I might have caused Tadpole, or Mr Frog, needless worry. 'You know how vague her notion of time is,' I said finally, in as casual a tone as I could muster. 'Yesterday can mean anything from five minutes to four months ago. I haven't cried in weeks, honestly. I'm surprised she even remembers I said that.'

'That's what I thought,' said Mr Frog as we marched Tadpole across the road and swung her over the stream of water gushing alongside the opposite gutter, carrying the debris the street-cleaners had swept off the pavement to some murky underground destination, a manoeuvre which always made her giggle. 'But she had me worried. You do seem a lot better, but then she had me wondering if you weren't just putting on a brave face.'

'I can see I'll have to be careful what I say!' I retorted, only half joking. Tadpole might be an unreliable witness, but she was a witness nonetheless. I'd have to bear in mind, as her language skills improved, that anything I said or did might now be reported back to Daddy.

The girl from the estate agent's was waiting for us in front of the entrance to the building, listening to a message on her mobile phone. She looked at least ten years my junior, and reminded me of Maryline, with her sleek dark hair and perfectly calibrated make-up. 'I've brought a friend along for a second opinion,' I explained as we drew to a halt as one, our hands still joined. Anyone could see that Mr Frog and Tadpole were related, that he wasn't just any friend, but I was still struggling to find a combination of words which summed up our current relationship to my satisfaction. 'My ex-boyfriend' left Tadpole out of the equation, making light of the ties which would bind us for life; 'my daughter's father' felt too impersonal, as though he'd never been *my* anything.

'A sensible thing to do,' the girl replied, tapping in the door code and clattering ahead of us up the wooden staircase to the first floor, where she unlocked the door. Tadpole raced inside without a moment's hesitation. It was our second visit, and she already seemed perfectly at home. '*Bon, je vous laisse faire un tour.*' She stepped aside to let us pass. 'I need to make a call, so I'll wait out here, unless you need me . . .'

Inside, a T-shaped corridor led to two rectangular rooms of a similar size: on the left 'mine', on the right 'Tadpole's'. In between, a narrow kitchen and an equally narrow bathroom nestled side by side. The bathroom was home to the smallest bath I'd ever laid eyes on; little larger than a shower basin, but big enough for Tadpole. The floorboards had been buffed and waxed, the walls were freshly painted and light flooded in through large windows. Half the size of our current home, with just one square metre for every year of my life so far, it was small, and there was no view to speak of, as all the windows looked on to an interior courtyard and a second building, identical to the one in which we stood. And yet something about this place felt right: I could visualize Tadpole and me living here. I could imagine making these rooms our home.

'Nice parquet floor,' said Mr Frog. 'Shame they've ripped out the fireplaces.'

'Yes, it's not a patch on the other place,' I said, matter of factly. 'The buildings are the same age, but this one is working class, not bourgeois.'

'I like it though,' Mr Frog hastened to add. 'I know it's a lot smaller, but that's the sacrifice you'll have to make if you want to buy your own place . . .'

'What do *you* think, sweetie?' I said, turning to Tadpole. 'Would you like to live here with Mummy?' There was no reply. Tadpole was too busy flicking the light switch on and off, delighted to find the button at toddler level, but puzzled that her actions were producing no tangible consequences, in the absence of any power. I kneeled by her side and repeated my question: 'Would you like to live here with Mummy? We could paint the walls a pretty colour, make this room into your bedroom . . .'

'We going to paint on the wall?' said Tadpole incredulously, gesturing at the huge white canvas all around us. I'm sure she pictured herself in a plastic smock making naïve art murals with finger paints, which was not exactly what I had in mind.

'I think that's clinched the deal!' said Mr Frog with a grin. '*Vendu!*'

'Right, well, if you don't think I'm mad, then I'm going to put in an offer,' I said, suddenly decisive. 'I've lived in this city for ten years. It's about time I put down some proper roots.'

Returning to the estate agent's that evening after work, I did just that, signing the paperwork with trembling fingers while Tadpole doodled on a business card with a blue biro. I was taking my life into my own hands and, although it was terrifying, it was terrifying in a good way.

I met Toby on the corner of rue Rébeval, outside Café Chéri(e), the only café I've ever come across with brackets in its name. I've always been convinced there should be a question mark too, as the name calls to mind a couple strolling down the street, pausing on a whim to peer inside, one saying to the other: '*Tu veux un café, chéri?*' Although I'd skirted past the *terrasse* with Tadpole on the way to the swimming pool several times, I'd never seen its transformation into a lively bar by night, and I had to admit the cheerfully mismatched second-hand tables and chairs looked very different now, under muted red lights. Tadpole was with her daddy for the evening, and the following day was one of the many *jours fériés* which fall in the month of May, which meant the office would be conveniently closed the next morning.

After exchanging self-conscious hellos and kissing the air next to each other's cheeks, Toby and I stepped inside and took a seat at the only available table, our knees rubbing together through the fabric of our jeans in the cramped space. The conversation was stilted at first.

'So. Been up to anything exciting?' Toby enquired.

'Oh, you know, the usual,' I replied airily, wishing I had something interesting to add to what I'd already told him in the emails we'd bounced back and forth since we met at the party. It was one thing flirting online, where I could choose my words with care and edit them to my heart's content, another thing entirely seeing him again in the flesh. 'Working, blogging, buying a flat . . . What about you? Are you around for long or is this just a flying visit?'

'A few days this time, I think,' he said evasively. I got the distinct impression that Toby didn't like to be pinned down. I'd only discovered he was coming to Paris the previous evening. Either he had a penchant for making whirlwind last-minute plans, or he enjoyed keeping people guessing.

Just as we managed to flag down a waitress to order one of the rum cocktails which seemed to be the house speciality, a band shuffled on to a small stage at the back of the room. A man with a mullet, the top buttons of his shirt open to reveal a mass of wiry grey chest hair, began to bellow out what I suspected was a cover version of a Johnny Halliday song. 'You're not telling me that the kind of people who come here actually like this sort of music?' I said, swivelling to stare at the *bobo* crowd draped nonchalantly over the chairs around us. 'This isn't what I expected at all!'

'One can only hope it's supposed to be ironic,' said Toby dryly. 'But apart from anything else, it's far too loud. How about we have one drink, then move on to a bar where we can actually hear ourselves think?' Right on cue, the waitress appeared and set down two tumblers with straws.

'Good idea.' I picked up my drink and took a long sip of sweet punch, the sugar numbing my front teeth.

'Any preference, *Mademoiselle*?'

'None at all.' My residual shyness was beginning to thaw. I'd eaten little that day, and I could already feel the effects of the alcohol as it entered my bloodstream. 'You choose. Anywhere will do. I'm easy.' Toby raised an eyebrow, and I smiled. After a shaky start, things seemed to be progressing nicely.

It probably wasn't a coincidence that the next bar Toby chose was on Place Sainte Marthe, seconds away from his apartment. The walls were painted red here too, but as we ducked through an arched doorway into the room behind the bar and took a seat in the corner, I was amused to see that two facing walls were decorated with a kitsch patterned wallpaper, punctuated by yellowing photographs in orange frames, as though someone's living-room wall had been grafted on to this unlikely setting. The long-haired, wild-eyed proprietor sat down by my side while he took our drinks order, putting his sandal–clad bare feet up on a chair, and I noted with pleasure that Toby looked impressed with my ability to hold my own in French.

Sipping ginger juice through a straw, idly wondering if it might have aphrodisiac properties, I sat cross-legged on the *banquette* and listened as Toby told anecdotes, ever the master storyteller, noticing how the timbre of his voice changed when he drew cigarette smoke into his lungs. I was captivated by his smile, his dark chocolate eyes, and had to suppress the urge once or twice to reach out and touch his thick, carefully tousled hair. All traces of awkwardness had evaporated now: banter ebbed and flowed effortlessly between us; time seemed unusually elastic.

'I haven't read your blog by the way,' Toby said, without apology, when the subject came up. 'I don't intend to actually. I'd rather get to know you instead.'

'That's probably no bad thing,' I retorted. 'There's a bit too much of me out there, and it would give you rather an unfair advantage.' In truth I found his lack of curiosity puzzling, even hurtful. I knew for a fact that if he'd had a blog, I'd have been all over it like a rash: hungry for more information, on tenterhooks to see whether I'd merit a mention, sifting through the evidence for clues about what made him tick. Did his lack of curiosity about me signify a lack of interest? Then again, after everything that had happened with

James, it would be refreshing to spend time with a man who didn't hang on *petite anglaise*'s every word.

It was only when the owner came over to chivvy us out that I realized we were alone in the bar, and probably had been for some time. As we were ushered towards the exit, I was surprised to see the plastic furniture from the *terrasse* neatly stacked inside the front door. I couldn't speak for Toby, but I for one hadn't heard the merest scrape of a chair across the tiled floor.

'*Un café, chérie?*' enquired Toby, his hand on my arm as we stepped out into the deserted square.

'Your place, or mine?' I replied, with a grin, knowing full well what the answer would be.

Toby walked me halfway home the next morning and we paused to say goodbye in front of the café where we had met twelve hours earlier.

'I had fun last night,' I said casually, as if I did this sort of thing all the time. 'Fun' was an accurate description of our night. It had been playful. Toby had exhibited none of James's intensity; none of his almost religious reverence. But despite my light-hearted tone, under cover of my coat sleeves I was digging into my cuticles with my fingernails. What was supposed to happen next?

He'd looked relieved when I explained, over coffee in his tiny flat, that I was raw from a recent break-up. As I'd suspected, he wasn't looking for a relationship either. He was a social butterfly flitting from city to city, elusive by design, reluctant to settle on any one bloom. Once we both knew the lie of the land, we seemed to have tacitly agreed to have some uncomplicated fun. I'd teased him about his chaotic apartment, the books stacked in teetering piles, but nonetheless moved willingly towards the mattress on the floor which served as his bed.

If we really can keep things light, I thought, casual might be just what the doctor ordered. But I'd never done anything like this before, and I hadn't a clue how we were supposed to behave the morning after.

'I'll be in touch,' said Toby, planting a goodbye kiss squarely on my lips, but withdrawing immediately.

Making my way up rue Rébeval, oblivious to the ungainly high-rise blocks towering above me on either side, still warmed by the afterglow of his attention, I decided that however fleeting, however short-lived these sensations might be, I was determined to savour them while they lasted, without pushing for more.

I liked him, and sensed I could grow to like him more. But I knew it was far too soon to beckon anyone inside the invisible circle I had drawn around myself. Too soon to risk allowing the firm ground beneath my feet to shake and tilt. Because even though, on the surface, I was beginning to feel more whole than I had in a long time, I was still conscious of my soft centre. Still unwilling to test the limits of my new-found strength.

'I don't want to see you get hurt again, that's all. Not so soon after James,' said Amy sharply as she unwrapped her sandwich and brought it to her lips. We'd bought lunch from a bakery close to the office and decided to take our picnic to the Palais Royal gardens, where, in the absence of any unoccupied metal chairs, we'd perched our buttocks on the stone lip of the fountain. 'It all sounds a bit too convenient for him – he's got you at his beck and call whenever he waltzes into town.'

If anything, my casual fling sounded uncannily similar to Amy's tortured long-distance relationship with Tom, but I kept that thought to myself and channelled all my energy into stamping my foot in the pale sand to disperse a crowd of over-enthusiastic pigeons. For a moment Amy and I remained silent, chewing thoughtfully on our sandwiches. The harsh midday sunlight was making my eyes water and I wished I'd had the foresight to bring my sunglasses.

'I know I'm on the rebound,' I confessed, between mouthfuls. 'And I know Toby isn't a serious candidate for anything long-term. Or even medium-term. But maybe that's precisely why he's so attractive to me, right now. Unsuitable is good. Temporary is good . . . And although he makes it seem like he's calling the shots, I don't actually have that much flexibility, so *he* tends to fall in with *my* plans.'

Toby and I had seen each other twice more in the past two weeks since our date at the Chéri(e) and each time I'd made sure Tadpole was absent for the night, safely across the road with Mr Frog. Tadpole still spoke about James sometimes – the letter 'J' was still for 'James' not 'jam' – and in some ways I regretted introducing her to him so early in our relationship. I wouldn't make the same mistake twice: my daughter would be spared a steady stream of short-lived 'Mummy's friends' passing through our home. The solution, I decided, was to lead parallel lives, making sure they were never permitted to overlap. On my nights off I could do precisely what I pleased. But the next morning, I'd wash the bar smoke from my hair, remove the smudges of the previous night's make-up from beneath my eyes and become a mother again. It wasn't so different from slipping into the role of the perfect secretary when I entered the office, or becoming *petite anglaise* at a bloggers' meet-up. I'd become extraordinarily good at playing multiple roles.

'And will you write about this on the blog?' Amy stood up and brushed the crumbs from her skirt, her sudden movement scattering the advancing pigeons once more. Still standing, she took a long drink from her bottle of Evian.

'I might,' I replied disingenuously. In fact, I'd spent some idle time working on a post that very morning, which I had yet to publish. 'Toby says he doesn't read it anyway, so I don't see what harm it can do. And it would be good to spice things up on the blog. I've been struggling to hold everyone's attention since James jumped ship. From the beginning, there was always a man in the picture, and now it's just me and my daughter, I'm a bit stuck for subject matter . . .'

'You might want to try putting yourself first, and not that blog of yours,' said Amy as we gathered up our bags and rose to leave. 'I know it's important to you, but don't live your life to please your readers.'

As we walked back to the office in silence, bracing ourselves for the icy chill of the air conditioning, I wondered to what extent I really was guided in my choices by the need to find material for *petite anglaise*. Was I living my own life or was *she* the master choreographer, nudging me in the directions where good stories lay? Would I be living my life differently if I wasn't writing about it on my blog?

Slipping into my ergonomic chair, glancing around to make sure the coast was clear, I opened up my draft blog post and re-read it before hitting the 'publish' key.

I choose my outfit, my undergarments with care, because I know from experience that a drink, with him, will lead to much, much more. In the bar, I bask in his attention, happy in this moment, knowing full well it will be fleeting. I lie in bed, his sleeping body curled around mine, his arm around my waist, marvelling that someone can be so close, skin against mine, but simultaneously seem so remote, so inaccessible.

When we part the next day and I hear the words I fully expect to hear – 'Well, I guess I'll see you when I get back' – I feel a twinge of something I was determined not to feel. A

brief pang of remorse that I may have been selling little pieces
of myself to the lowest bidder.

The next day, I trawled through the comments slowly, one
by one. Eighty-two people had felt the need to weigh in and
tell me how they felt.

'I don't know, *petite*,' Lost in France lamented. 'It just
sounds like a prescription for disaster.'

Many shared his reticence, begging me to exercise caution
to avoid getting hurt so soon after losing James.

'*Petite*, you decide what works for you,' urged Ingrid, 'but,
ultimately, hold out for adoration and respect. Please.'

The words which resonated with me the most came from
someone called Trinigirl.

'Ah yes,' she wrote, 'we've all danced to this particular tune
at one time in our lives. In my experience, the majority of
women are hopeless romantics, believing that, in time, he'll
realize how wonderful we are, and fall in love with us . . .'

Did she have a point? By writing this post, knowing that
there was a chance Toby might read it, I was up to my old
tricks. Was I not sending him an open letter and hoping for
some sort of response, in return?

33. Roquette

'I've got news!' I shrieked down the phone. 'The estate agent just called, and my offer on the flat has been accepted!' Mr Frog had now reverted back to being the person I invariably called when something happened that I simply had to share, and knowing that he had Tadpole with him, calling him before midday on a Saturday was perfectly reasonable, for once.

'Wow! That's fantastic news. Congratulations!' His script was word perfect, but something in his tone of voice suggested that his enthusiasm was tempered by other, conflicting emotions. I supposed it must feel strange to him that I should finally be taking this step alone, after all the apartments we'd visited together. It felt odd to me too, as though I were slamming a door shut in his face; foreclosing on any possibility of reconciliation.

'By the way, have you two eaten lunch yet?' I said, looking at my watch. 'Because if you haven't, I was thinking maybe we could go to the Chinese restaurant with the fish tanks. So you can see how well your daughter uses her chopsticks. My treat.'

'We haven't eaten yet, so yes, that would be great.' I sensed hesitation in his voice. 'The thing is, we'll need some time to get ready . . .'

'She's not watching TV in her pyjamas at this time of day, surely?' I said, feigning disapproval. I was far more relaxed about parenting these days, now that the tasks were shared more equally between us and, above all, I was more realistic.

All that mattered to me, really, was that Tadpole was spending quality time with her daddy.

'Do you have hidden cameras?' asked Mr Frog, mock suspiciously.

I snorted with laughter. 'Just give me a call when you're ready, okay?'

Two hours later I leaned back in my chair looking up at my reflection in the mirrored ceiling, feeling sated and somewhat giddy. I wasn't sure if it was the midday beer or the prospect of becoming a homeowner which was making me feel light-headed. Maybe a combination of both. 'I can't believe she managed to polish off a whole adult portion of chicken fried rice on her own,' Mr Frog said, shaking his head in astonishment. Our impassive waiter arrived to clear the plates I'd neatly stacked, and we ordered a scoop of vanilla ice cream for Tadpole, plus two espressos for ourselves.

'You do realize we'll be here all day now,' I said wryly. 'Have you seen how long it takes her to eat one spoonful? She won't put it in her mouth, she just licks the spoon.'

'I'm in no hurry,' Mr Frog replied. 'It's been great.' Tadpole had been on top form throughout lunch, peering into the fish tanks which flanked our table, struggling comically to master her huge varnished chopsticks before hunger got the better of her and she cast them aside in favour of a dessert fork and teaspoon. Waiting for dessert to arrive, she was now busy drawing a picture on the paper tablecloth with a pencil I'd found in the bottom of my handbag. The stick lady with hair reaching to the bottom of her A-line skirt was no doubt supposed to be me. The man by her side, his head like a pincushion, was Mr Frog.

'Well, if you feel comfortable with this, maybe we should do things together at the weekend more often?' I suggested. 'You know, when neither of us has any other plans . . .'

'I'd like that,' Mr Frog said, his eyes riveted to Tadpole's picture. A short, curly-haired stick figure now stood between us, an impossibly wide grin stretching from one side of its face to the other, where the ears should have been.

After bidding goodbye to Mr Frog and Tadpole, I caught a *métro* to Voltaire. By some miracle, I'd managed to secure a Saturday afternoon appointment with my bank manager when I'd called that morning, something that would usually have taken weeks to obtain. My account was still held by the branch closest to my very first Paris apartment, a Caisse d'Epargne on Place Léon Blum. I'd been banking with them for over ten years, which, come to think of it, was the longest I'd ever lived in a single town. Even as a child, back in England, I'd moved around the country, at the mercy of my father's job.

Emerging from the *métro* with half an hour to spare, I decided to take a stroll along rue de la Roquette, past my very first *chez moi*. The weather was indecisive: cloudy and menacing one minute, sunny and optimistic the next. Umbrella and sunglasses weather, I've always called it, because you never quite know which one you'll need. Wandering around my old neighbourhood under changing skies, I paused at a few of my old haunts, my moods mirroring the weather, my memories bittersweet.

So much had changed over the past decade, so many shops and restaurants had come and gone and, when I saw a place I recognized, I paused, grateful for some continuity. A faded sign in a *traiteur*'s window reminded its customers that, back in 1990, the shop had won a national prize for making the best *fromage de tête*. I'd never ventured in, unnerved by the concept of 'head cheese', which I suspected had more to do with 'heads' than 'cheese', but I was relieved to see the shop hadn't given way to another soulless sushi bar or garish Chinese takeaway. Peering into the window, it was as though the clock had been wound back ten years, and I half expected to see my twenty-three-year-old self reflected back at me.

A few paces further the air was filled with the pungent aroma of roast chicken. The prices were in euros, not French francs, but the white-overalled butcher's assistant tending to the plump chickens turning on their metal spits looked familiar. He called out to me as I passed, a jovial '*bonjour Mademoiselle*,' and I silently thanked him for not saying '*Madame*', allowing me to preserve the illusion of time-travel for just a few moments longer.

The tiny shop below my first apartment no longer sold records, now into its second or third incarnation as a mobile-phone discount store. Nonetheless, the front door of number 104, to the left, was still painted the same shade of brown, and I could have sworn the net curtains veiling the first-floor windows were the very same *voilages* my landlady had hung when I arrived – the gauzy material yellowed with age but the motif identical. I loitered for a moment in the doorway, trying in vain to remember the door code. Even if my memory hadn't failed me, the exercise was probably futile. It had been ten years: the code must have been changed countless times since I lived there.

In my mind's eye I saw a younger me striding out of the door, a copy of the *Rough Guide* in her hand, determined to cover every inch of the city on foot. I glimpsed the same girl, looking tired and slightly the worse for wear, meandering homewards from a nightclub in the early hours of the morning. She was carefree, sometimes reckless; still convinced that youth conferred some sort of magical immunity which would keep her safe from harm. And as for Mr Frog, she hadn't even met him yet.

Drifting along the road, as if in a trance, I neared the red and white laundrette – the *laverie* featured in *Chacun Cherche Son Chat*, the film which had made me cry when I'd seen it just as I was contemplating leaving Paris years before. A young man with a chequered laundry bag pushed open the door, releasing a gust of humid air and the scent of lavender fabric conditioner into the street. Inside, students flicked idly through magazines while the drone of spin cycles lulled them into a pleasant torpor.

The sight of the clock on the laundrette wall startled me out of my reverie, breaking the spell. It was nearly three. If I didn't get a move on, I'd be late for my appointment, and that wouldn't do. Retracing my steps, I promised myself a return visit another day, when I'd allow myself more time to linger before I yanked myself back into the present.

Soon, if everything went according to plan, I'd be moving into a new flat, not much bigger than my first foothold on rue de la Roquette, with my half-French daughter. I had responsibilities now. I was a mother, soon to be a homeowner. And I was, now more than ever, wedded to the city that the girl from rue de la Roquette had chosen to make her home.

If she could have peered into the future, curious to see exactly what Paris held in store for her, I hoped that, seeing me now, she wouldn't have disapproved.

34. Whole

Toby had returned from his travels once more, but everything had changed. Our conversation was hopelessly maladroit. We blundered around in ever decreasing circles, stripped of our usual articulacy, then lapsed into excruciating silences. Each time he attempted to describe how he felt, his words hung in the air uselessly, devoid of any actual meaning. We were supposed to be having a serious, meaningful conversation about where we were headed – or indeed why we were headed nowhere – but it was proving impossible. Banter was the only register we seemed capable of and, without it, we'd lost all means of communication. We sat side by side on the sofa, light-years apart.

It was my fault, entirely. The previous evening, emboldened by a couple of gin and tonics, I'd taken it into my head to provoke some sort of confrontation. We'd been chatting to each other by instant messenger while he'd been away, and the frequency of our contact seemed to be increasing, but when he announced his imminent return I realized I was tiring of our games, fed up with trying to second-guess his motives, weary of trying to hold myself aloof so that I wouldn't lose face.

I'd begun to suspect that something would have to give the last time we'd met. The transition from banter to bedroom had become awkward: sex felt like an unnatural transaction, tacked clumsily on to a friendship, with no affection to cement the two together. But despite all this, and despite the fact that Tadpole lay sleeping in the next room, I'd still applied nail varnish and moisturizer, and made liberal use of depilatory cream. These laborious preparations were the proof that some part of me was still hoping for something tonight: a turn-around, a declaration. Now I sat with my chin resting on my knees, my hair loose, tickling my calves, waiting for him to speak.

'I don't know what to say that won't sound clichéd,' said Toby apologetically.

'Well, please try to avoid "It's not you, it's me" if you want to get out of here alive,' I suggested, looking down at my ineptly painted toenails.

'I read your blog, finally,' he said suddenly. 'It was the weirdest thing.'

I cringed inside. There were two, maybe three posts about us, in total. I'd hinted that I was having a hard time with our unspoken pact of superficiality. I'd used that phrase about 'selling little pieces of myself to the lowest bidder'. I only hoped he hadn't read the comments. To say that some of my readers had been tough on him would have been putting things mildly. His treatment of me had been called 'shabby' and I'd been told I had 'all the wrong instincts with men'.

'And?'

'Well, it was very odd . . . I didn't recognize myself in your descriptions of me at all. I didn't recognize you. It was like reading about a couple of strangers. We only spent two or three nights together, and I was honest about my expectations from the start . . .' He shifted awkwardly on the sofa. The whole thing was so excruciating that I just wanted it to end, to push him out of the door.

'It was more like five or six times, actually,' I said quietly. 'And, obviously, *petite anglaise* can't resist playing to her audience a bit, I'll admit that. And I'm sure my speaking voice isn't the same as her writing voice. But isn't this more about how two people can read the same situation in two completely different ways? I've been busy resisting the urge to build castles in the air, like I always do, and you just saw whatever it was that *you* wanted to see . . .'

When he left, I closed the door behind him with an audible sigh. It stung, this new rejection, but it was also a relief to put an end to the ambiguity and incertitude, which had definitely begun to rankle. I had been deceiving myself the day I decided I could master the art of detachment, or maybe the mistake was to allow things to go on in that vein for as long as they had. Taking my pocket diary from my handbag, skimming over the past few weeks, I found the proof that I'd been wrong, but so had he. We'd seen each other exactly four times.

I'd played it up, he'd played it down, and the truth lay somewhere in the middle.

I heard the creak of a door the next morning, followed by the pattering of bare soles against the floorboards. Pulling the bedclothes up to my chin, I hastily closed my eyes, preserving Tadpole's illusion that she was responsible for waking me.

A hand grazed my cheek, and I braced myself for her 'WAKEY WAKEY, MUMMY,' the volume of which never ceased to amaze me. How could such a small pair of lungs produce such a booming voice? Surely it went against all the laws of physics?

Instead, to my surprise, I felt tiny fingers exploring the contours of my face, and it was all I could do to prevent my mouth twitching involuntarily. I kept my eyes tightly closed, savouring the moment, hoping to prolong it for as long as possible. 'Mummy got lovely eyebrows,' a sleepy Tadpole voice muttered as she traced the curve of my right eyebrow. 'And Mummy got beautiful lips,' she whispered, her fingers feather-light against my mouth. I basked in her unconditional love like a cat in a patch of sunlight. Toby had been disturbingly immune to my charms, but here was someone who thought I was special, regardless of my bed hair, the sleep in my eyes and my Miffy pyjamas, a Christmas gift from my mother.

My mouth was ajar, and I felt an intrepid digit venturing inside to probe my front teeth. I was sorely tempted to nibble on her finger, pretending to bite, but reluctant to break the spell. Before I could make up my mind, she spoke again. 'Mummy *have* very pretty yellow teeth . . .'

'Yellow?' I spluttered, eyes wide open, all pretence of sleep abandoned. Tadpole withdrew her finger, hastily. 'No, not yellow! Mummy's teeth are white. Not as white as your lovely baby teeth. A different white.'

'No, Mummy!' Tadpole frowned, patently unconvinced. 'They yellow, like your hair.'

'Could I have less of the brutal honesty and more of the unconditional love, please?' I groaned, pulling the bedclothes back over my head in mock protest. But as Tadpole slipped into bed beside me for our morning snuggle, begging me to scratch her back, '*avec tes griffes*', as though I were an animal with claws, rather than a mummy with mere fingernails, I had to admit that – yellow teeth or no – there were far worse ways a person could start her day.

Mr Frog lolled on his sofa, while I sat cross-legged in his new leather armchair, leaning towards the table from time to time to swipe a handful of crisps – salt and vinegar flavour, because in our time together I had managed to convince Mr Frog of the merits of certain English foods. Finding myself at a loose end on my night off, I'd slipped across the road for a chat. Tadpole lay sleeping in Mr Frog's bedroom. For a while we'd exchanged anecdotes about her, in a spirit of light-hearted one-upmanship, our naturally competitive streaks coming to the fore.

'You should have seen the tortoise she drew this morning before school on her magic board,' I said. 'It was fantastic, totally life-like. She patterned the shell and everything. Although it may have had five legs, now I come to think of it . . .'

Mr Frog stood and went over to his desk, rifling through a stack of papers, pulling out a sheet of A4 paper and bringing it over to me with a triumphant smile. 'Good, isn't it?' It was a perfect snail, complete with antennae poking out from under its hat at a jaunty angle, very reminiscent of Brian in the *Magic Roundabout*.

I decided to skip the yellow teeth anecdote, which was funny, and would no doubt make it on to the blog in some form, but smarted, and had even prompted me to make an appointment at the dentist's to investigate teeth-whitening procedures. Instead, I described how Tadpole had reacted to the blossom drifting down from the trees on the way to the childminder's house that morning. 'She said, "Mummy, it's just like confetti!" She's so poetic, our girl, don't you think?'

'Ah yes, I've heard her say it in French too,' said Mr Frog, not to be outdone. '*On dirait des confettis!*'

'It's funny,' I said, thinking aloud. 'I hardly ever hear her speak French these days. And I suppose you rarely hear her speak English.' Mr Frog nodded. Effectively, a language barrier had been erected all the way along the fault line of our separation. 'You getting out much?' I said, not wishing to dwell on the things which divided us. But when Mr Frog shifted uneasily in his seat, I wished I'd held my tongue.

'Yeah, quite a bit. Less than in the beginning though . . . I've calmed down a bit now.'

I wondered if there was a girl, or girls, but wouldn't permit myself to ask, not unless he volunteered more information first. There were lots of subjects I dared not broach with Mr Frog. I'd never asked him how he'd coped when I was seeing James. Whether he'd read my blog, back then, or whether Tadpole spoke about him. I had no idea how he felt about me, these days. Now that I was alone again, did he nurture any hope, however faint, that we might find a way to bury our differences and try again? Did I?

'Well, I suppose I ought to head home,' I mumbled when the conversation petered out. It seemed incongruous calling the empty apartment across the street home, while my daughter quietly snored in the next room. Ironic that I should have to leave, when the two people I cared about most in the world were right here.

We stood in the doorway, lingering for a moment, as though neither of us really wanted to part. Something about the way he looked gravely into my eyes and inclined his head, almost imperceptibly, made me think he was trying to decide whether to kiss me. Not *la bise*, which in itself would have been a huge departure from the friendly distance we'd been maintaining for the last few months, but a proper kiss. On the lips. I stared at him, mesmerized, my thoughts a blur. Would he go through with it? And if he did, would I return his kiss or pull away? Where would either of those outcomes leave us?

In the end, all he did was give my arm a squeeze, before closing the door gently behind me. I stood in the darkness on the landing outside his apartment for a moment, my heart pounding, wondering whether I'd imagined the whole thing. And even though it was one of those perfect moments of high drama that I loved to immortalize, lingering over its significance, I realized I had no intention whatsoever of including the scene in my blog.

Some moments had to be kept private: our continuing friendship was more important than full disclosure to a few thousand strangers, many of whom made no secret of their desire to see us reunited.

I plunge into the bowels of the *métro* the next morning, my steps perfectly in time with the music filling my head. Though I am lost in my thoughts, gliding along on autopilot, my hips instinctively know the height of the turnstile barrier, remembering precisely how hard it must be nudged. My feet lead me to the correct spot on the platform, aligned with the exit I'll need when I alight at my destination. I feel the familiar bumpy contours of the warning strip along the platform edge through the thin soles of my shoes.

A full calendar year has now gone by since I first laid eyes on James. The song playing on my iPod is our song, 'Gorecki', by Lamb. The very same song I'd listened to in the *métro* when I left the Hôtel Saint Louis, ecstatic tears streaming down my face.

I remember the woman I was before *petite anglaise* came along, that sleepwalker, deeply dissatisfied with her life, seething with resentment but unable to articulate what was wrong. I remember how by writing about the city around me, by writing about the people in my life, I began to see everything more clearly. I realized that being a mother, being in a relationship, shouldn't have to mean burying my own needs deep inside, denying their very existence. That way only bitterness lay.

When James fell in love with *petite anglaise* and came into our lives, I willingly clambered on to a rollercoaster. There were moments when I doubted the wisdom of my actions. Moments when I worried that the blog was living my life for me, or pushing me to reveal more than I should to satisfy my thirst – and my readers' thirst – for drama, for material, so that the show might go on. *Petite anglaise* looked on with interested detachment, using me as a guinea pig, a lab rat, placing me in ever more unexpected situations to see how I would react. All the while furiously scribbling, documenting my emotions, recording my every move.

Maybe it wasn't really James I fell in love with, I think to myself with a sudden blinding flash of clarity. Would it not be fair to say that I fell for my own words, or the image of myself that he reflected back at me, the carefully constructed, larger than life version of me: *petite anglaise*? Everything she wrote was in some way calculated to charm and seduce, and hadn't James been the most tangible proof of her success?

I take a long look at my face reflected in the window of the *métro* carriage as it rattles and sways through the dark tunnels. I look different somehow, more knowing. In a single year I've done more living than in the entire decade that went before it. Rising from the ashes of two failed relationships, I'm a single mother now, and a woman who is well on the way to owning her first home.

I've formed one half of an ill-matched couple for most of my adult life but now, alone, I feel whole, at peace with myself. The desire for flight has finally left me. No shadowy figure runs alongside the train. Given the chance, I wouldn't trade places with the old me. Nor do I wish that *petite anglaise* had never existed. She brought me here. And I really like where I've wound up.

My phone vibrates, announcing the arrival of a text message from one of my new blogfriends, asking me if I fancy going for drinks in the Café Charbon at the weekend. I smile, and shake my head. 'I think it will be a while before I'm ready to face that place again,' I text back. 'But I hope, for my sake, it never closes down!'

As the train pulls into the station, I raise the handle so that the double doors spring open while the carriage is still in motion, allowing me to alight at the precise moment it reaches a standstill. I walk along the platform, still accompanied by my soundtrack. Sometimes I feel like I own this city. Whatever lies in store for me, whoever may be waiting around the next corner, I feel sure of one thing: my future is in Paris.

Ahead of me I see blank pages, inviting me to cover them with bold, lurid strokes.

Acknowledgements

With thanks to Simon Trewin, Sarah Ballard and Katy Follain for their invaluable help and guidance and to Angela Sanderson and Meg Zimbeck for their feedback and support.

CATHERINE SANDERSON

RENDEZ-VOUS

Sally is a thirtysomething single mum who lives with her daughter Lila in Belleville, criss-crossing Paris by *métro* to give English lessons to the corporate clients of a language school.

Sally left Nicolas, her French partner of ten years and Lila's father, after she discovered, quite by chance, that he was having an affair with his secretary. Six months have now passed and she's beginning to bounce back, with a little help from her friends, and also from a French online dating site called *Rendez-Vous*.

But making a new start is fraught with complications and Sally finds herself pulled in different directions. Can she find a way to reconcile motherhood with single-womanhood? To what extent can she keep Lila and her love life separate? Is she truly ready to turn her back on Nicolas?

To be published in summer 2009

WIN a trip to
Paris with Eurostar!

Fall in love with Paris like Catherine Sanderson in *Petite Anglaise* …

We are offering one lucky winner the chance to sample the delights of the world's most romantic city with a prize courtesy of Eurostar. Travel to Paris in style on the Eurostar – your ticket will include a celebratory glass of champagne, a delicious meal on board and spacious, comfy seats. When you arrive in this wonderful city you will be put up for one night in a 4★ hotel in the centre of the city, which will be the perfect base for seeing all the sights. Whether it's going up the Eiffel Tower, taking a boat trip up the Seine or taking advantage of the magnificent shopping, Paris has something for everyone.

To enter the prize draw and for terms and conditions, please visit
www.penguin.co.uk/petite

**Closing date:
31st March 2009**

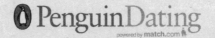